THE BEN LINE
1825-1982

THE BEN LINE

1825-1982

An Anecdotal History

MICHAEL STRACHAN

MICHAEL RUSSELL

© Michael Strachan 1992

First published in Great Britain 1992
by Michael Russell (Publishing) Ltd
Wilby Hall, Wilby, Norwich NR16 2JP
Typeset in Sabon by The Typesetting Bureau Ltd
Church Street, Wimborne, Dorset
Printed (on acid-free paper) and bound
by Biddles Ltd, Guildford and King's Lynn

Indexed by the author

ISBN 0 85955 197 3

Contents

Introduction

The long, and continuing, history of the Ben Line has been partially covered in previous publications, notably George Blake's *The Ben Line, 1825-1955* (Edinburgh, 1956), and Graeme Somner's *Ben Line Fleet List and Short History* (Kendal, 1980), for the short historical preface of which I myself was largely responsible.

Chapter 1 of the present book compresses the first 120 years into a few pages. The facts are, however, presented in a fresh light, and entirely new material is included about the years between the two World Wars. All the other chapters deal with the period 1945-82.

I joined the Ben Line as a clerk in November 1946 and retired from being its chairman and chief executive in March 1982, so any account of the company's activities written by me is bound to be coloured by my own experiences and observations.

Money, inevitably, is a recurring theme, but this is not a 'business history', which must be left to some future, detached, economic historian. So, while giving due prominence to the major developments that occurred, I have tried to record what life was like, ashore and afloat, not ignoring some of the hilarious incidents – even trivia – that an 'insider' is privileged to recollect.

This book could not have been written without the help of members of the company, both those who have retired and those still serving. Among so many it is invidious to cite names, but I must asknowledge the support and encouragement I have received from Mr W. R. E. Thomson and his colleagues on the board of the Ben Line Group Ltd, and the contributions made by Captain W. O. Atkinson, Captain J. Liston, Sir Roderick MacLeod, Captain A. P. Paterson, Messrs H. Paton, A. M. Peill and the late A. J. Rait, and Sir David Thomson, Bt.

Ms Lynn Heath patiently and expertly translated successive manuscript drafts to word processor.

M.F.S.

Edinburgh, January 1992

THOMSON GENEALOGICAL TREE

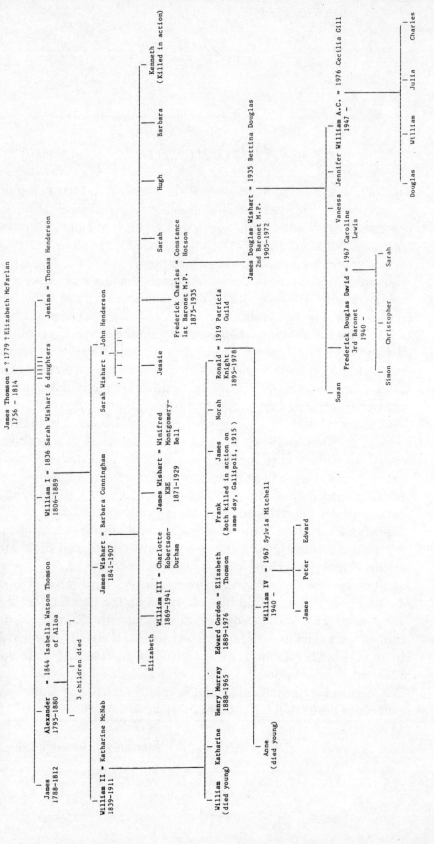

I

The Story So Far

1825 – 1945

The origins of the Ben Line go back to 1825 when two young brothers, Alexander and William Thomson, set up a shipbroking partnership based in Leith, the port of Edinburgh. At that time William was still only nineteen but it seems probable that he was the prime mover in the new venture. He was the more forceful character, his the ardent enthusiasm for ships and the sea.

William had been only eight and Alexander was still a minor when their father James (1756-1814) died, leaving a building business which had a particular interest in the importation of marble to adorn the fine new houses of Edinburgh. This interest was shared by other members of the family. Thomas Henderson, the young brothers' trustee during their minority, who became their brother-in-law by marrying their sister Jemima, was active in shipping and exporting from Leghorn, the outlet for Carrara marble. Their uncle, another Alexander Thomson, was the owner, or chief partner, of the Leith Marble Works.

William served an apprenticeship with Robert and John Cockburn, wine merchants of Leith, and then joined Alexander in the family business. While Alexander extended the marble business to Glasgow, William acquired experience of ships' husbandry. He also obtained an auctioneer's licence, enabling him to conduct sales, mainly timber, on the Sands of Leith. Shipbroking, however, seems not to have been a money spinner in those early years and difficulties with wily Italian merchants resulted in low profits from the marble trade, so it was not until 1839 that the brothers managed to finance the building of their first ship, at Buckhaven in Fife. She was a little broad-beamed barque, 88 feet long. They named her *Carrara* and put her on the Italian run, carrying coal and woollen goods from Leith to Leghorn and returning home with marble.

[1]

Business and matrimonial interests went happily hand in hand in those days. In 1836 William married Sarah Wishart, daughter of a Leith merchant dealing in the textiles then produced in the Forth basin, which found a ready market in Italy. Eight years later Alexander, then aged forty-nine, married Isabella Thomson, daughter of Captain Watson Thomson of Alloa who had been a master mariner before 'swallowing the anchor' and involving himself in the woollen business and the importation of timber. These Alloa Thomsons and another Alloa family, the Mitchells, played an important part in financing the early ships and providing them with cargo. Coal was supplied by the prosperous Alloa Coal Company of which the head of the Mitchell family, William, was a founder-partner. He was also a brewer, miller, grain merchant and supplied meat from his farms to victual the ships. His daughter Janet married one of the Thomsons of Alloa.

The cost of *Carrara* and how she was owned are unknown, but these details are available in respect of William Thomson's next acquisition in 1840 when he bought a fifteen-year-old, full-rigged ship, the *Australia*, for £3,500, towards which Andrew Thomson, head of the Alloa family, put up 30/64ths and his younger brother Captain Watson Thomson took 12/64ths, leaving 22/64ths to be owned by A. & W. Thomson.[1]

Australia enabled the brothers to engage in a trade more profitable than Italian marble and it has previously been suggested that henceforth prosperity reigned. However within a year *Australia* was wrecked and lost in the approaches to the St Lawrence River and it was not until 1844 that the brothers acquired a replacement, *Joanna*, already fourteen years old. She was bought at auction in Glasgow for £800, but a further £350 was spent in repairs and new gear. William Mitchell of Alloa took one half of the 64th shares, Andrew Thomson of Alloa had twenty-one and the rest were held by A. & W. Thomson.

1 The Merchant Shipping Act of 1854 settled the sixty-fourth as the invariable unit of ownership of British ships, which it still is. This Act gave statutory recognition to a practice which existed long before, and has been variously traced back to Viking or even Roman times. I am indebted to David R. MacGregor for referring me to Ralph Davis, *The Rise of the English Shipping Industry*, London, 1962, pp.82-3 and *The Mariner's Mirror*, vol.45, no.4, 1959, pp.302-3.

The real turning point came in 1847 when Alexander retired from the partnership, (though he continued to hold varying shares in individual ships) and the firm's style was changed from 'A. & W. Thomson' to 'Wm Thomson & Co.' under the able direction of William.

II

It is interesting to analyse the origins and careers of the sailing ships managed by William Thomson and his successors from the first acquisition in 1839 to the last disposal nearly sixty years later in 1898. There were twenty-three vessels in all, of which twelve were built on the eastern seaboard of Canada, usually by small family yards, as speculative ventures. The ships were launched, loaded with timber, and sailed to Britain for auction. The Thomsons bought four such new vessels, the remaining eight of Canadian origin being acquired second-hand after they had traded for other owners. Overall thirteen vessels were bought new and ten second-hand. This high proportion of second-hand tonnage and the willingness to sell when a ship had outlived its usefulness, or could command a good profit, were characteristic of Thomson ship management right down to the 1980s. Thus eleven out of the twenty-three were eventually sold to other owners and twelve were lost in service.

The number in service at any one time reached a peak of twelve in 1875 when the steam revolution was already well underway, just as a hundred years later the conventional cargo fleet reached a peak when the container revolution had already begun.

Apart from the Canadian ships, all the new acquisitions were products of Scottish yards, but there were only two from the same builder – the famous yard of R. Steele & Co. of Greenock. Two were built by different Leith firms and one came from each of Alloa, Brucehaven, Glasgow, Kincardine and Stirling. In a rapidly expanding market competitive pricing and nearness to the headquarters in Leith seem to have outweighed the advantages which might have accrued from a measure of standardisation and continuity with one or two chosen builders.

Twelve total losses in under sixty years are evidence enough of the hazards then suffered by sailing ships, particularly if they were engaged in the North Atlantic. From the late 1840s to the mid sixties

[3]

this was the staple trade, carrying Alloa coal out to Canada and timber on the return voyage. Four ships were wrecked in the St Lawrence and its treacherous approaches.[2] One was lost by fire in 1862 while carrying coal on passage from London to Rangoon, and two years later two more, bound for Canada, were destroyed by spontaneous combustion in their cargo of coal.[3]

Sailing north about Scotland en route for the St Lawrence, seemingly the usual practice, involved traversing the difficult Pentland Firth where the Skerries claimed another ship outward bound from Leith to Quebec with coal: nine of her crew perished,[4] and so did the entire crew of eighteen men when the ill-named *Golden Pledge* sailed from Liverpool for the East in January 1864 and was never heard of again. The *Alexandra* was wrecked south of Madras in 1869 and three years later *Ocean Chief* foundered off Calcutta. The last sailing ship casualty was the fine iron ship *Benan*, wrecked off Western Australia in 1888.

The locations of these latter disasters reflect changes in the patterns of trade. The Canadian run was varied by voyages further afield: some of these voyages were on charter, others were independent trading ventures starting with a cargo of coal and then relying for their itinerary and financial result on the resourcefulness of the Master, who was always encouraged to take one or more 64th shares. In the early 1850s two ships were diverted from Canada to carry prospectors hoping to make their fortunes in the Australian Gold Rush. At the end of that decade the first *Araby Maid* made an exploratory voyage to Singapore, China and Japan, returning via Peru and Cape Horn, a circumnavigation lasting just short of two years. This dipping of the toe into Far Eastern waters was to prove the harbinger of the most far-reaching development in the company's trading pattern.

By this time trade between Europe and the Far East, particularly China, was more free than it had ever been. The East India Company's monopoly of all British trade with Asia, which had existed since 1600, was finally terminated in 1834. By the Treaty of Nanking in 1842 the uninhabited island of Hong Kong with its superb natural

2 *Australia, Araby Maid* I, *Adriatic, Algiers.*
3 *May Queen, Joanna, Wanderer.*
4 *Vicksburg.*

harbour had been ceded to Britain, and the so-called 'treaty ports' on China's mainland: Canton, Amoy, Foochow, Ningpo and Shanghai were opened to international trade. Before that the only foreign entry had been through Macao, the Portuguese colony established in 1557, and the East India Company's base, a few miles away at Canton. As a result of the Treaties of Tientsin (1858) and Peking (1860) a further twelve 'treaty ports' were opened, including two in Taiwan, and the mainland area of Kowloon was added to the British colony of Hong Kong.

The foremost company to exploit the new opportunities was P & O, founded in 1837, who developed an Overland Route across the Isthmus of Suez. Cargo and passengers, transhipped at Alexandria and Suez, were carried across the desert by camel and horse-drawn vehicles. Depots and workshops were established at both ends of the route along which there was a chain of resthouses. P & O's main service with sail-assisted steamers to India was extended in 1844 via Galle in Ceylon to Penang, Singapore and Hong Kong. An average of 170 sailing ships,[5] including some Thomson vessels, were employed carrying coal to P & O's Eastern refuelling depots. These found their way home with tea, spices, rice and other produce, or continued to Japan and across the Pacific as *Araby Maid* had done. Thomson sailing ships participated in the China tea trade, but did not compete with the crack 'clippers'. The opening of the Suez Canal in 1869 wiped out most of P & O's enormous investment in the Suez Overland Route and made many of its ships obsolete because some were designed for European waters and others for the tropics beyond Suez.

Meanwhile in 1865 Alfred Holt, the great Liverpool shipowner and engineer, had founded the Ocean Steam Ship Company and in the following year his *Agamemnon* became the first steamship to sail from Europe to China. She set out from Liverpool and arrived at Shanghai in seventy-seven days via Mauritius, Penang, Singapore and Hong Kong. *Agamemnon* and her sisters *Ajax* and *Achilles* were all 10-knot ships of 2,820 grt, and by 1879 had become part of a fleet of twenty ships.

---

5 Eric Jennings, *Cargoes*, Singapore, 1980, p.20.

William Thomson I took into partnership his sons William II[6] (1839-1911) and James Wishart (1841-1907) as soon as they reached their majority. The two new partners assumed their responsibilities at a time when the challenge of steam was beginning to make itself felt. The opening of the Suez Canal in 1869 made it imperative for a line with expanding interests in the Far East trade to change from sail to steam in order to keep pace with its competitors, but the first Thomson steamship did not join the fleet until 1871, the year after William Thomson I retired from day-to-day business. This first steamer, *Benledi*, built and engined by Barclay Curle in Glasgow, was propelled by compound steam engines of 800 indicated horse-power (ihp), giving her a maximum service speed of nine knots in fair weather, one knot slower than Alfred Holt's famous trio. She was 1,557 tons gross, partly rigged so that she could make port if her engines broke down, or save coal if the wind was favourable. Her first cost, ready for sea, was £26,000 and this was cleared by profits from her first five voyages which occupied exactly three years.[7]

However, doubts about the viability of steam propulsion, like those which beset the company nearly a century later at the onset of the container revolution, resulted in a very cautious transition. These doubts were, moreover, well founded. Steamers by no means had it all their own way. British yards continued to build more and more sailing ships, and this boom did not reach its peak until 1875. Sail could hold its own against steam until the mid-eighties.[8]

So there was no headlong plunge into steam propulsion. On the contrary, after *Benledi* I five second-hand sailing ships[9] were purchased and two more, *Benan* (1875) and *Bencleuch* II (1875) were specially commissioned. *Bencleuch* II was 1,418 gross tons, 247 feet long with a beam of 37 feet and depth to main deck of 22 feet. Only marginally smaller than her steam driven 'aunt', *Benledi*, she was

6 His biography by T.E. Milne appears in *Dictionary of Scottish Business Biography 1860-1960* (A. Slaven, S. Checkland eds.) Aberdeen, 1990, vol.2, pp.315-16.
7 David R. MacGregor, *The China Bird*, 1986 edn, p.129.
8 *Ibid.*, pp.118, 131.
9 *Palmyra* (1873), *Mic Mac* (1873), *Royalist* (1895) (which had been under Thomson management but wholly owned by the Mitchells of Alloa since 1846) *Adriatic* (1875) and *Algiers* (1875).

also the last sailing ship to be disposed of, by sale in 1898, and continued in service under two more owners until she was wrecked off the Dutch Coast at the ripe age of thirty-three.

Thus it was not until 1876 that a second, slightly larger and more powerful steamer, *Benarty* I was delivered by Barclay Curle, and a third, *Bengloe* I, from the same yard came into service two years later. In 1880 the famous yard of Alexander Stephen & Sons, Glasgow, delivered *Benalder* I, the first Thomson ship to exceed 2,000 gross tons.

By this time Wm Thomson & Co. had become sufficiently involved in the Far East trade to be taken into account as a competitor by Alfred Holt & Co. and P & O. There was additional competition from the steamers of the Glen and Shire Lines. Rates of freight became so low that these companies, minus P & O initially, were persuaded to enter into an 'Agreement for the working of the China and Japan Trade, Outwards and Homewards'. This was signed in August 1879 and became the forerunner of the Far Eastern Freight Conference.

The Thomsons advertised their early steamships as 'The Clipper Line of Steamers'. By 1881 the service to China and Japan was advertised as 'The Ben Line of London and China Clippers'. Though maintained primarily by steamers, this was not really a contradiction in terms, since the early steamships were also equipped with sail, and between 1881 and 1914 the company built twenty steamers whose fine lines and clipper bow, equipped with bowsprit and figurehead, lent them much of the grace of the sailing ship.

Not many of 'the Leith Yachts', as they were nicknamed, were sisters, other than in name and the unmistakable outward appearance: a 25-feet bowsprit with figurehead, black hull and yellow funnel. Size and engine power continued to increase: *Benlarig* I (1881) was only 2,265 gross tons with compound engines developing 1,300 ihp; *Benmohr* I (1893) attained 3,000 gross tons and had triple expansion engines of 1,500 ihp. The first Thomson ship to exceed 4,000 gross tons was *Bencleuch* III (1901), 1,600 ihp, built and engined by Ramage & Ferguson, Leith. The last of the clipper-bowed steamers, *Benrinnes* I (1914), was 4,798 gross tons and her triple expansion engines of 2,150 ihp, gave her a service speed of 12½ knots,[10] still

10 Blake, p.94, gives her 11½ knots.

slower than the fastest among her main British competitors in the Far East trade. She remained in the fleet until she was sold in 1937, but sank the following year after an air attack off Valencia in the Spanish Civil War.

So far as the Thomson fleet was concerned, iron hulls began to replace wood in the mid 1860s. Iron was in plentiful supply at home, whereas most timber had to be imported. Steel did not replace iron until some twenty years later. *Benlawers* I, (1886) and all subsequent vessels built for the company had steel hulls.

After *Moscow* I (about which ship more below) was wrecked off Spain in January 1890 no ship managed by Wm Thomson & Co. was lost until *Bengloe* II stranded in the Philippines in September 1914. This record of nearly a quarter of a century compared extremely well with that of the sailing ships, which suffered twelve total losses in under sixty years – four of them in a single year, 1864. The great boon of steam was that a ship could use her power to steer away from a lee shore and could, at last, go astern.

IV

The transition from wood to iron, the gradual demise of sail in favour of steam and the removal in 1867 of the fiscal advantage previously enjoyed by Canadian timber put an end to the Canadian trade. In its place the Thomsons developed a trade with the Baltic. This owed much to a longstanding friendship between William Thomson I and John Jordan, a Leith merchant who was a partner in James Miller & Co., merchants and millowners in Russia. The new service was inaugurated in 1878 by *Bencleuch* II, but she was the only sailing ship employed in this trade. In the same year two small second-hand steamships were purchased, Jordan being the majority shareholder. One already possessed the appropriate name of *Petersburg*; the other was *Stirling* built in 1856. These were joined by *Czar* (1879), and *Moscow* I (1881), both new ships built by J. Laing of Sunderland. When *Moscow* I was wrecked and lost in 1890 she was promptly replaced by *Moscow* II (1891) from Ramage & Ferguson, Leith. She and her near sisters *Petersburg* II (1891), *Reval* (1898) and *Cronstadt* (1907) were exceptionally shallow-drafted, enabling them to pass through the canal between Cronstadt and St Petersburg (Leningrad). The depth of the first three was fourteen feet and of the last only thirteen, about ten feet less than the ships constructed for the Far East trade.

By 1889 the ships serving the Baltic had been incorporated as The Leith and St Petersburg Steam Shipping Company[11] with its registered office at 63 Constitution Street, Leith, which was also the office of Wm Thomson & Co. Both companies moved to 28 Bernard Street, Leith shortly thereafter, probably in 1889, certainly by 1890.[12] In the latter year Wm Thomson & Co. were advertising sailings from Leith and Granton to St Petersburg, Reval and Cronstadt, departing every ten days during the ice-free season, which lasted from about the end of April to about the end of November. Later other ports on the east coast of the United Kingdom were added and, as Baltic connections strengthened, the range of foreign ports was extended to Libau, Kiel, Copenhagen, Aarhus, Riga and others. To the basic outward cargo of coal was added machinery for the Miller mills near St Petersburg, while the homeward cargo included timber, grain, flax, hemp, linseed and oilcake. Passengers were regularly carried with stewards and stewardesses to look after them. The latter did a remunerative contraband trade in ladies' underwear and stockings. British bowler hats were also sold profitably on the black market.[13]

Each ship performed between seven and ten round voyages during the ice-free season. All these voyages were taken into a single reckoning and profits rarely fell below £1,000 per ship for a season's trading, though that was scarcely a gold mine when set against the first cost of *Czar* (1879), for instance, at £19,506. More money might be made during the five remaining months of the year when such time as was not required for repairs and refitting was spent on charter voyages, typically coal to Italy, returning via North Africa with esparto grass for the Scottish paper-making industry.

A fifth ship, *Ladoga*, delivered in 1914, was in Russian waters on the outbreak of hostilities, as were *Moscow* and *Petersburg*. Three of the five survived the war; George Blake has described their extraordinary adventures in some detail.[14]

11 The name was changed to The Petrograd Steamers Ltd in 1921.
12 *Edinburgh & Leith Post Office Directories* 1889/90 and 1890/91.
13 Black, *op.cit.*, p.62.
14 *op.cit.*, pp.64-7.

Meantime the Russian Revolution in 1917 had put paid to James Miller & Co., John Jordan died in 1918 and though some half-hearted attempts were made to increase the fleet with a second-hand vessel and two new ships which had been ordered by the British Government before the war ended,[15] it was decided to abandon the service. The last of the Baltic steamers *Onega* II was sold to Japan in 1927 and the company under its changed name, The Petrograd Steamers Limited, was finally wound up in 1941. Part of its funds were used to finance at least one Ben Line ship.

At the outbreak of the First World War the Thomson fleet consisted of fourteen clipper-bowed Ben Line steamers and the five Baltic ships. Four of the Baltic ships were requisitioned by the Government and employed as colliers; no doubt the fifth, *Moscow* II, would have been similarly employed, but she was laid up in St Petersburg at the outbreak, taken over for Russian Government service in 1916 and finally scuttled either by the Bolsheviks or by British agents, in 1918.

In 1915 three Ben Line ships were requisitioned and were joined the next year by two more. These five ships all served as colliers and only one was lost. The rest of the fleet went about its usual business, but suffered two losses from enemy attacks.

Benmohr II was captured and scuttled by the German cruiser *Emden* in the Indian Ocean in October 1914 and the following year *Benvorlich* I was torpedoed by a U-boat, but in that early part of the war the crews of both ships were given time to take to the boats. The requisitioned *Benlarig* II serving as a collier was less fortunate. She went missing with all hands in the Indian Ocean: sabotage was suspected. Many other Ben ships had remarkable escapes: four beat off U-boat attacks[16] – one with the help of the Royal Navy. *Benalder* II was torpedoed but managed to make Alexandria where she was repaired. A few weeks before the war ended *Benrinnes* I was fired at by two torpedoes but both missed.

With the loss of slightly over one quarter of the fleet – three Bens and two Baltic steamers, Wm Thomson & Co. were fortunate compared with some other British companies. The British Merchant Marine as a whole lost one third of its tonnage.

15 *Twilight/Onega* I (1918-19), *Cramond* (1919-21), *Onega* II (1920-27).
16 *Benledi* III, *Benavon* I, *Benlomond* II, *Bendoran* I.

William II and James Wishart, the sons of William I, died before the outbreak of the First World War. Both had large families (see genealogical table). William II had two daughters and six sons (of whom the first born died as a child, two were killed in action, and two more wounded); James Wishart had five sons (of whom one was killed in action) and four daughters. Two sons from each branch came into the partnership; Henry and Edward, William III and James Wishart II.

A major constitutional change took place in 1919 when The Ben Line Steamers Limited was formed, thereby ending 'one ship accounting' and the distribution of profits at the end of each voyage to the holders of shares in each ship, to the detriment of reserves. The first directors were William Thomson III, chairman, his brother Sir James Wishart Thomson (who had been knighted for his services as wartime Shipping Controller for India and Mesopotamia), Alexander Mitchell of Alloa, Henry and Edward Thomson. Almost immediately, however, a rift between Henry and Edward resulted in Henry resigning from the board. He also resigned from Wm. Thomson & Co. of which he, Edward and Robert McArthur (who had worked his way up the company) had been partners since 1911. McArthur died in 1925 and in 1928 the partnership was augmented to five by the admission of A. M. Mitchell (son of the above Alexander) and J. D. W. Thomson (see Appendix listing the partners and directors).

During the war Henry had looked after the business. That all four of his brothers were either killed or wounded while he did not fight left him with a permanent feeling of guilt. The business disagreement did not prevent amicable discussion and shared holidays with Edward and other members of the family, but it did result in him setting up as a successful independent shipowner. He lived with his spinster sister Norah, occupying a combined house and office in Drumsheugh Gardens, Edinburgh, though latterly they permitted themselves the extravagance of a house separate from the office in Belgrave Crescent. He conducted operations virtually single-handed. Relying on trusted brokers and agents, hiring in marine and engineer superintendents on a part-time basis, he owned up to three ships at any one time and tramped them round the world. His minimal correspondence was conducted in longhand, he did his own book-keeping, and took all his own decisions.

He was still very much in business after the Second World War and it was occasionally my duty to inform him by telephone of the text of a cable intended for him which had arrived addressed 'Thomson Edinburgh', the Ben Line's telegraphic address. This he would acknowledge in a low, dour, voice. He never wasted words – or anything else – but his voice was at variance with the old-world charm displayed to visiting business representatives, whom he received at the front door, and after discussions in his study, let them out himself. During the Great Depression he was concerned for the welfare of his crews and when trade picked up again in the mid-thirties he shared his ships' profits with them, thereby facing expulsion from the Shipping Federation which regulated the supply and pay of officers and ratings. Eventually he sold up and retired in his middle seventies. His older contemporary, Sir William Burrell (1861-1958), whose spasmodic shipowning, assisted by an able brother, was on a larger scale, gave himself plenty of leisure to acquire superlative art collections and achieved a measure of immortality by bequeathing them to the City of Glasgow (leaving his immediate descendants in relative poverty). By contrast an evening playing bridge was all that Henry Thomson needed as a relaxation, or indeed could spare because of his extraordinary methods of work. His probably unique individual achievement as a shipowner was based on unremitting hard work, astute decisions, and experience gained with Wm Thomson & Co.

During his lifetime many people had cause to be grateful for unobtrusive acts of generosity. The major part of his fortune was eaten up by death duties; he left the residue amounting to about £350,000 to the Church of Scotland, RSPCC, RSPCA, and to various seamen's charities at the discretion of his executor.[17]

The company's first new ship after the First World War[18] was built by Charles Connell & Co. on the Clyde, thus beginning a relationship which lasted until 1970. *Benvorlich* II, delivered in August 1919, was of standard Government design, just over 5,000 tons gross, with

17 Henry Thomson's executor was his nephew, William Thomson IV.
18 Blake p.117 states erroneously that *Benreoch* I (1921) was the first such ship.

triple expansion engines of 2,500 ihp and a speed of 12 knots. She was followed between 1921 and 1930 by a series of nine purpose-built nearly identical ships,[19] all slightly under 6,000 tons gross with an overall length of around 430 feet, powered by quadruple expansion engines of 3,000 ihp giving them a speed of 12 knots. There were no more clipper bows and raking masts; these new ships were stout workhorses with straight stems and overhanging counters. Eight were built by Connell; the penultimate of the class, slightly smaller and less highly powered, came from Lithgow's. There was a gap of five years between delivery of the first in 1921 and the second in 1926, during which time the fleet was supplemented by the purchase of five second-hand vessels.

Seven of the new class were delivered between 1927 and 1930. This hitherto unprecedented spate of new ships could not have come at a less auspicious time since it coincided with the Great Depression of 1928-32. No wonder that any further expansionist plans were shelved and that not one more new ship was delivered for a decade. What is remarkable is that the entire fleet was kept trading when nearly one fifth of Britain's ocean-going tonnage was laid up, and more than three million people were unemployed. The fact that no Ben Line ship was laid up at that time has always been remembered with pride.

While the financial repercussions of the Great Depression were undoubtedly a major factor in causing the ten-year hiatus in new building there were other considerations. The trade between Europe and the Far East was becoming increasingly competitive, and subject to complicated controls arrived at by negotiation between the participating lines: more will be said about this aspect in chapter xii. Next, mention has already been made of the company's practice of selling off ships, usually for continued service with other owners, and buying in second-hand, even third- and fourth-hand tonnage as replacements. This practice continued throughout the inter-war years; between 1931 and 1939 seven such ships were acquired. The Great Depression itself resulted in some extraordinary bargains: *Bendoran* II, ex-*Indradeo*, ex-*Eurybates*, ex-*Cambrian Princess*, was

19 *Benreoch* I (1921-51); *Benarty* III (1926-40); *Benvenue* III (1927-41); *Benmohr* IV (1928-42); *Bencruachan* I (1928-41); *Benwyvis* I (1929-41); *Benledi* IV (1930-50); *Benavon* II (1930-40); *Benlawers* III (1930-40).

[13]

a Connell ship already twenty-one years old when she was bought from the Westminster Bank for £6,000 in 1931. The sale was, as usual, subject to the drawing and inspection of her tailshaft. The tailshaft was condemned and she had no spare, so the vendor had to spend a sum equal to the purchase price in order to provide her with a new one. This ship traded until 1944 when she was bought by the Government and sunk as part of the artificial Mulberry Harbour off the Normandy beaches. Even that was not the end of her career because she was refloated in 1947 and towed to Blyth for breaking up.

In 1932 the company bought its biggest ship yet, the 6,869 tons gross *Benmacdhui* II built on the Clyde in 1911. She was third- hand; the total costs of bringing her out of lay-up, drydocking, and making her ready for sea amounted to only £10,000. The last three fourth-hand or second-hand purchases in 1938 and 1939 were all around 6,500 tons gross, between sixteen and eighteen years old, with speeds of about 12 knots.[20]

One gets the impression from George Blake that ships and crews were very well found and looked after. Standards on such matters are relative, and judgements tend to be subjective. Those who went to sea in the thirties remember the stringent economies, poor pay and indifferent victualling. In 1931 a first-year cadet earned £2 per month. This was raised nominally to £4 in the second year, but in 1932 all sea and shore staff including the partners took a 10% cut.

There were of course Board of Trade regulations prescribing precise minimum rations, but the translation of the printed word into the food which appeared in the mess room varied quite widely from ship to ship. Some chief stewards were better managers than others, and the skill of some chief cooks did not find favour with the consumers. As one veteran said to another, reminiscing about those days: 'We only had pudding once a week.' 'You were lucky' was the reply, 'we had it every day!'[21] In those days a man's butter ration was issued to him by the tin, whose contents had to suffice for several days but quickly liquefied in hot weather. Eggs were something of a luxury, but it was standard practice to serve egg and bacon on

20 *Benlomond* IV, *Benvannoch* III, *Benvrackie* III.
21 Captain A.P. Paterson and Captain W.O. Atkinson, who first went to sea as cadets in 1931 and 1934 respectively.

Thursdays and Sundays. To make up for the paucity of fresh fruit and vegetables there was an issue of limejuice – a practice which persisted until after the Second World War. Prices of fresh food at ports of call around the world could be expensive, and they varied with the seasons of the year. At the end of each voyage a master had to produce a figure representing the victualling cost per man per day, which was carefully scrutinised by the managers, who may not always have been aware that the price of a Siamese pig, bought at Kohsichang and fattened up on galley refuse in a pen on deck until deemed ready for slaughter, might have been entered in the portage bill as 'dunnage' – the low-grade timber needed in large quantities to separate and secure parcels of cargo. Lean times continued throughout the thirties: an officer[22] who joined *Dakarian*, renamed *Benvannoch* III when she was bought in May 1939 from T. & J. Harrison, who had a reputation for extremely thrifty management, remembers how delighted he and his shipmates were to find that the stores on board, purchased with the ship, included quantities of chicken and grapefruit, delicacies unknown to Ben Line crews.

Throughout the period between the two World Wars the Ben Line's eastbound sailings on the liner berth were approximately twice as frequent as the westbound sailings, reflecting the overall imbalance between outward and homeward cargo, and Ben's inability to compete with the faster vessels of P & O and Alfred Holt's Blue Funnel and Glen Lines, which creamed off much of the higher-rated more valuable cargo. Ben's outward-bound sailings loaded sulphate of ammonia, steel and coke from Middlesbrough, iron, steel and sheet glass from Antwerp, cement in bags loaded hot from Bevan's Wharf on the lower reaches of the Thames. Ben Line carried much of the cement used in the construction of the naval base at Seletar on Singapore Island, and the sixteen-inch guns and ammunition to defend it from a seaward attack that proved useless against the Japanese landward assault. Sulphate, cement, iron and steel formed a bottoming on which more profitable cargo from London and elsewhere might be stowed if and when it could be obtained.

About half these eastbound sailings had to be traded home on time charters, or more frequently on voyage charters. They ballasted across the Pacific to load lumber from North American and

22 Captain J. Liston.

Canadian ports on the west coast. They loaded full cargoes of rice from Kohsichang at the mouth of the Bangkok river, and full cargoes of copra from the Philippines. If they were capable of maintaining a speed of twelve knots some ballasted to New Zealand during the wool season and loaded for Dunkirk and Hull. Another possibility was a full cargo of bulk sugar from Cairns in Queensland to UK.

During the Great Depression a full cargo of soya beans from Dairen (Talien) in North China paid as little as fourteen shillings per ton for the voyage to Europe. If this cargo was loaded in the winter months it remained so cold that when the ship arrived in the high temperatures of the Red Sea a bottle of water suspended down a ventilator into the hold would in an hour or two provide a luxuriously cool drink.

Groundnuts from the Madras coast were loaded in bags from surf boats. Their high stowage factor could be reduced in the evening after the day's work had ended by steaming full ahead and full astern to shake them down and make room for more. The last bags were loaded two tiers higher than the hatch coamings. The wooden hatches were laid on top and after twenty-four hours steaming the hatch boards had settled firmly in position. These unorthodox practices might not have been disclosed to the owners but ensured that the ship was indeed full and earning her maximum freight.

Ships with forecastles and aftercastles, normally used for storing paint, ropes and other stores might be filled with a space cargo, such as bagged groundnuts, but prior to arrival at the Suez Canal these would be piled on the hatches for the Canal transit to avoid paying extra dues. 'In winter it could be a frantic rush to restow the cargo before clearing the long breakwater at Port Said, since it was not unusual to be shipping green water as soon as you entered the Med.'[23]

VI

The company's experiences during the Second World War have been recounted at some length by George Blake. One of his major sources was *The Ben Line: The Story of a Merchant Fleet at War 1939-1945*, which is mainly a record of tragedy, and the testimonies of eye-

23 Captain W.O. Atkinson.

witnesses. This book was inspired by Sir Douglas Thomson (who had inherited his father's baronetcy in 1935), and much of the editing was carried out by J.M. (Ian) Miller, a member of staff throughout the war. Well printed and produced in hardback by the Edinburgh publishers Thomas Nelson for private circulation in 1946, it had the distinction of being the first such history from any British shipping company.

At the outbreak of war in September 1939, the Ben Line fleet consisted of twenty ships, only one more than in 1914, though the carrying capacity had more than doubled from 64,500 to 145,750 deadweight tons.[24] Their average age was between fifteen and sixteen years; ten were purpose-built and ten had been bought second-, third-, or fourth-hand. Of these twenty ships all but seven were lost by enemy action. The first losses occurred on consecutive days, 10 and 11 September 1940. *Benarty* III was captured by a German surface raider in the Indian Ocean and sunk by time bombs after the crew had abandoned ship. Next day another surface raider, also operating in the Indian Ocean, sank *Benavon* II by gunfire, killing twenty-three of the crew.

The greatest loss of life occurred in *Benalbanach* I, delivered by Connell's in October 1940. She was the first new Ben since 1930, and the first to exceed 10,000 tons deadweight. Under her master, Captain D.K.C. Macgregor, she played an outstanding role in Operation Torch, the initial North African landings. On a subsequent voyage, laden with troops and supplies for North Africa, she was sunk by aerial torpedo in the Mediterranean. No less than 410 men, including Captain Macgregor, lost their lives. Her first officer, A.P. Paterson, was among the few survivors; soon afterwards he was promoted to master at the age of twenty-six and later became a marine superintendent. Captain Macgregor's beautiful Belgian wife never married again; she lived, worked and eventually died in Scotland, always maintaining close contact with the Ben Line, especially since her sister had become the wife of Captain A.P. Paterson.

Of the fourteen Bens lost by enemy action, six were sunk by German submarines, one was sunk by an American submarine (but by that time she had a Japanese crew as she had been captured in

24 Blake, *op.cit.*, p.129.

December 1941 off Hong Kong); two were destroyed by German surface raiders, two were mined, two succumbed to air attack and one burned out, probably as a result of sabotage. In addition, four of the thirteen ships which the Government entrusted to Wm Thomson & Co.'s management were sunk by U-boat, air attack or mine. Of the managed ships which outlasted hostilities more will be said in the next chapter.

In *The Ben Line: The Story of a Merchant Fleet at War 1939-1945* and in George Blake's history, attempts have been made to chronicle the extraordinary endurance and heroism of the Ben Line crews. It was beyond the scope of these publications to deal with the impact of the horrors of war both physical and psychological on those who survived. The crew of *Benarty* III, imprisoned in Italian Somaliland, were liberated by British troops after a few months, but the life of her master, Captain J. Watt, was shortened by his privations. The crew of *Bennevis* I, captured off Hong Kong, spent nearly four years as prisoners of the Japanese during which four of them died, three from malnutrition. One of the survivors, R.D. Robb, a promising young cadet, on his first voyage, later became one of the very few Ben Line officers to achieve an Extra Master's Certificate, and was appointed an assistant marine superintendent.

Another individual's appalling ordeal ended happily. Poon Lim, a young Chinese steward, was the sole survivor of the crew of *Benlomond* IV, commanded by Captain J. Maul,[25] which was torpedoed in November 1942 750 miles east of the River Amazon. How Poon Lim contrived to stay alive and sane, alone on a life raft for 133 days before being rescued, has become the subject of a whole book and numerous other accounts in a score of languages.[26] His physical and mental resilience were such that after only a fortnight in hospital in Brazil he was fit enough to return to UK where King George VI personally awarded him the British Empire Medal 'for exceptional

25 Captain Maul's son, John, went to sea with the Ben Line but had to come ashore after being attacked by poliomyelitis. He joined Head Office in 1950 and became one of the longest-serving members of staff, retiring as manager of the Ben Line Crew Department at the end of 1991.
26 Ruthanne Lum McCunn, *Sole Survivor*, San Francisco, 1985, which was condensed, with new illustrations, in *Reader's Digest*, March, 1986. See also *The Ben Line: The Story of a Merchant Fleet at War 1939-1945*, Edinburgh, 1946 and *Ben Bulletin*, no.33, April 1987, pp.18-19.

courage, fortitude and resource'. Eventually he became a US citizen and tried to join the US Navy, but was declared physically unfit because of flat feet. He married in 1952, brought up four children and, forty years after his long, successful fight against extinction, retired in 1983 as chief steward in United States Lines.

2

Life at Head Office

1946 – circa 1950

It may be worth recording how I came to join the Ben Line, since chance – luck – played such an important part. My ambition before the war had been to try to enter the Diplomatic Service. Towards the end of 1945, while still in the Army, I sat a Civil Service written examination held in Trieste for candidates from the forces serving in Italy and Austria. This was followed by a weekend of assessment at a country house in England and appearance before a final Selection Board at Burlington House in London, after which I was informed that I was classed as a 'reserve'. Meanwhile the President of my Cambridge College, Sir Kenneth Pickthorn, had been asked by his fellow MP and friend Sir Douglas Thomson to recommend a likely young graduate to enter the family shipping business. The Ben Line selection procedure was neither so protracted nor so painstaking as that of the Civil Service. Early one morning, while Sir Douglas was still in his shirtsleeves, I was interviewed by him and his partner James Grieve at the house of Constance, Lady Thomson in Ennismore Gardens, which her son used as a base when attending Parliament. After about half an hour of question and answer on both sides they offered me a post as a shipping clerk in Edinburgh, starting forthwith, working five and a half days a week with two weeks' annual holiday. Admittedly they were not taking much of a risk; there was no security of tenure, no clear indication of promotion, nobody in those days dreamed of offering – or inquiring about – a pension, and the salary was only £400. This was considerably less than the lieutenant-colonel's pay I had been receiving, but I still had over £1,000 saved from my six years as a soldier. I asked for a few hours to consider this proposition and then sent a telegram saying I would start on the following Monday. A few weeks later the Foreign Office informed me that I had been upgraded from 'reserve' and they could offer me a job immediately. By that time it was too late: I had made a decision which gave me no cause for regret and much to be thankful for.

The Ben Line Office had moved from Leith in July 1943 to 10 North Saint David Street, next door to the Edinburgh Stock Exchange in the centre of the city. The move was carried out in the course of a day by the office staff: one or two able-bodied men in reserved occupations, the rest young women or men too old or infirm to be otherwise employed, about a dozen in all. There were no rare or valuable pieces of office furniture, few pictures or other artefacts, and the chairman and senior partner Edward Thomson (variously known as 'The Major', or more usually 'Mr Ted') saw to it that a great deal of accumulated paper was destroyed. He had small appreciation of a future historian's needs, but fortunately the leather-spined books, each devoted to a separate ship, showing her expenditure and earnings voyage by voyage, did survive intact from the 1840s onwards, to form the backbone of George Blake's history.

The office at 10 North Saint David Street was a substantial Victorian stone-faced building with a narrow frontage, on four floors and a basement, connected by a central stairway and an unreliable lift. On the ground floor, to the right, was the General Office in which Charles Watson, the cashier, occupied a glass-partitioned cubby-hole in the furthest corner. The opposite corner, looking on to the street, was likewise partitioned off for one of the company's major assets, the charmingly soft-spoken widow[1] who operated the telephone exchange. Most of the rest of the space was taken up by a large table from which mail was sorted out and dispatched by an elderly retainer,[2] who smoked a foul pipe and was more conversant with the works of Sir Walter Scott and James Hogg than with the shipping business. He was assisted by two cadets, when they were not engaged on their other duties as office boys, a clerk who was hard of hearing,[3] and the office chauffeur[4] who had trouble with his eyesight, being permitted to drive only when nobody else was available.

1 Mrs Mary E. McAnsh.
2 D.D. Wilson
3 Atholl Forbes.
4 William Jamieson.

Still on the ground floor a passage led from the front door to the office of the marine superintendent, Captain J. P. Drummond, fortunate to have survived numerous wartime adventures and extremely unlucky not to have been decorated for gallantry. His office adjoined the crew department which for some time consisted solely of a pretty, shy, very efficient young woman[5] who had been with the company in Leith when the office hours were 8.30 a.m. to 6 p.m. (8.30 a.m. to 1 p.m. on Saturdays) with half an hour for lunch. She says she never had any trouble from seamen or their dependants, but in 1947 it was deemed more appropriate to recruit a man to cope with potentially rough seafarers. Alan Dodds became manager of the crew department and in due course his lady predecessor became the wife of Captain W.O. Atkinson, of whom more later.

On the first floor one front room was occupied by the engineer superintendent, Major A.C. Hill. The rest of the frontage was taken up by the board room. No board meetings ever took place there. All decisions were made in the room shared by Mr Ted and Sir Douglas on the floor above. Off this holy of holies led another room from which J.M. (Ian) Miller, no relation of the millowners in Russia, was primarily responsible for running the homeward berth. He was assisted by a clerk[6] who wrote up the homeward manifest ledgers in beautifully legible handwriting and in his spare time took leading parts in amateur light opera productions. A back room was shared by two hard-worked secretaries,[7] one for the two senior partners and one for Ian Miller.

The top floor was largely occupied by the accounts department headed by James Grieve, who had worked his way up in the company and had become a partner in 1943. As assistants there were two recently demobilised officers: Norman Galbraith, ex-Royal Navy, the youngest son of Sir Douglas Thomson's fellow MP, Commander Galbraith (later 1st Lord Strathclyde), and Micky Mathers, an Old Merchistonian like James Grieve, who had recently joined after serving in the Indian Army. So I was not the only one to be recruited 'on the old-boy net'. The rest of the department were female: two clerkesses and a secretary. The younger clerkess

5 Margaret Innes (Mrs Atkinson)
6 R.W. Sharp.
7 Miss Nancy Yule (Mrs Gracie), Miss Margaret Imrie.

possessed a magnificent bosom, usually displayed to advantage in a close-fitting jersey. It was confidently predicted that she would ensnare her bachelor boss, who was already well past his first youth, – but he escaped, to marry some years later a lady[8] who shared many of his enthusiasms, including old Bentleys and the Ben Line.

In the basement lived a small, aged caretaker, and his wife[9] who did the office cleaning. He had at one time played football for Heart of Midlothian, but had long since exchanged his boots for carpet slippers, which he appeared to wear at all times, whether in the building or outside. At the end of the day's work, cloth-capped and carpet-slippered, he would potter up the street with a large envelope marked 'EXPRESS' containing outgoing mail on the first incongruous stage of its journey.

When I started in November 1946 there were four partners: Mr Ted, Sir Douglas, James Grieve and Alec Mitchell, one of the Mitchells of Alloa, who was a substantial Ben Line shareholder. He and his secretary occupied a room on the top floor where he devoted himself to his private affairs and took no part in the shipping business. Excluding these two, but including the two cadets, who were at this time employed for a year or eighteen months as office boys before being sent to sea, the total Ben Line staff was twenty-two. One attribute was shared by all of them – the old stagers, the infirm, those few who were fit but had been in reserved occupations with the company during the war, male and female – all took an immense pride in the company, and I soon discovered that the seagoing staff were similarly imbued. This quite remarkable company spirit was fostered both consciously and unconsciously by the two senior partners, Mr Ted and Sir Douglas, who were also at this time the only directors of The Ben Line Steamers Limited of which James Grieve served as company secretary.

In 1947 the Ben Line board of directors was increased to three by the appointment of Andy Hill, the engineer superintendent, who had joined the company after the First World War, during which he had been awarded the Military Cross for gallantry as a tank officer.[10] Tall, slightly stooping, cleanshaven and ruddy, usually dressed in

8 Miss Nina Rae.
9 Mr & Mrs Kennoway.
10 Not recorded in Blake, *op. cit.*

a brown tweed suit, with sparse fair hair, he was quietly spoken and well-mannered. Meticulously honest and conscientious, a good judge of the technical abilities and characters of the fleet's engineer officers, he was regarded by them with a mixture of awe because of his seniority, and amusement because of his straitlaced frugality.

Verses written in the thirties by a radio operator, who had ample experience of listening to ill tidings, and maybe of transmitting some, offer an insight into the tribulations which might beset the Superintendent Engineer during a night of bad dreams in which he is rung up by the Marine Superintendent, Captain J. H. Cole.[11]

> 'Is that you Hill?' said Captain Cole,
> 'I fear we're in a nasty hole,
> *Bencruachan* lost her tail-end shaft
> The crew's just landed on a raft.
> *Benvrackie*'s six weeks overdue,
> The 'fridge is bust on *Benvenue*.
> *Benmacdhui*'s gone ashore,
> *Benreoch*'s on fire in No.4.
> *Benavon* lost her bronze propeller,
> Made Walvis Bay on the mate's umbrella,
> What's more, *Benvorlich* lost an anchor,
> And the Chief's in jail for playing Banker.
> *Benledi* rammed and sank *Bengloe*.
> *Benrinnes* has bust her dynamo,
> *Benarty*'s bunkers are on fire,
> *Bendoran*'s boilers tied with wire.
> I have their store lists in my hand,
> They stretch from Leith to Newfoundland,
> So just before you go to bed
> You'd better phone and tell old Ted.'
> And now you know why poor old Hill
> Scrutinises every bill.

The author of the verses, George Godfrey, was killed in *Benalbanach* I when she was sunk in 1943.

11 Captain Cole, holder of the Distinguished Service Cross, Lloyds Silver Medal for meritorious service and the Bronze Medal of the Royal Humane Society, was Marine Superintendent from 1928 until his death in 1942. Some of his exploits are described in George Blake, *op.cit*. His son Harry joined Wm Thomson & Co. in 1951, succeeded Charles Watson as cashier in 1965 and retired in March 1992

Benan *(1875-88), from a painting by Captain A. Cromarty in Head Office.*

Bencleuch II *(1875-98), from a painting by Captain A. Cromarty in Head Office.*

ABOVE, LEFT *William Thomson I (1806-89), oil painting by Hugh Collins,
1884, in Head Office* ABOVE, RIGHT *Alexander Thomson (1795-1880)*
BELOW, LEFT *James Wishart Thomson (1841-1907)* BELOW, RIGHT
William Thomson II (1839-1911).

Benledi I *(1871-87): builder's drawing of the first steamship.*

Moscow II *(1891-1916) at Reval.*

ABOVE, LEFT *William Thomson III (1869-1941)* ABOVE, RIGHT *Sir James Wishart Thomson, KBE (1871-1929)* BELOW, LEFT *E. G. Thomson, MC, DL ('Mr Ted') (1889-1976)* BELOW, RIGHT *Captain J. H. Cole, DSC, marine superintendent 1928-42.*

Benavon I (1905-30), loading and discharging in Japan, 1908.

Detail from advertisement in The Handy Shopping Guide, *1 January 1910.*

Benvorlich I (*1896-1915*) *being torpedoed by U28, after the crew had abandoned ship, 1 August 1915.*

Benlawers III (*1930-40*), *typical of the ships built between the two World Wars.*

Benlawers IV *(1944-68), the first turbine ship, armed and in war paint.*

Merchant Aircraft Carrier (MAC ship) Empire Macalpine, *managed 1943-46.*

ABOVE, LEFT *Sir Douglas Thomson, Bt (1905-72)*
ABOVE, RIGHT A. C. Hill, MC, *chief engineer superintendent 1930-64, director 1947-68*
BELOW, LEFT *Captain J. P. Drummond, marine superintendent 1942-51*
BELOW, RIGHT *J. M. Miller, partner 1947-64.*

I expect that this imaginative tale of woe reached Andy Hill. I hope so, because he had a sense of humour. He could tell a good story too, after which he would applaud himself with heaving shoulders and a repeated hissing titter, which was the nearest he got to a laugh. He was a remote relation of the Thomson family through, I think, Barbara Cunningham (Hill's second name was Cunningham) who married James Wishart Thomson (1841-1907). Hill was a bachelor and lived for many years with his mother in an Edinburgh hotel. Unlike most of the male staff he did not smoke, and he drank only sparingly. At Christmas time he would tour the office dispensing boxes of cigars and bottles of spirits presented to him by grateful, or hopeful, suppliers and contractors. He retired as superintendent in 1964 after which he took little part in the business, though he remained on the Board until the end of 1968. I went to see him shortly before he died in his eighties and we talked of the things he had helped to accomplish for the Ben Line, since he exercised a considerable influence on the development of the fleet. Only after his death did I discover something about his inconspicuous acts of charity, including the provision of £12,500 to enable the Church of Scotland to set up an eventide home in Edinburgh, and the establishment of a trust with the aim of training young Hong Kong Chinese in marine engineering.

The office stood on the west corner of the T junction where York Place becomes Queen Street. The slope of North Saint David Street lay on the carters' uphill route with laden waggons from the Port of Leith. This slope was specially laid with two smooth granite tracks for the waggon wheels, between which slightly raised, transverse granite setts gave the horses' hooves a purchase. After a short rest in York Place the carters would urge their teams – two, or even three, harnessed in tandem – round the corner at a trot with a great clatter, ready to apply the brakes if they failed to surmount the hill, which sometimes happened.

There were very few cars in Edinburgh and I could not possibly afford one. You could travel a fair distance by tram for a penny, but I concluded that there were distinct advantages in being housed within walking distance. This I continued to do for some years, first by taking a small room in a boarding house at 10 India Street run by a naval officer's half-French, half-Irish widow from whose grimy kitchen delicious breakfasts and dinners were carried up to the communal dining-room by a little daily girl. For my room, meals and use of the communal sitting room I paid £3 per week. Later I moved to 66 Great King Street, where for an extra ten shillings I had my own large sitting-room and separate bedroom. After I was married in 1948 we lived in a ground-floor flat at 21 Drummond Place, which was a pleasant seven-minute walk through the gardens of Drummond Place and up Dublin Street to the office.

I spent my first few weeks with the cashier, Charles Watson, learning the rudiments of book-keeping and how to handle cash. We had to account for what appeared to me alarmingly large sums, particularly since two ships managed for the Government were at that time sold off to new owners. *Empire Macalpine* and *Empire Mackendrick*, MAC ships or merchant aircraft carriers, were built on the north side of the Forth at Burntisland. The original idea of this class of ship and its design were shared by Sir Douglas Thomson at the Ministry of War Transport, Commander Brewer of the Trade Division of the Admiralty and Sir Amos Ayre, Chairman of the Burntisland Shipbuilding Co. Ltd. *Empire Macalpine* was the first to be built and proved successful in protecting North Atlantic convoys, equipped with four Swordfish aircraft armed with depth charges, whose intrepid pilots could take off and, with luck, land again on a deck which measured only 417 feet in length and 57 feet in breadth. Some vessels of this type were subsequently built to carry oil, but the two MACs managed by Wm Thomson usually sailed westbound in ballast and returned full of grain. Ships with a similar wartime role, though larger and faster, were subsequently built in the United States and two such 'Woolworth' aircraft carriers, converted already to peacetime merchant ships, became valuable units of the Ben Line Fleet.[12]

From Charles Watson I learned that in balancing the books at the end of each day it was far more difficult to trace the errant penny than the apparent discrepancy of several thousand pounds which could usually be traced to one or more errors in my arithmetic.

Charles Watson had been with the company since boyhood, apart from a break for service with the Royal Navy in the First World War.

12 *Bardic* (*Bennevis* III 1957-73); *Gallic* (*Benrinnes* IV 1957-73).

An extremely kind, generous man, and a practising Christian, he was the unofficial staff manager to whom men and women turned for advice and help. We lunched together most days in Crawford's basement coffee shop very adequately for 1/6d.

To add variety to office routine Sir Douglas employed me as a general factotum. One of my first outside jobs was to go by train to Middlesbrough in order to bring back to Edinburgh the office car, an old and unreliable Jaguar which Sir Douglas with his wife drove down to join *Bencruachan* for their passage to Antwerp. I was allowed briefly on board to admire this new pride of the fleet commanded by Captain Eyton-Jones and then started back on a snowy afternoon. It was a somewhat fraught journey during which I had to put on the spare wheel because of a puncture, the door handle broke in my hands and the windscreen wipers decided to cease functioning. I ran out of petrol a few yards from a garage and the helpful garage owner, who thought it would be easier to tow me to the pump, succeeded in pulling off the bumper. This was not, I felt, a very auspicious beginning to a career in shipping. Other tasks were more straightforward. One day Sir Douglas handed me a dead chicken and told me to take it to the Royal Dick Veterinary College. On the label round its neck his wife had written: 'This fowl looked poorly so I wrung its neck. Can you please tell me what it died of.' He invited me to spend a weekend at his large house, Holylee, near Walkerburn, mainly, I suppose, to make sure that I did not eat peas off my knife, but I was able to make myself useful by plaiting the manes and tails of his wife's and daughters' hunters. Later I acted as groom when his eldest daughter ran in her first point-to-point. There followed regular invitations to shoot pheasants and grouse. By foregoing a pint or two of beer – in itself a luxury rarer than I would have wished – I could still afford a few cartridges.

Air-conditioning had just begun to appear in the Far East. Offices, if they were cooled at all, relied on long-bladed, slowly-rotating electric fans in the high ceilings, but in some staff houses those occupants who felt that they could afford the luxury equipped their principal bedroom with a noisy, rectangular box. Sir Douglas brought back one of these machines from Singapore and told me to get it installed in a window of the senior partners' office on the second floor of 10 North Saint David Street. Its manufacturers,

Electrolux, had an Edinburgh branch, so I asked them to send an engineer. Having unpacked and walked round it with a professional eye, he observed: 'Man, I reckon that's an air conditioner.' The Edinburgh climate was reason enough why he should be unfamiliar with this particular product of his firm. It did extract some of the cigarette smoke from the senior partners' office, but it also produced icicles that dropped off into the street to the danger of passers-by, and was soon shut down.

The same window was the scene of another experiment. Concerned by the quantity of crockery broken on board, Sir Douglas ordered samples of a new range of unbreakable plates, cups, saucers and dishes. These he dropped, one by one, out of the window and they all smashed on the pavement.

After doing my stint in the cashier's cubby-hole I was sent upstairs to Ian Miller's office where I spent a lot of time encoding and decoding cables and radio messages. Like other ex-servicemen, I had had a good deal to do with codes of various kinds, used to deprive the enemy of information. The Ben Line fleet and the company's agents used the Lombard Code, not to preserve secrecy but to save expense. Lombard consisted of sequential permutations of five letter groups. These were arranged in chapters, or sections, dealing with different aspects of commercial shipping business. There were spare groups against which the users could place any phrase not occurring in the printed work, which was the size of a large dictionary. I perceived that permutations beginning with 'x', 'y' and 'z' with the fourth letter 'q' remained entirely unused and could form the basis of a handy Ben Line Private Code to be employed in conjunction with Lombard. In my spare time I extended the permutations – a purely alphabetical process – and arranged much-used phrases against them in some logical order. The Private Code was printed and distributed about the end of 1947. Henceforward an agent could report 'Bencruachan (or any other ship in the fleet) arrived and expected to sail on...' as a single five-letter group, while a crew member could receive 'Merry Christmas and a Happy New Year. Love from all at home', that text costing one shilling, via Portishead Radio, which would have cost thirteen shillings (including the full stop) if transmitted in clear language. I was gratified by the success of my first, anonymous, printed product, but the proprietor of Lombard, a

Mr Quick, who visited us as one of his more important customers, was not best pleased on being shown this modest display of independent enterprise, which he regarded as poaching on his preserves. However I knew, and he realised, that there was no infringement of copyright. We continued to be purchasers and users of Lombard for many years, and the Ben Line Private Code went into a second revised edition in 1961.

Encoded incoming messages were transcribed in the lefthand column of the company's own face sheet with the decoded translation written in longhand against each group. This gave rise to some harmless fun. I devised a message purporting to come from Bangkok saying that there had been a military coup and the deposed leader had taken refuge on a Ben Line ship; what should the master do next? I presented this to my senior partners, but before surprise gave way to serious consternation I pointed out that it was April Fools' Day. Fortunately they had a sense of humour.

One disadvantage of using Lombard and the Private Code was that Cable and Wireless, and the General Post Office which handled all radio messages, could not be given discretion as to what was urgent and what was routine, so the two or three members of staff who were responsible for receiving messages outside office hours were often woken in the middle of the night merely to learn that a ship had arrived or sailed. I escaped this chore so long as I lived in 'digs' but when I got married and had my own telephone I was saddled with my share of it and remained so for some years after I became a partner. Sometimes of course the message was urgent, usually reporting trouble. If this was of a mechanical nature valuable hours might be saved by planning immediately how the crisis was to be dealt with.

In December 1951 the newspapers gave prominence for some days to the fate of the *Flying Enterprise* and her valiant master. The same storm which crippled that ship also badly damaged *Bennevis* outward bound fully loaded, including large amounts of explosive and a deck cargo of army vehicles. She was one of the first Bens to be equipped with a radio telephone. Her master, Captain R. L. Chalmers, rang me up several times on consecutive nights to report the extent of the damage. There was in fact little I or anyone else could do except listen, and try to give him some encouragement. For a time there were fears that the ship might be lost, but she managed to limp unaided into the shelter of Falmouth, where she had to lie well off the shore because of the explosives.

The official office hours were 9.30 a.m. to 5.30 p.m. with an hour for lunch, 9.30 a.m. to 1 p.m. on Saturdays, that is a 38½ hour working week, excluding one hour for lunch from Monday to Friday. I had long since recognised that there are 168 hours in a week and that it was easily endurable to extend the official hours. In practice I and many other Ben Line staff worked over 50 hours a week willingly, without complaint – and without overtime payments.

The day started shortly before 9 a.m. with the opening and sorting of incoming mail. In those days the partners expected to see every incoming letter and invoice, everything except crew allotment notes – dependants claiming a weekly, fortnightly or monthly sum, which were passed directly to the crew department. Masters reported at least once from each port of call and enclosed an abstract of their log; a daily batch of circulars was received from the Far Eastern Freight Conference; there were important letters from our London loading brokers, Killick Martin & Co. Ltd, one dealing with the outward berth and another covering the homeward trade. Galbraith Pembroke & Co. Ltd, who were our agents in London as well as being our sale and purchase, insurance and chartering brokers, reported on these separate markets daily by letter, mainly summarising the previous day's telephone conversations. These telephone conversations took place at set times: Killicks rang punctually at 11.45 a.m., Galbraiths reported on the charter market each afternoon at 4 p.m. Their sale and purchase calls were unpredictable: if a ship was being bought or sold there would be frequent calls reporting bid and counter-bid until the parties had arrived at a settlement – or broken off negotiations. Vernon Fullforth, the director in charge of Galbraith's sale and purchase department, was a virtuoso about whom more later.

Opening and reading all the mail gave one a good overview of the business, and the partners' practice of gathering to read the mail and swap comments was a very useful exercise which continued right up until after I retired from the chairmanship.

Before the Second World War urgent mail for Hong Kong, China and Japan was sent via the Trans-Siberian Railway, with a second copy by sea. After the war airmail was gradually developed, but was considered unreliable, with some reason. When the Comet crashed off Elba in 1954 some charred fragments of our letters were returned to us by the GPO. For many years after the war outgoing mail to the Far East was prepared in quadruplicate – original by airmail, copy by surface mail, copy for the file and one on pink paper. All outgoing letters had a pink copy and these (except the most interesting ones of a confidential nature) were gathered together and circulated among the operational staff.

We did not adopt a five-day week until the seventies. Saturday morning was usually a busy time because many ships were scheduled to leave port. Sometimes a difficult decision had to be made between incurring expensive Sunday overtime, if dock labour was available, holding the ship until Monday morning, or sailing her and shutting out some cargo, which could antagonise valued customers. Sailors said that if a ship lay in port idle on a Sunday the owner would put nothing in the collection that day. This is most likely to have been apocryphal in so far as the Thomsons of my acquaintance were concerned, if only because their churchgoing was usually confined to baptisms, marriages and funerals. This did not preclude many deliberately unpublicised acts of generosity to help various organisations and individuals, particularly by Mr Ted.

When I joined, Mr Ted was still in his late fifties. He was an impressive figure, tall, erect, broad-chested, ruddy-cheeked, with a good crop of nearly white hair. In order to avoid the inconvenience of going to a barber, he insisted, to his wife's despair, on trimming this himself, none too expertly, with a razor. He appeared in the office regularly, but only on Tuesdays and Fridays, wearing a blue serge suit, white shirt and black tie, protected from the weather by a battered grey trilby and a mackintosh of some antiquity. Under his arm an old army mess tin contained his lunch, to be eaten at his desk, washed down with a cup of coffee which he brewed for himself. A newly joined trainee, who later became a director of the company,[13] recalls seeing this singular figure arrive and make for the lift. He thought he had better inquire what his business was. Mr Ted had a deep booming voice, quite out of character with his self-effacing nature. His response on this occasion was 'Who the hell

13 R. Thorman.

are you?' His enthusiasm for Scotland and Scotsmen prejudiced him against most of those unfortunate enough to be of other nationality. I sensed that, at first, I was somewhat suspect, having been born in England and educated there, but I did enjoy the redeeming feature of a Scottish surname. He proclaimed that anyone could join the Ben Line, except Old Etonians (Sir Douglas was one) – and black men. He might have added to his excluded categories anybody whom he regarded as cleverer than himself – and Germans. The scars of the First World War would not heal. So many of his contemporaries had perished; two of his younger brothers had been killed in action, both on the same day, and a third, Ronald, was badly gassed. He himself had been wounded and awarded the Military Cross for gallantry. In extreme old age, when he lay in delirium, his confused thoughts were preoccupied by anxiety for the safety of his teams of draught horses hauling the heavy artillery with which he served.

He was an extraordinary mixture of ultra-conservatism and ultra-nationalism on the one hand, and topical modernity on the other. He was rather proud of the fact that he had never flown in an aeroplane (and he never did), but he was an early television addict and one of the first to own a Mini Morris car, from which his massive form would disengage itself outside the office every Tuesday and Friday about ten o'clock. His wife Betty also drove the Mini and had a tendency to keep the choke out, so he connected it to the horn. The Mini was only the tip of the iceberg. A large outhouse at his home, Callands, near West Linton, contained his collection of vintage cars. Famous makes such as Alfa-Romeo, Aston Martin, Bentley, Bugatti, Delahaye, Hispano-Suiza and Rolls-Royce were kept in running order, and sometimes subjected to highly unorthodox modifications, with the help of a resident factotum, Jock Anderson, who had been his army batman. After the outbreak of the Second World War Lord Beaverbrook appealed for high-powered cars for the services. The RAF was presented by Mr Ted with an 8-litre Bentley, made about 1930, which had been owned by the Duke of Kent, who drove it on his honeymoon. After being used as a staff car in North Africa it was returned to him in almost perfect condition in 1946. Ten years later this and eighteen other cars from the collection were licensed so that they could travel on the public highway instead of being confined to the roads on the Callands estate, to take part in a rally organised by Mr Ted and James Grieve. A few weeks later the Suez Canal was closed by war and petrol rationing was introduced. He was showered with coupons for the nineteen cars which bore current licences. His partners – and other staff members – could well have used some additional petrol, but Mr Ted's sense of public duty prevented him from transferring any of this unexpected largesse. Eventually he sold his collection at auction and gave the entire proceeds to the Royal National Lifeboat Institution.

Interest in cars and in the promotion of Scottish achievement were combined in the help he gave to Ecurie Ecosse, a motor-racing concern based in Edinburgh which, with his financial support succeeded in winning the Le Mans Twenty-Four Hour Trophy.

Besides Callands he acquired the neighbouring estates of Castlecraig and Netherurd, but gave the mansion at Castlecraig to Glasgow City Council and rented the big house at Netherurd to the Girl Guides for half-a-crown a year, giving it to them outright some years later. There was a family connection with the Girl Guides because his brother Ronald (who became Lord Lieutenant for Peeblesshire and was knighted), married Patricia Guild, a Girl Guides Commissioner. Ronald never entered the family business but his only son, William IV, became Mr Ted's heir, and succeeded me as chairman in 1982.

In his benefactions Mr Ted sought to avoid publicity and never looked for any public recognition, though he did agree to become a Deputy Lieutenant for Peeblesshire and served for a time on the County Council.

The two senior partners were united in their aim of creating a bigger, better, more prosperous, and thoroughly independent Ben Line, but they by no means always saw eye to eye, mainly because they had different conceptions of how that aim was to be achieved. Sir Douglas's ambition was to vie with the most powerful of our competitors, particularly P & O and Alfred Holt & Co., whose numerous and faster cargo liners offered more frequent services with shorter passage times, which creamed off much of the high-paying cargo. Mr Ted on the other hand was quite prepared to abandon the liner berth and put vessels on the tramp market when he could see an attractive profit, and he was much interested in buying and selling second-hand ships. He felt that the company should concentrate on doing difficult things well: carrying very heavy or awkward pieces of cargo for example. In the matter of carrying explosives his and Sir Douglas's views happily coincided. Large quantities, both commercial and military, were moving from the UK to the Far East; our competitors were not specially interested, the freight was high and good discipline ensured that we never had any serious mishap.

Neither of the two seniors consulted their junior partners overmuch on strategic issues, though there was plenty of dialogue on day-to-day operational matters. James Grieve reported mainly to Mr Ted. I do not think James possessed any professional accountancy qualifications; Mr Ted was a chartered accountant and felt he could provide all the expertise required in that direction, and so far as James was concerned his chairman could do no wrong. As already mentioned, in addition to sharing Mr Ted's passion for old sports cars – particularly Bentleys – James was an angler, golfer and keen cricketer. Each summer he took his own cricket team, the 'Fireflies', on a Yorkshire tour. One could not accompany James down the street without encountering a crony connected with one or other of these sporting activities, but his prime interest was the Ben Line, and he worked as hard and conscientiously as anybody.

Ian Miller, admitted to the partnership in 1947, also worked extremely hard. He had spent his whole working life with the company. During the war years, while Sir Douglas was much preoccupied with his duties at the Ministry of War Transport and in the House of Commons, Ian had borne the brunt of the day-to-day operational duties in the office. Sensitive, ambitious, and full of nervous energy, he was now primarily responsible for the Homeward Trade from the Far East to Europe while Sir Douglas controlled the Outward Trade. Unfortunately the two did not get on well together. Even after Ian became a partner Sir Douglas addressed him by his surname, which was not unnaturally resented. I soon discovered that quite a lot of my time was spent in keeping the peace between them.

Any successful partnership needs a diversity of talents, and those talents usually bring some weaknesses with them. The grit in the oyster produces the pearl: some friction and irritation can be productive. This was a successful partnership because its members were united by pride in the Ben Line's past achievements and by determination to make the company prosper.

[34]

3

Development of the Fleet

1945 – 1970

The seven owned ships which survived the war did not represent a very promising foundation on which to rebuild the fleet. Four of them, *Bengloe* III (by then serving as a coal hulk at Taranto), *Benalder* IV (repaired after being torpedoed), *Benrinnes* II and *Benvannoch* III, were very elderly ladies, none built later than 1921, and all bought second-, third- or fourth-hand. Antiquated and slow, they were reaching the end of their useful lives, but with foreign owners hungry for tonnage it was possible to sell them all for further trading between January 1946 and December 1949. The other three survivors had been built for the Ben Line, all by Charles Connell. *Benreoch* I, already twenty-four years old, and *Benledi* IV, built in 1930, had quadruple expansion engines giving them a speed of 12 ½ knots. Only *Benlawers* IV, the first turbine ship built for the company, completed in 1944, was capable of 15 knots.

The owners were pleased with the performance and reliability of *Benlawers*'s turbines and this preference, against less efficient quadruple expansion and high maintenance costs of the diesels of those days, was maintained for many years. Two new ships both conceived in wartime were delivered in 1946. Connell produced the biggest vessel yet owned by the company: *Benvorlich* III, 12,120 dwt. She was built to a standard Government 'Empire' design, with substantial modifications made by the owners during her construction. Three months later, in June 1946, Joseph L. Thompson of Sunderland completed the marginally smaller but faster *Bencruachan* II. Like *Benlawers* IV, both were powered by two turbines, high pressure and low pressure, developing 7,500 shp which gave the former a speed of 15 knots and the latter, because of her finer lines, 16 ½ knots. *Benvorlich*'s first master, Captain Riddle, initially thought she was 'ower big and ower fast' but all three ships had long and very successful careers in the Far East trade.

In those days a ship's identity was still closely associated with her master who commanded her for many succeeding voyages. Thus *Benvorlich* III was commanded until his retirement by Captain W.F. Riddle, who had served with great distinction in command of a MAC ship during the war. He was an unlikely-looking seafarer. Out of uniform, in a neat tweed suit and bowler hat he might have been taken for a country solicitor. He was a keen bridge player – and a highly expert shipmaster. Captain W.E.R. Eyton-Jones, OBE[1] was also unusual; he was Welsh and proud of it, but his first loyalty was always to the Ben Line in which he took infinite pride. Wm Thomson & Co. never copied other companies in appointing a commodore. It was supposed that conferring such a title might give the recipient an unduly inflated idea of his own importance. However Eyton-Jones, and his successors, were allowed to be know informally as the senior master. He survived into his mid-eighties and regularly sent me, the young man he had first met in Middlesbrough in 1946, a Christmas card, reminding me that the Ben Line was the finest shipping company in the world.

Between May 1946 and October 1947 six[2] standard wartime ships were bought from the Government for about £150,000 apiece. All but one[3] had been managed by Wm Thomson & Co. since their delivery and, as it happened, all came from yards in the USA, though ships of similar design had also been built in the UK and Canada. No money had been spent on frills; their equipment and accommodation were very basic. All were powered by triple expansion engines, developing only 2,500 ihp in the earlier models, raised to 3,000 ihp in those built during the latter part of the war, giving them a service speed of between 10 and 11½ knots. They were good cargo carriers, with a capacity of something over 10,000 dwt and around 500,000 cft

1 Eyton-Jones was appointed to command the new *Bencruachan* II in 1946. He transferred to the new *Benreoch* II in 1952 and stayed with her till his retirement.

2 A seventh, *Benwyvis* II, ex-*Samsacola*, ex-*Silvercedar* was bought in 1949, and yet further standard, wartime-built vessels were subsequently acquired.

3 The exception was *Bennevis* II, managed by Turnbull Scott & Co. as *Ocean Gallant*. The others were *Benlomond* V, ex-*Ocean Valentine*; *Benarty* IV, ex-*Ammla/Samvard*; *Bendoran* III, ex-*Samdauntless*; *Benvrackie* IV, ex-*Samaffric*; and *Salmonier/Benmhor* V, ex-*Sammont*.

of space. Though they were not built to have long useful lives many, like the British 'pre-fab' houses, survived for longer than had been envisaged by their original designers. During the late forties and early fifties they were an important part of the Ben Line fleet. All were in due course sold off for further trading to other owners. One, *Benvrackie* IV, realised the top price ever paid for a ship of her class. She had been considerably improved by Wm Thomson & Co., but her sale in 1952 for £600,000 to Italian owners represented a very handsome profit, which was ploughed back to help pay for new ships. The last to go, *Bennevis* II, continued in the fleet until 1959. This ship had a varied career. In the early fifties Mr Ted, accompanied by his wife and his sister Norah, took her out to Australia, his only postwar journey to foreign parts, and in 1955 she was chartered to carry Government stores to Christmas Island, where the British nuclear experiment took place. On the Australian voyage *Bennevis* called at Singapore. Arthur Kinnear, newly appointed to head the Singapore office, met the ship and conducted the Thomsons to his recently acquired office car, an American-built Ford, of which he was extremely proud. Mr Ted disapproved: 'American isn't it? Get rid of it, and buy a British make.'

Mention has already been made of Mr Ted's predilection for doing difficult things well. He was attracted by the heavy lift ships of which several had been under construction in British yards for the Ministry of War Transport when the war ended. The first such ship, *Benalbanach* II, was purchased in may 1947 and three more were added between July 1951 and April 1956.[4] They were all turbine ships, though in the case of two, *Benwyvis* III and *Benarty* V, they were turbo-electric, the turbines being connected to electric motors which gave them a service speed of 14½ knots, *Benalbanach* II and *Benledi* V with two turbines developing 6,800 shp (shaft horsepower) were half a knot faster. All had derricks capable of lifting up to 120 tons.

These ships were well suited to their original purpose of carrying bulky equipment, landing craft, army tanks and vehicles, and during their time in the fleet they carried in addition a wide range of

4 *Benalbanach* II, ex-*Empire Athelstan*; *Benledi* V, ex-*Empire Admiral*, ex-*Peter Dal*; *Benwyvis* III, ex-*Empire Byng*, ex-*Peter Dal* II; *Benarty* V, ex-*Empire Wallace*.

heavy and awkward lifts including locomotives, railway carriages, launches, and large pieces of machinery.

Their weakness was the absence of tween decks. The company fitted them with collapsible steel and timber 'shelves' which could be erected at one end of each of their three enormous holds, but these provided a total of less than 50,000 cft. The problem of providing adequate ventilation, vitally important to prevent dangerous over-heating in a parcel of bulk copra, for example, was partially over-come by equipping them with patent 'Cargocaire' forced draught and extraction systems. Great logs from North Borneo weighing twenty tons or more might present no problems, but bales of rubber stowed beneath other generals could arrive so misshapen, stuck to each other and to the ship's stanchions, that much of the freight was eaten up by the cost of discharging them and meeting damage claims.

These shortcomings were remedied in the only heavy lift ship built for the fleet – *Benarty* VI, delivered in February 1963 from the Dundee yard of Caledon Shipbuilding and Engineering Co. Ltd. She was Mr Ted's pet lamb and he with Captain A.P. Paterson largely controlled her design. Captain Paterson recalls that, after a rough specification had been drawn up, Mr Ted asked Mr Parker, chair-man of the Dundee yard, to indicate a price, which he did. 'Too much – I'll give you a week to sharpen your pencil,' replied Mr Ted. They soon came to mutually acceptable terms and when he took delivery after the successful trial trip he produced from his pocket a rather crumpled cheque for the precise amount needed to complete the transaction. By this time considerable strides had been made in the reliability and efficiency of diesel engines, particularly by the Swiss firm Sulzer. *Benarty* was powered by a 6-cylinder Sulzer engine built under licence by David Rowan & Co. Ltd, Glasgow, develop-ing 9,000 bhp for a speed of 17½ knots. She was fitted with tween decks to make her suitable for general cargo and, at Mr Ted's request, her hatch covers and tank tops were specially strengthened for the carriage of Centurion army tanks. Her outstanding charac-teristic was a gigantic derrick, designed by the German firm of Stülcken, capable of lifting 180 tons. She continued in the fleet until sold to Singapore owners in May 1981.

Sir Douglas once wrote in response to an inquiry from the Secretary of the Far Eastern Freight Conference: 'Poaching cargo from Uncle Alfred is a sport for which there is no close season.' When this letter was circulated to the Member Lines of the Conference, the partners of Alfred Holt & Co. and the directors of their wholly-owned subsidiary, the Glen Line, did not think it particularly funny. Wm Thomson & Co. were equally keen to meet formidable competition from P & O. The question was what kind of ship should be built. That they should be turbine-engined was agreed without argument, but what should be their speed and carrying capacity? Every extra half knot added alarmingly to the fuel bill. The company owned only one ship capable of more than 15 knots.[5] Furthermore there was a deeply entrenched view that the most profitable condition for a ship was to be full of cargo and down to her marks for as much of her voyage as possible. A vessel which was much in excess of 11,000 dwt and 550,000 cft might well carry a lot of fresh air around the world. These were certainly the views of Andy Hill, the superintendent engineer and a director of the Ben Line, supported by Mr Ted. Sir Douglas would have liked to be more adventurous and in due course he got his way. In the meantime the specification was fixed at maximum 11,500 dwt, around 550,000 cft, with a service speed of 16 knots. Five such ships were delivered between February 1948 and December 1949 – *Benmacdhui* III, *Benvenue* IV, *Bencleuch* VI, *Benalder* V, all from Connell, with two turbines, 7,500 shp, by David Rowan & Co. Ltd, and *Benavon* III, from Joseph L. Thompson of Sunderland, powered by three turbines, high, intermediate and low pressure, by Parsons Marine Steam Turbine Co. Ltd of Wallsend, which developed only 6,800 shp but gave her the same speed as her near sisters. Their combined first costs represented an outlay of £2,584,908. *Benvenue* IV was the cheapest at £490,240 and *Benavon* III the most expensive at £562,663. All had very successful careers, though it was often wished that they had been bigger and faster. All survived until the container era; eventually three were sold for breaking up and two for further trading.

5 *Bencruachan* II.

A special feature of this Benmacdhui class was the provision of single-berth cabins for the crew, and for six passengers (though a second passenger could be comfortably accommodated on a settee, as I discovered when my wife and I travelled from London to Aden in *Benvenue* in the later fifties). The only exception was a double-berth cabin for two cadets, which had an interconnecting room that served as a study.

It was no coincidence that in December 1949 the Ben Line tweaked Uncle Alfred's nose by introducing a homeward service with Liverpool as first discharge port, thence Glasgow, Dublin, Le Havre and Antwerp. Simultaneously a monthly service from Japan was advertised, but had to be discontinued owing to lack of cargo, until it was re-inaugurated in August 1951.

Sir Douglas's expansionist, competitive aims received powerful support from his close friend, and former colleague at the Ministry of War Transport, Percy Rogers. Percy had joined Killick Martin & Co., Ben Line's London loading brokers, in 1920 while still in his teens. In 1936 he had been loaned to the Sea Transport Department of the Board of Trade and two years later was made its liaison officer with the Admiralty. During the war he became Director of Allocation of Tonnage in the Ministry of War Transport. Although appointed a partner of Killick Martin & Co. in 1940 it was only in 1948 that he was released, with a CBE. Portly, balding, with blue eyes and a heavy black moustache, later a grizzled Edwardian beard, he was immensely enthusiastic and energetic. He liked fast cars and smart restaurants, and was always delighted to entertain. He prided himself on knowing all the 'right people' who could be lobbied and persuaded to help solve every problem. His staff were driven hard, and they regarded him with a mixture of awe and affection. These sentiments – at any rate the former – were shared by his broker competitors, Escombe McGrath (P & O) and McGregor, Gow & Holland (Glen). His fierce loyalty to the Ben Line sometimes made his partners in Killick Martin a bit apprehensive, since a large part of their livelihood consisted of looking after the London interests of Elder Dempster, owned by Alfred Holt & Co., though there was no immediate conflict of interest since Elder Dempster concentrated on the trade with West Africa.

It took some time to persuade Wm Thomson & Co. to place orders for bigger, faster, purpose-built vessels, rather than relying on buying second-hand. In 1950 four[6] of the latter were acquired, all but one slow, standard wartime ships.

At length a single order was placed with Connell for a 17-knot turbine ship of over 12,000 tons dwt. *Benreoch* II was delivered in October 1952, costing £802,543. She was given some time to prove herself and then between March 1955 and July 1957 Connell delivered three near sisters which had six hatches instead of five, *Benvrackie* V, *Bendoran* IV, *Benlomond* VI. *Bendoran* was the first new ship in the fleet to cost over £1 million[7] and *Benlomond* cost £1,138,052. The usual practice was for Mr Ted, Sir Douglas and Sir Charles Connell to sit round a table on board the ship which had just been delivered and haggle over the price of the next one.

With these ships a revolutionary experiment was made. In 1955 *Benvrackie* V inaugurated the 'Star Service' out and home between London and Singapore. Each sailing was scheduled to spend a fortnight straddling two months in Singapore and was thus able to offer bills of lading dated in the month of arrival or the month of departure. This was particularly attractive to rubber shippers, who could choose which date gave them the better return, depending on the market. Because the ships stopped only at Aden for a few hours to bunker they offered the fastest passage time, twenty-two days, which gave them access to high-paying general cargo in both directions. They sailed with vacant space, but the profitability of the service finally disproved the old concept that a ship must ideally be full and down to her marks.

In terms of power these ships were not revolutionary, our competitors had excellent vessels capable of 17 knots or even a fraction more. So the next step was to design a ship which really could outpace them.

The building of *Benloyal* II was deliberately shrouded in secrecy. It was supposed that our competitors might wish to copy us, though initially this was far from the case. Alfred Holt & Co. and P & O with their large in-house staffs of ship designers were entirely

6 *Benvannoch* IV, ex-*Empire Tudor*, ex-*Grandyke*; *Benattow* I, ex-*Pegu*; *Benloyal* I, ex-*Empire Swordsman*, ex-*Granrock*; *Benrinnes* III, ex-*Ocean Volunteer*, ex-*Alcyone Union*.
7 *Benmhor* VI, ex-*Penrith Castle*, was bought in 1952 for £1¼ million.

assured that they knew what was best, and what was economically viable. When *Benloyal* II was delivered in January 1959 with a service speed of 20 knots, the first cargo liner of this speed ever to appear on the run between Europe and the Far East, they proclaimed that such a ship was economic lunacy. She could never justify her fuel bills at 75 to 85 tons of oil a day. Way back in 1882 Thomas Skinner & Co.'s *Stirling Castle* had averaged 18.41 knots on her trials and on her maiden voyage made the passage from Hangkow to the Royal Albert Dock London, in 29 days 22 hours, but she burned at least 150 tons of coal a day and needed 8 engineers and 52 firemen.[8] No wonder that she and her owners had short, though spectacular, lives. Since those days there had of course been great advances in the efficiency of steam propulsion, but, said her critics, there must be doubts as to whether *Benloyal* was sound from an engineering point of view. These doubts seemed to be confirmed when she shed a propeller blade outward bound on her maiden voyage. The shock was so violent that Chief Engineer J. Young thought at first she had broken her back. She limped into Singapore where she was fitted with *Benvrackie*'s spare propellor as *Benloyal* had none of her own. This makeshift enabled her to steam home at 10 knots. Thereafter every new Ben carried a spare, usually in a tweendeck aft, sacrificing around 3,000 cft of cargo space.

Benloyal's design was mainly the work of Connell's naval architect, Mr William A. Paterson. Her exceptional speed was achieved by a combination of very fine lines comparable with those of a naval destroyer, and two turbines built by David Rowan which developed 15,500 shp. At 550 feet overall she was over 40 feet longer than her immediate predecessors and presented a more graceful appearance than had been seen in the fleet since the days of the 'Leith Yachts'. To maintain stability she had to carry nearly 500 tons of permanent ballast in the form of concrete blocks,[9] and the forepart of the ship was so narrow that it had limited usefulness for the stowage of cargo. Nevertheless she had a highly successful career and was finally

8 David R. MacGregor, *The China Bird*, London 1986 edn., pp.128-9.
9 Other subsequent ships, developed from *Benloyal*, needed permanent ballast. Chunks of armour plate from warships broken up locally at Inverkeithing were efficient – and, unlike concrete, commanded a scrap value at the end of the ship's life.

sold for breaking up in 1978. *Benloyal* is important in the history of merchant shipping because she was the first of a new generation of high speed cargo liners, evolved not only by Wm Thomson & Co. but by their competitors in the Europe-Far East trade, who felt compelled to revise their early scepticism.

In 1960 Holt's ordered four 20-knot motor ships for their Glen Line. This Glenlyon class was delivered between 1962 and 1963. Though the rivalry was intense there were elements of mutual trust and magnanimity between them and us. Sir Douglas took the unprecedented step of inviting a Holt representative to attend the trials of *Benvalla* in September 1962. This was accepted, and Holt's reciprocated with an invitation to attend *Glenogle*'s trials which were to take place a few days later. There was then an exchange of correspondence between Sir Douglas and Sir Stewart MacTier, Holt's engineering director (and a fellow Old Etonian):

I am glad that you enjoyed your trip on *Benvalla* and Mr Hutton [Ben Line engineer superintendent] is looking forward to the trial trip of *Glenogle*. I am sure that neither of us can lose anything by having a look at each other's ship.

I wonder if you would think of swapping prices. The only condition that I would like to make is that none of my Partners convey to any outside person what your price was, nor would any of your co-Directors tell anyone outside what our price was.

You may not wish to exchange this information and it might embarrass you if I put it in this letter, but if you will do a swap then our figures are in the enclosed envelope.

The sealed enclosure read:

Our fixed price contract was £1,550,000 to which various subsequent 'good ideas' have probably added £75,000. This excludes wireless, radar, echo sounder, etc, but I doubt if all of this would amount to more than £20,000.

MacTier replied on 26 September:

Thank you for your letter of 22 September. We were very glad to have Mr Hutton with us on the second day of the Builders' Trials of the *Glenogle*, and I hope he felt that his time was well spent.

I showed your letter to John [Nicholson, Chairman of Holt's] and we are perfectly happy to swap prices as between your Benvalla and our Glenlyon class.

As we really do keep these matters pretty confidential, we would be grateful if you would restrict your circulation to your Senior Partner [Mr Ted].

On our side John and I only will see your price, and we shall not inform our London Colleagues [the Glen Line Board].

As far as the Glenlyon class is concerned, we bought the four sets of engines direct from Sulzers, Winterthur, and we contracted for several other items independent of the Builders. In the circumstances, the best thing I can do is to give you a consolidated average price for the four ships [two from Fairfield, two from Dutch yards]. This is likely to be £2.13 fixed price, and taking account of my estimate of extras and credits.

The substantial difference between our respective ships can be accounted for, at least in part, by two major items:-

1 The cost of the insulation and corresponding machinery to provide about 2,000 tons of 40 cubic feet of refrigerated space, which I imagine involves an investment of about £150,000 per ship.

2 The premium which we deliberately pay arising from the fact that we operate our ships both in respect of hull and cargo uninsured. This chiefly emerges in the form of a considerable amount of belt and braces treatment in the engine room, and in the fire-fighting facilities.

Sir Douglas answered by return of post: 'I shall only show your letter to my cousin.' He faithfully observed this undertaking and this correspondence came to light recently in a safe at Edinburgh Head Office. Sir Douglas continued:

We have always kept our prices quite confidential so I am just as glad that the information is confined to you and John. Actually when I think about it, if I were put into a witness box and examined about why I wanted to keep my prices private, I do not know that I should be able to think up a very good explanation. I had talked about the relative values to Charles Connell and his guess was very near the truth, although I shall not tell him that.

We are probably rather small to do complete self insurance but I have no doubt that it has paid you. You pay extra for belts and braces on which you get an investment allowance and we get no investment allowance on the premiums we pay to Lloyd's.

By casting his bread upon the waters Sir Douglas had allowed Cecil Hutton a good look at the Glenlyon class (which resulted in some useful modifications to *Benvalla*'s successors), had obtained the cost price of the four Glen ships in return for disclosing the price of *Benvalla*, and had assured himself that Ben were getting good value for money. He probably felt some satisfaction in passing on some potentially important information, which might further increase the price differential:

Mr Hutton much enjoyed his trip which he found most interesting and there is one place where we have both belt and braces and you have not. You only have one jacket cooler so I imagine that you have not suffered any breakdowns of this cooler in your other ships in the past. I think if the cooler stops, then your main engines practically stop too.

Bettina [Lady Thomson] says that she would love to see the furnishings in *Glenogle*. She does our passenger furnishings and she has hardly seen anyone else's passenger accommodation. The *Queen Mary* on which she has travelled is not an exact parallel.

The experience gained from *Benloyal* II was used in the design of three more 20-knotters, all built by Connell: *Bengloe* IV delivered in June 1961, *Benvalla* I, September 1962 and *Benarmin*, July 1963. Stability was improved by reducing the length of the centre castle and forecastle, and they had an increased deadweight capacity of around 13,000 tons compared with *Benloyal*'s 10,400 tons, though their cubic capacity was in fact slightly less than *Benloyal*'s.[10] *Bengloe* was engined with the same turbines as *Benloyal*'s but as already noted in the case of the heavy lift ship *Benarty* VI, the Sulzer-designed diesel engines were now considered to have the edge over turbines for efficiency and economy and these, built under licence by Fairfield and by Barclay Curle were installed respectively in *Benvalla* and *Benarmin*.

III

There were further evolutions in this late flowering of high-speed cargo liners. Three ships were built capable of 21 knots or over, about 750,000 cft and over 14,000 dwt, even longer and broader in the beam, though their depth was unchanged at 34 feet. Few ports could accommodate vessels drawing more than 32 feet and even at that draught a ship might be limited as to the amount of cargo she could bring alongside the wharf. The first, *Benledi* VI, was delivered in June 1965, followed by *Benwyvis* IV, December 1966

10 *Benloyal* 10,400 dwt, 656,174 cft; *Bengloe* IV 13,270 dwt, 632,780 cft; *Benvalla* I 12,545 dwt, 624,760 cft; *Benarmin* 12,475 dwt, 609,890 cft. These figures varied marginally over a ship's life owing to modifications. The above are taken from a copy of *Ben Line Ships Particulars*, amended up to November 1965.

and *Benalbanach* III, July 1967. They were all built by Connell and engined by Barclay Curle with 9-cylinder Sulzer diesels of 20,700 bhp. There were four holds forward of the engine room and accommodation, and only one aft. Numbers 3 and 4 holds had triple hatches which could be worked simultaneously, though not in London, where the dockers under their Communist unofficial leader Jack Dash preferred to take another step towards making themselves dispensible. Each of these ships became more sophisticated than her predecessor. Each also became more expensive, but that did not allow Connell to escape the disastrous decline of Clyde shipbuilding which by this time was well under way. Denny of Dumbarton had gone into liquidation in 1963, Harland and Wolff closed their Govan yard and Simons- Lobnitz shut down, followed next year by Blythswood and Hamilton. In the autumn of 1965 Fairfield, with a work force of over 3,000 and more than £30 million worth of orders called in the receiver. It was thought that salvation might lie in a grouping of yards and large-scale Government assistance through grants and loans, so by 1968 Connells had merged with John Brown, Fairfield, Stephen and Yarrow to form Upper Clyde Shipbuilders (UCS). This amalgamation proved short-lived and totally unsuccessful – UCS was wound up in 1971 – but meantime the last two 21-knot Bens, which had been ordered before the merger, were delivered from the Scotstoun yard that had been the birthplace of so many of their predecessors.

These two ships, *Bencruachan* III (1968) and *Benlawers* V (1970), were the first Bens to be fitted with engine room control rooms. In other respects their design was strongly influenced by the first moves towards the most radical revolution in sea transport since steam superseded sail. In September 1965 Holt's Blue Funnel and Glen Lines together with P & O, our three major British competitors in the Far East trade, joined with two other powerful liner companies which did not have rights in the Far East, British & Commonwealth and Furness Withy, to form Overseas Containers Limited (OCL). We were not invited to join this consortium, whose plans were kept secret for as long as possible and certainly included clipping the Ben Line's increasingly powerful wings, maybe even wringing its neck.

The members of OCL, particularly P & O might have appreciated that in any case such an invitation, with its concomitant surrender of independence, would have been declined, since a year or so previously an unprecedented event had taken place. Sir Donald Anderson, chairman of P & O, announced that he and his managing director, Michael Thwaites, wished to visit us in Edinburgh. Such a thing had never happened before. The partners gave them lunch in our poky diningroom, which did not compare favourably with the splendour of theirs at 122 Leadenhall Street, and we waited to hear what they wished to talk about. Sir Donald said that P & O and other British shipping companies, unspecified, were contemplating a major far-reaching development, unspecified, which might be to Ben's advantage. He wanted to know whether we were interested in cooperating. When they had left we debated this extraordinary démarche. I and, I think, Ian Miller and Roderick MacLeod were in favour of finding out more about what they had in mind, but Mr Ted and Sir Douglas were united in deciding that any form of cooperation with P & O would compromise our independence and must be resisted. If this visit was indeed a veiled invitation to participate in a joint venture which was to crystallise in the formation of OCL, and if I had known the likely terms, I would have agreed with Mr Ted and Sir Douglas.

Shortly after the formation of OCL we received an invitation from Mr A.F. Hull, chairman of Ellerman Lines, to discuss the possibility of forming a rival consortium. There is nothing more powerful than a mutually recognised threat from an outside source, such as OCL, to spur hitherto prickly antagonists into amicable cooperation. Our previous relations with Ellerman had not been entirely harmonious. Ben and the Danish East Asiatic Company had fought an expensive and time-consuming freight war against them when they had attempted to enter the trade with Thailand. We now found that we had a number of common interests with them. More will be said about the formation of Associated Container Transportation Co. Ltd (ACT) in a later chapter. It was set up in 1966 and in the following year Ellerman approached us with a novel proposition. They wished to reduce the scale of their activities in the trade with India and Pakistan while we needed more ships to compensate for longer sailing times round the Cape of Good Hope after the Suez Canal was closed by war in October 1967. We also needed ships suitable for serving the smaller ports in Indonesia. Ellerman were anxious to avoid redundancies in their seafaring staff, while we needed officers and men to crew the five ships which we agreed to buy from them. By February 1968 those 14/14½-knot motor ships, complete with crews had been transferred from Ellerman to the Ben Line fleet.[11]

We now realised that at least some of our customers would wish to ship some of their cargo in containers, so the construction of *Bencruachan* III was interrupted while she was redesigned to make her more suitable for that purpose. We all had doubts as to whether containers would be ultimately successful. Sir Douglas felt pretty sure that they would not, but there was certainly a move by shippers towards presenting cargo for shipment on pallets and flats. The last and biggest of the 21-knot ships, *Benlawers* V was therefore designed to be as versatile and flexible as possible. Captain W.O. Atkinson's long experience as a cargo superintendent was called upon and he had a big say in her specification. She was 600 feet overall with a beam of 82 feet providing 1 million cft of space and 14,750 dwt. *Bencruachan* was powered by a Pametrada turbine but for *Benlawers* we reverted to a 9-cylinder Sulzer built by Barclay Curle.

Sir Douglas's achievements have been well summed up by one of his main business rivals, Sir John Nicholson:

During the 1930's, when I was training with Holts, Ben, though a founder member with unrestricted rights, played a negligible part in the Far Eastern [Freight] Conference trades for which their semi-tramp ships were ill suited. And when in 1935 Holts acquired and rebuilt Glen Line from the wreckage of Lord Kylsant's Royal Mail empire it seemed likely that Ben would be squeezed to extinction between P & O and Holts who dominated the UK trade. But by 1971 when I left the chair of Ocean (as Holts had then become) Ben were recognised as major participants throughout the Far East. None of their competitors doubted that the chief architect of this extraordinary metamorphosis was Douglas Thomson.

Immediately after World War II Ben set about building up a modern fleet and a dependable agency structure. And because rival fleets were in tatters or temporarily eliminated, and the trade was recovering fast, Ben were able to exploit their new found strength with early effect on the main routes and in subsidiary areas previously neglected by established operators. Their rapid expansion was aided by concentration on defined objectives and by Douglas's skill in handling Conference negotiations.

11 *Benedin*, ex-*City of Winnipeg*; *Benalligin*, ex-*City of Khartoum*; *Benkitlan*, ex-*City of Swansea*; *Benarkle*, ex-*City of Poona*; *Benratha*, ex-*City of Newcastle*.

He spoke little in general debate [at Owners' Meetings of the Far Eastern Freight Conference] but his character and good sense always commanded respect. So having a clear view of his own needs and a shrewd perception of others' strength and weakness he usually got his own way by stubborn determination allied with natural and appealing charm which brought him many friends. And as they advanced Ben's standing was strengthened by the aura of his personality and the impact of his sudden shafts of originality. I never knew him intimately but though we were often jealous business rivals I shall always retain warm affection and much admiration for this remarkable man who was almost the last in a long and honourable tradition of British shipowners prepared to risk their private fortunes in a hazardous business to the great benefit of their fellow citizens.[12]

The point about putting a private fortune at risk was fair enough in respect of Sir Douglas, since a large part of it was tied up in Ben Line shares. Otherwise he was not a particularly wealthy man. During the Second World War he had bought a country house and estate in Peeblesshire, at the bottom of the market, and was never happier than when working on his farm. 'Why is it', once asked an observant oriental millionaire, 'that, as soon as you British can afford it, you go into the wilds of the country and play at being peasants?' He did have other irons in the fire besides the Ben Line, and some of these had to do with ships. In 1947 in collaboration with cousins in Newfoundland, he set up the Salmonier Shipping Co. Ltd at St John's which bought *Sammont*, one of the US standard ships, which Wm Thomson & Co. had managed since 1943 and continued to manage until she was profitably sold in 1951. She traded for a time on the tramp market as *Salmonier* and was then transferred to the Ben Line berth as *Benmhor* V. His next venture was less successful. In 1961 a syndicate was formed to own *Benlarig* III, ex-*Javanese Prince*. She turned out to be the unluckiest ship in the fleet, and as the owner of 5/64ths (acquired with money borrowed cheaply from Wm Thomson & Co.) I was only too well aware of the financial worries she caused until we sold her for breaking up in 1969. Meantime Sir Douglas had formed a fresh syndicate, which included the Connell family, to own *Bendearg*, a big new ship, far less sophisticated than the Benloyal class and one knot slower, but with a capacity of over 800,000 cft and over 16,000 dwt. She came into

12 Letter and memorandum dated 9 March 1983 from Sir John Nicholson, Bt, KBE, CIE, to the author.

service in June 1964 and was so successful that an improved version, *Benstac*, also built by Connell with Sulzer engines by Barclay Curle, speed 19 knots,[13] was delivered in 1968.

In that year Sir Douglas became seriously ill. As befitted a former Oxford rowing Blue, he fought on doggedly and regularly came into the office, but was clearly unwell and not really able to make decisions. So, although I did not become chairman until he retired in October 1970, I became the chief executive over two years earlier.

13 Incorrectly stated as 22 knots in *Ben Line Fleet List and Short History*.

4

Launches, Ships' Names and Trial Trips

Like human beings a ship is conceived as the result of a shared experience, in this case between the owner and his advisers on the one hand and the builder, with many specialists' assistance, on the other. During their infancy, before they have been fitted out ready for life at sea, ships are given names at a ceremony permeated by superstition and well-wishing. Whatever that name may be, the ship acquires a feminine gender because the predominantly male humans most closely involved need her cooperation, and know that she needs their constant protection and support. During her life the ship develops a character of her own, capable of inspiring the deepest devotion, if she is lucky and happy, or exasperation, mistrust and positive dislike if she is not. Unless she is exceptionally preserved as a showpiece, like Drake's *Golden Hind* (which was not well enough looked after), Nelson's embalmed *Victory*, or *Cutty Sark* at Greenwich, a ship comes to the end of her useful life more quickly than most of the humans who have cosseted, cursed or loved her, and she moves out of their ken to be broken up, sold off – or, alas, lost in some disaster. Enough has already been said in the preceding chapters about why and how particular ships were conceived, so let us move on to the ritual of launching and naming.

The owners' choice of a lady sponsor might be the wife, sometimes the daughter, of one of the partners or directors, or the wife of someone closely involved with Ben Line business. Mrs Walter Godin, wife of the chairman of Killick Martin until he retired in 1951, launched *Benavon* III and when we were opening up a new trade with North Borneo in the fifties the privilege was bestowed upon the wife of A. L. P. F. Wallace of Candacraig, chairman of Wallace Brothers. My wife launched *Benlomond* VI, built by Connell in 1957, and *Benhope* II from Sunderland Shipbuilders Ltd in

1977. The builders of *Benavon* III were surprised not to receive a telegram from Wm Thomson & Co. in response to theirs announcing that the ship had been safely launched; the following morning however they received a polite acknowledgement – on a postcard.

On the Clyde the date and time of a launch was governed by the elements as well as by the ship's state of readiness. The tide must be high and preferably assisted by a following wind. Very high winds could cause an expensive postponement. The launching party, all dressed in 'Sunday best', consisted of senior staff of the shipyard and of the engine builder, the owners and their marine and engineering superintendents, the master who was to command the ship and his chief engineer, wives, children and one or two close friends. Latterly a busload of office staff came through from Edinburgh for the occasion and mingled with the craftsmen, who had worked on the ship and were now assembled on either side of the slipway, to the sound of the shipwrights' hammers knocking away the wooden chocks between the supporting cradle and the ship's hull. The front of the launching platform at the head of the slipway was only a foot or two from the ship's stem, towering high above. The sponsor was led on to the platform by the builder and given the beribboned bottle with which she was to perform the ceremony. There was then a pause. The shipwrights' hammers were still thwacking away. The atmosphere was tense, conversation muted, despite the builder's assumed nonchalance. Not every launch goes smoothly. Ships have been known to slip away prematurely, or refuse to budge. Bottles have been known not to smash at the first attempt so the neck, besides being attached to the ship, was also attached to a trusted member of the builder's staff who could quickly haul it in and hand it back for a second shot. At the wartime launch in Baltimore of a ship,[1] which was to be managed by Wm Thomson & Co., the sponsor's elastic gave way as she was about to throw the bottle and she was photographed with her knickers round her ankles. The superstitious might have regarded this as a bad omen, but the sponsor did not transmit her ill fortune to the ship, which became a very happy and lucky member of the Ben Line fleet.

At last the signal is given, the sponsor says in as loud a voice as

[1] *Ammla,* so named because she was sponsored by the American Marine Library Association, acquired in 1947 and renamed *Benarty* IV.

she can muster for the awesome occasion 'I name this ship *Ben-lomond*. God bless all who sail in her.' She hurls the bottle, it shatters, there is a pause and then, very slowly at first, the ship begins to move. Everyone cheers and waves, those on board wave back; hooters sound. She must not enter the water too fast for fear of damaging herself by hitting the opposite bank of the river, so her gathering speed is restrained by tons of heavy chain attached to the hull which uncoil with a thunderous roar in clouds of red brown rust.

The liquid in the launching bottle for Ben Line ships built by Charles Connell was cold tea. The owners stipulated that the bottle should contain whisky, more appropriate for a Scottish ship than the traditional champagne. However at Connell's yard the task of shrouding the bottle's nakedness in red, white and blue ribbon was entrusted to the youngest apprentice who had helped to build the ship, and it was an open secret that his elders and betters made sure that the contents were not wasted. Nevertheless I have been present at Connell launches where I caught a distinct whiff of the real stuff after the bottle had been smashed, so some Bens at least were launched with a judicious mixture of what the workforce brewed up in their billy-cans and what they most liked to consume in the pubs.

After the launch, while the ship was being nursed into her fitting-out berth by tugs, there was a short reception in the shipyard office at which her prosperity was toasted and the sponsor was presented with a memento by the builder. Later, before the ship sailed on her maiden voyage, the sponsor gave the ship a picture, clock or other adornment, bearing a commemorative plaque. At *Ben-lomond*'s launch my wife was given a diamond and pearl bracelet. Over twenty years later, after it had long lain unworn, it was 'popped' and provided her with most of the wherewithal to make a longed for trip to the interior of China.

Only three sailing ships received 'Ben' names: *Bencleuch* I (1853) was named after the highest peak in the Ochil Hills overlooking Alloa, which was both her birthplace, in the yard of J. Duncanson, and her port of registry. That name was handed on to the largest Thomson sailing ship, built by Steele of Greenock, in 1875. Her sister delivered in the same year by Steele's equally famous and longer lived competitor, Barclay Curle of Glasgow, was named

Benan, a variant of Ben Avon in the Grampian Mountains. Why that particular name was chosen is lost in the mists of time, but the reason for always merging the two words of the name of the mountain into one is not hard to understand: the ship's name could be transmitted by cable or radio message for half price.

The first steamer was named *Benledi* after the picturesque peak in the Trossachs, and thereafter all steamships, except those trading with the Baltic, were given 'Ben' names. Once a name had been adopted the tendency was to hand it on; as one ship left the fleet her name was given to the replacement. Thus up to 1982 no less than eight had been named *Benledi*, seven *Bencleuch, Benlomond, Benmohr* (or *Benmhor*)[2] and *Benvannoch*, six *Benalder, Benarty, Benvrackie*, and *Benwyvis*, five *Benalbanach, Bendoran, Benlawers, Benrinnes* and *Benvorlich*.

There were reasons, apart from sentimental attachment, for this continuity. In the first place the company did not have a free choice. To ensure a ship's individual identity each name had to be approved by the Registrar of Shipping and if that name was already carried by another ship it was not available. In the early 1900s when the Thomson fleet was already trading as the Ben Line, some of the more attractive names were being used by Watson Brothers of Glasgow who were managing and developing a rival Ben Line. Litigation between the two concerns seemed probable, but in August 1905 Watson Brothers undertook to abandon the title of The Ben Line Steamers Co. Ltd in return for the payment of £275 by Wm Thomson & Co.[3]

Long coveted names such as *Benloyal* and *Benhope* were held for many years by a trawler company. When we did at length secure *Benloyal* the laird on whose land the mountain stands recognised the connection by sending the ship each year a haunch of venison which had been stalked on its slopes.

Names had to be reasonably easily and unambiguously pronounceable by Asiatics, as well as by Sassenachs. The latter tended to render *Bencruachan* as *Ben-crew-ackan*, or *Ben-crooshen*, consonant with the once popular nostrum Kruschen Salts. It was also important to

2 Mr Ted changed the spelling for *Benmhor* V (1947) and subsequent ships on the grounds that this approximated more closely to the original Gaelic.
3 Letter from Watson Brothers, 4 August 1905.

ensure that a name did not mean something offensive or obscene if translated into Chinese, Japanese or some other oriental language. Despite diligent combing of the gazetteer the problem of satisfying all these requirements became progressively more acute. We cheated slightly with *Benvalla*, a fine and successful name adapted from Penvalla, the hill overlooking Broughton in Peeblesshire. We thought we had invented *Benveg* meaning 'Little Ben' for the coaster which traded between Singapore and Bangkok, but later discovered a hill of that name in Ross and Cromarty. Inevitably, perhaps, *Benveg* was known usually and affectionately as 'The Vegetable'. By 1968, when the number of Ben ships reached a peak of thirty-six, I was in a position to ordain that, in order to avoid argument and waste of time, the choice of names would be delegated to a committee of one – David Thomson – subject only to final approval or veto by me. Names new to the fleet were *Benalligin*, *Benarkle*, (popular because contemporary with the famous racehorse), *Benarmin*, *Bencairn*, *Bendearg*, *Benedin*, *Benhiant*, *Benkitlan*, *Bennachie*, *Benratha* and *Benstac*.

The first *Benlarig* (1881) was a sail-assisted steamer with a clipper bow which was sold to Japan when she was twenty-two years old, but her successor *Benlarig* II had gone missing with all hands in the Indian Ocean in 1917. Some felt it was an unlucky name, but it was argued that other lost ships had handed on their names to happy and prosperous successors, so the name was revived in 1961. However *Benlarig* III had an extraordinarily unfortunate career and her name was never used again. A wise owner respects sailors' superstitions – and may share them!

Connell, and other British shipbuilders of the period, were generally very over-optimistic about delivery dates. It was unusual for the contract between builder and owner to contain a penalty clause for late delivery which could be enforced in the case of demarcation disputes, go-slow tactics or outright strikes. The builder had to rely on supplies from a host of sub- contractors, who could find themselves beset with similar problems. A further tiresome impediment was the Clydesiders' extreme difficulty in distinguishing between *meum* and *tuum*. Anything removable – lightbulbs, lavatory rolls, towels, curtains, carpets – tended to disappear. The builder's inability to coordinate the work of all the different tradesmen so that they finished on time meant that joiners, plumbers and electricians would still be working on the ship when she was finally handed over. Before then the ship did a builder's trial, and if that proved successful the owner's trial was held as soon as possible thereafter.

Those attending the owner's trial sometimes slept on board the previous night, ready for an early start in the morning. Mr Ted was persuaded to do that, with Sir Douglas and me, in June 1961 on *Bengloe* IV, 20 knots, an improved version of the first 20-knotter, *Benloyal* II. *Bengloe* had spacious accommodation, including cabins for twelve passengers. She was the first to have a passengers' lounge complete with a bar decorated by a rather daring mural which featured an alluring mermaid.[4]

Mr Ted was allotted the master's large suite of bedroom and day room. At breakfast next morning he was asked how he had slept. He indicated his disapproval by answering: 'Well; but I spent some time calculating what all that space would make if it was filled with copra.'

The ship was usually berthed at Gourock whence she moved off at slow speed down the Firth of Clyde. The highlight of the day was the full speed and manoeuvring trials on the measured mile, indicated by white markers on the east coast of Arran. These had to be carried out between fixed times which were reserved in advance. After several runs she would cruise back up the Firth or round Arran, up the Kilbrennan Sound and so to her berth, where her Ben Line crew and stores were waiting. When she was safely berthed the builder's flag was hauled down to be replaced by the Ben Line houseflag and thereafter she became the owner's responsibility.

4 By 1978, when *Bengloe* was broken up, the artist, Sue Crawford, had achieved fame. She gladly accepted as a gift from the company this mural which was the first of her many commissions.

5

Life on Board

circa 1945 – *circa* 1970

In the fifties and sixties crews were large in comparison with later standards and averaged slightly over fifty men. Masters came from many walks of life. Some had joined the Ben Line as apprentices or cadets (the difference is explained below) and worked their way up. Others had joined as deck officers after serving with other companies. One[1] had been a soldier and an airman before going to sea, and another[2] had started life as a miner. It was possible to join the company as a deckboy at fifteen and by hard work, with some aptitude for learning, pass the successive examinations needed to obtain a master's ticket.[3] Some of the Ben Line's best masters 'came up through the hawse pipe' in this way. In the sixties and seventies that became more and more difficult as the Merchant Navy Training Board in its wisdom rendered the examinations increasingly theoretical, with the avowed object of making a master's ticket the equivalent of a university degree. What we needed was practical knowledge based on first-hand experience and the grit and strength of character required by the captain of a ship.

During and after the Second World War all ships carried a chief officer, who was second in command of the ship and had to hold a master's ticket so as to be able to take command, should the master become incapacitated. It was usual for the 1st officer also to hold a master's ticket. Besides supervising the work of the 1st, 2nd and 3rd officers, the chief officer was responsible for training the cadets, both in practical and book work, and he worked the deck crew

1 Captain E.D. Copeman.
2 Captain T. Sutherland.
3 Captains Copeman, J.M. Macleod who was chosen to command the dynamically positioned drillship *Ben Ocean Lancer* and A.M. Watters who became senior marine superintendent, among others, all 'came up through the hawse pipe'.

consisting of the carpenter, bosun, bosun's mate, six ratings (able seamen, ordinary seaman, junior ordinary seamen and deckboy) and four Chinese painters. In some ships the entire deck crew including the carpenter were Chinese.

In addition the chief officer was responsible for all life-saving appliances and for drawing up a fire-fighting scheme for the whole ship, which had to be coordinated with the fire-fighting drill for engine room personnel organised by the chief engineer. The medicine chest was likewise in his charge; he was responsible for treating any sick or injured, and for making an entry in the medicine chest log detailing the date, name of patient, nature of illness or injury, and the treatment given.

He was expected to be fully conversant with the cargo being handled and in the case of bulk liquids, such as latex or palm oil, he supervised the preparation of the tanks, the pumping in, and eventual discharge, and the recording of temperatures. He supervised the ship's fresh water supplies, which needed careful control to avoid waste. In order to conserve the ship's electricity generating capacity, which came under increasing pressure as more and more labour-saving machinery was introduced, he had to ensure that the chief steward opened the refrigerated stores once only each day. He supervised the stewarding of the ship with periodical checks on stock and cash, and was similarly responsible for the management of the ship's canteen. He had to take particular interest in the cleanliness and tidiness of the accommodation, alleyways and decks, which were inspected by the master and chief officer every Sunday morning when the ship was at sea. He kept the Factory Act Record Book up to date and assisted the master with his accounts and other paperwork. Before the introduction of calculators and decimalisation, when the Malay dollar stood at two shillings four and one eighth pence and the Hong Kong dollar one shilling three and three sixteenths, there were conversion tables and the rates did not change frequently, but the preparation of the 'Portage Bill', in which the master submitted his account of receipts and expenditure to the owners at the end of each voyage, was a time-consuming exercise.

The chief officer's signature was required on overtime statements and boat notes, though the latter might also be signed by the 1st officer. In the days of cargo liners boat notes, or mate's receipts, tendered in duplicate when the cargo was loaded, were proof that the goods were on board. The condition and tally of the goods had to be carefully noted and any clauses intended for insertion on the bill of lading were entered on the mate's receipt; one signed copy was then returned to the shipper and one was retained by the chief officer. A claused as opposed to a clean bill of lading might protect the carrier from a claim; it might also affect the value of the goods. Killick Martin displayed an unusual claused bill of lading in their office for '3 elephants, 1 in dispute, if on board to be delivered', but the origin and outcome of that disagreement are shrouded in mystery.

In recognition of his multifarious duties the chief officer did not stand a watch, unless one of the three deck officers was sick, or otherwise unavailable, and he was excused having a duty night on board when the ship was in port, though that did not mean that he enjoyed any more free time than the 1st, 2nd and 3rd officers, who did night duties on a rotational basis. Night duty ensured that at least one deck officer, probably in addition to the master, was on immediate call if weather or any other crisis should endanger the ship, her crew or her cargo.

The advent of containers and containerships in the early seventies revolutionised the roles of the chief officer and 1st officer. As a result of the size and power of the containerships navigational skills were even more vital, while stowage and care of cargo became the prime concern of shore-based staff. The diminishing number of cargo liners still carried four deck officers, but in the containerships and bulk carriers it was possible to cut these down to three, so the chief officer stood a watch and was supported by either a 1st or 2nd officer and a 2nd or 3rd officer.

Besides taking the 4 to 8 watch at sea the 1st officer's prime responsibility on a cargo liner was the stowage and good out-turn of cargo. On the eastbound voyage he usually joined the ship when the responsibility for loading had been largely met by the relief 1st officer in collaboration with shore staff, but on the homeward run his job was a hectic blend of science and art. Science because he had to know the properties and stowage factors (number of cubic feet occupied by one ton weight) of all the commodities to be loaded. Were they liable to spontaneous combustion or otherwise hazardous? Did they produce odours which could taint other cargo, or moisture which might damage parcels with different characteristics stowed in close proximity? His art was to plan the stowage in a way which would avoid such dangers, ensure the ship's stability and distribute cargo for the same destination between different hatches so that discharging could be completed in the shortest possible time. A plan which had been well thought out could be jeopardised by unexpected bookings or last-minute cancellations. As a last resort some cargo already loaded might have to be shifted to a new position, which cost money and increased the risk of damage. He practised 'art' in a more literal form by producing a master cargo plan of the whole ship showing each parcel of cargo, with marks and numbers, on coloured grounds, one colour for each port of discharge. This might be further complicated by parcels on so called 'optional bills of lading' for which the shipper paid extra in order to delay declaring where his cargo should be discharged. The cadets made and coloured additional copies working from the master plan and further copies were reproduced ashore.

The 2nd officer besides his watch-keeping duties was responsible for all navigational instruments, charts, navigational books and sounding machines, while the 3rd officer had the care of all signalling equipment and was responsible for the efficient operation, maintenance and recordings of the mechanical hold ventilation systems, which were progressively introduced during the sixties.

Each ship carried between two and four cadets depending on the available accommodation. Prior to about 1920 the company took on indentured apprentices,[4] whose parents paid the owners a premium to have the young man trained as a deck officer. During the years between the wars this practice was discontinued and the company employed cadets who paid no premium, but they had to supply their own mattress, bedding, soap, linen, crockery, cutlery, even lavatory paper. Their hours at sea, like seamen, were '4 on, 4 off' that is 84 hours a week, and they were paid no overtime. They did not receive any formal training, but were expected to pick up knowledge by experience. After the Second World War much more attention was given to cadet recruitment and training. They still had to provide their own uniforms, both cold weather and tropical, but

4 The last surviving apprentice, Captain J.D. Wilson, joined the Ben Line in September 1918, retired in 1966 and died on 13 March 1982, aged 79.

received Ben Line buttons and cap badges at the company's expense. The company also sponsored competitions and prizes for British branches of the Sea Cadet Corps, and offered a scholarship voyage on a Ben Line ship to prizewinning Singapore Sea Cadets.

The sponsorship of cadets on the engineering side was inaugurated in the late sixties, although most junior engineer entrants served an apprenticeship on shore with a marine engineering company and then went to sea as uncertificated officers. Engineer cadets were carefully selected and about twelve were recruited each year. They were sponsored by the company on a four-year course of which the first two were spent at a nautical college, either Leith, Glasgow, South Shields or Aberdeen. They spent their third year at sea in a Ben Line ship and went back to the same nautical college for the final year. Provided that they passed their examinations they were then employed as junior engineer officers.

The uncertificated junior ranks were 7th, 6th, 5th, 4th and 3rd engineers. In many cases the 3rd engineer was the backbone of the engine room, highly skilled with years of experience, but unwilling to sit for a 2nd engineer's ticket and assume additional responsibility. The 2nd engineer, the senior engine room watch-keeper, might already hold, or aspire to hold, a certificate of competency as first class engineer, or 'chief's ticket'. This was gained by a prescribed minimum period of service at sea followed by a Ministry of Transport examination. There were separate certificates for steamships and motorships. The company did its best to arrange for an officer to serve at sea on each type, so that those who wished to do so could qualify for both.

To complete the engineering complement there were one, sometimes two electricians, six, usually European, ratings (of whom the senior was the storekeeper, and the others retained the old title of donkeymen), two Chinese fitters and one Chinese painter.

The engineering staff saved a great deal of expenditure on shore labour by themselves carrying out much of the maintenance and repair work needed to cover statutory surveys of main and auxiliary machinery and makers' recommended overhauls. Work which could not be carried out during the voyage was done while the ship was in European waters, and relieving staff were supplemented with extra engineers for this purpose. The engineer superintendent and his assistants were responsible for planning and progressing a programme which had to be crammed into a limited time scale. This Ben Line system was one of the company's strong points and was probably more highly developed than in any other shipping company.

Some ships carried a Chinese laundryman who occupied a steamy space in the bowels of the ship. He had to keep the company's bed and table linen clean but could charge the crew for washing overalls, and officers' white tropical shirts and shorts.

One member of the crew without whom the ship could not sail, by law, was 'Sparks', the radio officer. A few British shipping companies employed their own, but the Ben Line always relied on hiring them through the Marconi Company, whose highly efficient office in Chelmsford seldom let us down. Though technically employed by Marconi, these officers tended to regard themselves as Ben Line men and returned to the same ship for voyage after voyage. They were an interesting breed, intelligent, skilled, often 'loners' by nature and inevitably very much their own masters. 'Sparks' had to keep his statutory individual watches day and night at set times which, of course, varied as the clock changed during a Far East voyage. On a long sea passage he was the link with the outside world, the purveyor of instructions from Head Office, information from agents, and news from home. These duties nevertheless gave him quite a lot of free time which some occupied by keeping the canteen accounts, in return for an honorarium from the company.

The canteen was managed by the chief steward and provided all on board with goods ranging from toothpaste, talc and boot polish to sweets, nicotine and beer. The chief steward also had charge of the ship's catering arrangements supported by a chief cook, 2nd cook and baker, 2nd steward (whose special role was to look after the master) and three stewards, who waited at table in the saloon reserved for officers, cadets and passengers, and kept the accommodation clean. The most junior in the catering department was the galley boy who cleaned the galley, fetched and carried stores, and spent a lot of time peeling potatoes until latterly mechanical peelers were installed.

We tried in successive ships to reduce the temperature in the galley, where heat from the cooking apparatus was compounded by tropical weather, but we never achieved an air-conditioned environment, and those who worked there seemed to take being roasted as a matter of course.

A British foreign-going ship of 1,000 tons gross or more could not sail without a certificated chief cook. For this reason we insisted that the chief steward should hold a chief cook's ticket so that the ship should not be delayed if the chief cook became a casualty. When in 1967 the Merchant Navy Training Board introduced the new rank of catering officer, the necessary qualifications were a chief cook's certificate and a St Andrew's or St John Ambulance medical certificate, so he was able to take over the care of sick or injured from the chief officer.

The owners well understood the importance of appearances in promoting efficiency and good discipline: 'Juniors in the catering department [that is all stewards other than the chief steward who wore a blue jacket] will wear white jackets when serving table.' 'It is expected that on all important occasions masters and officers will wear uniform. Entering and leaving port will be regarded as one of these occasions, particularly when passengers are being carried.'[5]

In practice all officers wore uniform on watch and at meal times. For cargowork the deck officers wore overalls which bore their rank on the epaulettes. Engineer officers on duty in the engine room wore white boiler-suits without epaulettes. Both deck and engineer officers wore blue serge trousers, and jackets with gold braid on the sleeves according to rank and 'gold' metal company buttons what did not need polishing, with a white shirt and black tie. Outward bound as the weather became warmer the master ordained when tropical kit would be worn, usually after reaching Port Said. This consisted of a white or khaki open-necked shirt with epaulettes, white or khaki shorts and knee-length stockings.

Deck and catering crew came mainly from the Edinburgh and Aberdeen areas. Orcadians and Shetlanders were excellent seamen, but many took a voyage off at harvest time. Engineers came from Glasgow and Dundee, also from the Tyne and Tees and Sunderland areas but otherwise there were few English until we bought some Ellerman ships in 1968 complete with mainly English officers and Indian ratings.

5 *The Ben Line Steamers Limited, Instructions for Sea Staff*, October 1952 edn., pp. 18 & 19.

Wang Kee, our shipchandler and stevedore in Hong Kong, also supplied most of our Chinese crew, many of whom served twenty or thirty years with us. The Chinese bosuns, chief stewards and No.1 firemen gathered together their own picked ratings, no doubt exacting 'squeeze' in return. Discipline among the Chinese was very good and they also got on well with their predominantly Scottish shipmates.

The Ellerman ships gave us our first experience of Indian ratings. More of these were required to do the same amount of work as their European or Chinese counterparts, and as most of them came from the south of India they found it more difficult to cope with winter weather in European waters.

The time eventually came in 1974 when we employed our first female officer, a fully qualified 2nd mate.[6] We were not front runners; many years previously Alfred Holt & Co. had boasted a formidable woman chief engineer. But part of a 2nd mate's duties is to supervise Muslim stevedores in the hold: what problems might that cause? When I went to London I often breakfasted on a ship then loading or discharging there. I and the master were walking round the deck of the recently joined officer's ship when I spotted a slim, longhaired figure in overalls and hard hat coming towards us. 'Is that our new lady officer?' 'No, sir, he's the junior cadet.' Muslim stevedores may have had similar difficulties in differentiating the sexes; at any rate our apprehensions about their reactions proved entirely groundless.

As ships' speeds increased and their itineraries were streamlined a Far East round voyage seldom exceeded five months, compared with six months or more before the Second World War and immediately after it. European crew were relieved shortly after arrival home in UK and a fresh crew took the ship round her discharging and loading ports in UK and on the Continent. Sometimes the British voyage crew were relieved at the ship's first Continental port of call; in such cases we chartered an aircraft to transport the relief crew and bring the voyage crew home. Chinese crew were relieved in Hong Kong, though some were happy to remain on board and continued in the same ship for voyage after voyage. Voyage masters and chief engineers tended to remain with the same ship thus, as already

6 Miss Sheila Edmundson.

[64]

noted, becoming identified with her. Some masters, chief officers and chief engineers specialised in relief work. This could be extremely arduous, usually navigating in busy and confined waters, discharging and loading going on simultaneously at some ports, always under pressure to keep to schedule within the overriding precaution that the safety of the ship, her crew and cargo was always paramount.

II

The voyage crew joined, usually in London, shortly before the ship sailed outward bound. The first problem was to get the ship safely out of her berth at C Shed, down the length of Royal Victoria Dock, through the lock and into the river. The pilot who helped the master to accomplish this feat was for many years a chubby, imperturbable character named Bowen, who had an extraordinary appetite for ham sandwiches and mugs of coffee. Once in the Thames he took the wheel and handed over to the river pilot for the passage to Gravesend. Here the Channel pilot boarded and took the ship to Dungeness if outward bound, or The Sunk if making for a Continental port. On the inward voyage the same procedure operated in reverse.

These three stages of pilotage were rightly compulsory, though this did not prevent quite frequent narrow escapes from collision, and some accidents. Trinity House, which organised pilotage in the Thames and its approaches was an autocratic body but allowed us to have our own choice dock pilot and choice river pilot. For a long period after the Second World War the latter was a former Ben Line officer, Ian Macmillan, whose father, Captain George Macmillan, trained in the sailing ship *Bencleuch* and spent his entire career with the Ben Line.

Pilots around the world were – probably still are – just as prone to promote their own supposed self-interests by restrictive and arbitrary practices as other skilled professions, such as union-dominated stevedores and Conference-minded shipowners. When President Nasser nationalised the Suez Canal in 1956 it was confidently predicted that he would never find replacements for the large band of highly paid French, British, German, Scandinavian and pilots of other nationalities whom he put out of work. When the Canal reopened in 1957 it was found after a transitional period that the professed exceptional skill of the foreign pilots could be assumed without other than normal hazard by Egyptians.

No Ben Line ship berthed in Singapore after dark or sailed before daylight because, according to fleet gossip, the Singapore Pilot Association, a powerful partnership of exclusively British master mariners, thereby ensured that its members always got a reasonable night's sleep. This was a calumny on more than one count. The pilots did indeed refuse to berth any ship before daylight for reasons of safety, including the non-availability of suitable tugs at night. Apart from darkness and bad visibility in heavy rain, dangerously strong tides ran through the harbour.

It was possible to sail up to midnight (the stevedores' night shift ended at 11 p.m.) if the same pilot who had berthed the ship deemed it safe to take her out. Some of our competitors sailed in darkness, but all Ben Line ships waited until daylight, probably originally on Mr Ted's instructions, which were not subsequently countermanded. As regards the 'reasonable night's sleep', Captain K. H. Hardie, who joined the Singapore Pilot Association in 1953, recalls that work began at 5.30 a.m. (which meant rising at 4.30 a.m.) and finished between 6.30 and 7.30 p.m., unless it was his turn for duty on the night roster which was introduced that year. A Government survey at this time showed that the average working day for a Singapore pilot was 11½ hours. Hardie's extensive experience of navigating many ships with varying characteristics in difficult conditions was put to most welcome use when he rejoined the Ben Line and became the first to command the first containership, *Benalder* VI, which was so much larger and more powerful than any previous Ben Line ship.

Pilots in the Philippines expected a present for the satisfactory performance of their duties, usually a packet of 200 cigarettes and a bottle of whisky, which the ship could well afford from the duty free stores. But an uninitiated master ignorant of the unofficial tariff could be milked for far more and even old hands would find themselves hindered by customs officers who insisted that it was part of their duty to stay on board, eat large meals at frequent intervals and depart with liquor and tobacco for not having delayed the sailing of the ship on some fabricated irregularity.

'Squeeze' in Hong Kong was understood to the extent that the

Chinese wished it to be understood, and it seldom transgressed good manners by obtruding itself, but various forms of corruption in other Eastern ports, particularly in the Philippines, Thailand and Indonesia was far more open and widespread.

Masters were often constantly on the bridge in the busy Channel waters. The Bay of Biscay usually obliged by sorting out those prone to seasickness from those who continued to eat hearty meals in the saloon, where the chairs were tethered to the deck and a removable fiddle round the table and a moistened tablecloth prevented most of the crockery from sliding to destruction. The master was invariably on the bridge while the ship passed through the Straits of Gibraltar, where traffic in both directions was always a potential hazard. Lloyd's Agent maintained a signal station on the top of the Rock and if a ship signalled her name the station would radio the time of her passing to the owners. The more open waters of the Mediterranean could be very rough but it was usually possible then to get down to routine work on deck, which included maintenance of lifeboats, fire-fighting and life-saving equipment, overhauling and greasing all steel and wooden cargo blocks and shackles and the wire ropes which connected winches to derricks, repairing canvas hatch covers and awnings. The never-ending battle against corrosion was resumed by painting exposed surfaces, chipping and resurfacing the metal decks. Some of the slow drudgery of chipping decks with hammers and scrapers was alleviated by using chipping machines, though these were themselves in frequent need of maintenance and repair. Grit blasting was eventually introduced; this proved more successful but more costly. A great deal of time, paint and inconvenience was saved by using the newly invented hard plastics to protect alleyways and cabin bulkheads. With care and a periodical wash down these materials could last the life of a ship.

'We look to Masters and others to maintain a high degree of efficiency all round. Only by their so doing can our vessels continue to create a favourable impression in the minds of shippers and receivers, who are often as much influenced by the appearance of vessels as they are by good outturn and adherence to schedule.'[7]

In 1946, when the ships which had survived the war came out of camouflage, they were given a new set of colours which persisted

7 Ben Line Instructions for Sea Staff, Oct. 1952, p.19; May 1965, p.18.

into the containership era. The pre-war yellow funnel was reinstated, but the hulls were painted grey instead of black, and dark green was used instead of red for the boot-topping. Metal decks were coated with a black bituminous solution. Masts, derricks and samson posts became a light stone colour. For a time lifeboats were no longer painted white, but had their timbers varnished. This proved expensive because sea spray soon broke down the varnish and set up a chemical reaction on the copper nails which made the timber black and soft. We therefore reverted to white paint until timber hulls were superseded by fibre glass of a light stone colour.

The imitation of timber by painting the upperworks in grained panels had been a feature of the 'Leith Yachts' and was retained until the arrival of containerships and bulk carriers, when it was finally abandoned. The Chinese painters, indeed the whole company, took great pride in this unique hallmark which was achieved by applying successive layers of paint and varnish divided into panels by stencilled black lines, with conventional Scots thistles at the corners.

It would have been much less time-consuming to paint the upperworks a uniform colour, but the same argument applied to other aspects. The new ships delivered in the immediate postwar years preserved the tradition of brass fittings which were polished most days as a routine.

During the twenty-five years after the Second World War many other changes took place: the heavy sisal or hemp towing springs and mooring ropes were replaced by nylon, gleaming white when new. Steam-driven winches gave way to electric power and later ships were equipped with their own cargo cranes. In the sixties new Bens were fitted with hydraulically operated, steel, watertight hatch covers, so that a hatch could be uncovered, or covered, in a minute. Previously, having removed the tarpaulin, the hatch boards, each about 10½ feet long and 20 inches wide had to be manhandled, and the steel beams supporting them winched off. When heavy rain came down some protection of the hold's contents was provided by hatch tents but these might take some time to rig and got in the way of cargo operations if left ready suspended near the hatch.

At Port Said there was usually a delay of some hours to allow the northbound convoy to complete its passage or to enable the southbound convoy time to get organised. Rowing boats came alongside offering all manner of wares from hookahs and fake antiques to rugs and flywhisks. Any purchases were hauled up and the price let down on a cord as none of these hopeful merchants were allowed on board. They were prevented from doing so by our Agent's[8] watchman, who wore a white floppy hat, and a sailor's blue jersey bearing the Ben Line flag and his adopted name 'Jock Mackenzie', 'Jock McGregor', 'Jock McTavish' – one succeeded another, but all had a fund of news and gossip about officers on other Ben Line ships: who had been promoted, and who had not!

On encountering a warship of any nationality a Ben Line ship dipped her ensign, and when two Ben Line ships passed each other at sea the junior master dipped his ensign and the senior then dipped his in acknowledgement. Other companies observed a similar custom and on one sad occasion the Dutch passenger liners *Oranje* and *Willem Ruys* passed too close to each other in the Red Sea and collided.

In the fifties the Union Jack still flew over the old coaling station at Perim, but by then bunkering took place at Aden, using the products of the adjacent BP refinery.

In 1949 the Ben Line inaugurated a service from London to Singapore direct in twenty-five days but before then the usual rotation was Penang, Port Swettenham (Port Kelang) then Singapore. As all three ports were only a few hours' steaming from each other cargo operations were almost continuous and before the Second World War a deck officer was permanently stationed in Malaya to stand the watch between these ports and give the ship's deck officers some much needed rest. After the war this role was taken on by the chief officer.

Perhaps the most popular port with both European and Chinese seafarers was Hong Kong. Here loading and discharging usually took place in the anchorage using lighters and junks. Shore labour for maintenance and repairs was skilled and cheap. Jewellery, jade, watches, wireless sets, clothes, carved teak chests with camphorwood linings could be bought more cheaply than anywhere else, so Hong Kong was popular with passengers too.

III

Since the termination of the Baltic service brought about by the

8 Until the Canal and the agencies at Port Said and Suez were nationalised in 1956 we were represented by Worms & Co., French owned but with British managers.

First World War no attempt had been made to encourage passengers, and few were carried in the twenties and thirties. After the Second World War Sir Douglas introduced a change of policy. The Benmacdhui class which came into service from 1948 had four staterooms designed to carry one passenger, though roomy enough for a second, sleeping on a settee. In subsequent classes of ship the accommodation was increased with some double staterooms, providing for up to twelve passengers, but never more because that could have involved carrying additional life-saving equipment and a qualified medical officer by law. Sir Douglas's wife, Bettina, chose the fabrics and furnishings for the cabins and lounge, working in collaboration with the marine superintendents. She threw herself into this task with great enthusiasm and the result was both comfortable and attractive. Free fresh fruit and free tissues were supplied in the stateroom; cots were provided for children.

The canteen was stocked with table wines and cigars, and passengers were offered dinner at about 7 p.m. instead of an hour and a half earlier. Some masters thought such pampering was doomed to failure. Captain D. B. ('Sugar') Anderson, a magnificent, craggy figure well over six feet tall, who was an excellent master but did not take kindly to passengers, told the partners, 'Yer wine will go soor in the bottles and the worrrms will eat yer one-and-saxpenny cigars.' In fact the passenger service was well patronised. It was attractive to embassy staff, whose leave period did not start until the ship reached UK, so they could enjoy several weeks of paid holiday with free board and lodging. Colonial civil servants in Hong Kong, British North Borneo, Singapore and Malaya, rubber planters and relatives of personnel in the armed forces initially outnumbered those who were simply tourists. If you had time on your hands and could amuse yourself by reading, writing and card playing it was a very cheap and pleasant way to travel with ample supplies of duty free alcohol and tobacco. The company never expected to make much, if any, money from passengers but used the service as a form of advertisement. In the mid fifties fares worked out at slightly over three old pence per mile,[9] all found, except for canteen and laundry bills, and tips for the stewards at the end of the voyage. In 1966 the return fare between London and Singapore was £360 to £400 and it

9 In June 1956 the fare from London to Singapore (8,280 miles) was £129.

was possible to make a round trip to Japan and back lasting about ten weeks for £500.

There were inevitably some difficult passengers, those who drank more than was good for them, those who got bored and amused themselves by carrying on a vendetta with other passengers. One lady wrote an irate letter to the company from Port Said outward bound to say that she had been looking forward to good fresh sea air and was most displeased to find that her cabin was air-conditioned. If she changed her mind in the Red Sea she did not tell us.

When planning the design of the containerships we decided to exclude passenger accommodation, partly to save costs and partly because we thought, perhaps erroneously, that no passengers would want to be whisked round the world at 26½ knots with very little opportunity to go ashore.

The passenger service was finally abolished in 1975 by which time we did not have enough ships to offer a reliable service, that is to provide a sailing to the desired destination on a scheduled date.

The stewards served tea and hot buttered toast in the cabin at about 7 a.m. Breakfast was usually at 8 a.m. when the 4 to 8 watch came off duty. This was a substantial meal with fruit or juice, porridge or cereal, kippers, eggs, bacon, sausage and black pudding; a few stalwarts worked their way through most of the alternatives. A favourite breakfast dish was curried tinned salmon with rice.

If anyone felt peckish about 11 a.m. they had to make do with coffee and biscuits. Lunch at 1 p.m. might consist of soup, roast beef, mutton or pork with potatoes and vegetables, a steamed suet pudding with custard (even in the hottest weather), cheese, and coffee, usually not well made. The Chinese were able to produce added variety with chow mein, noodles with diced chicken and vegetables including bean sprouts, bamboo shoots and water chestnuts.

Afternoon tea with biscuits was followed by the evening meal, no less substantial than lunch but usually including more cold meats to give the galley staff a break. All meals were announced by a steward marching round the alleyways ringing a little glockenspiel.

IV

Until the mid sixties only the master (apart from passengers) was formally allowed spirits – whisky, gin and rum – in virtually unlimited quantities free of charge, paid for by the company and intended mainly for the entertainment of visitors to the ship, particularly those on official business. Most masters invited the chief officer, chief engineer and selected passengers for a drink in his day room before lunch on Sundays. Passengers could buy spirits, sherry, table wine, whatever the ship's canteen had in stock, by the bottle. Officers and ratings had to make do with canned beer likewise bought from the canteen.

Canteen prices were fixed by the company and were periodically reviewed, the general policy being to make a small profit on each item. This profit was divided between the ships for the purchase of sports or other welfare equipment and seamen's charities such as King George's Fund for Sailors, The Missions to Seamen and the Royal Alfred Homes. An annual statement was displayed on ships' notice boards showing how the money had been distributed in order to emphasise that serving crews had benefited as well as seamen's charities, and that no part of the profit had been retained by the company.

Until the mid sixties any seafarer with a drink problem was dismissed. Then Sir Douglas persuaded Mr Ted to agree to a change of policy, which I was delegated to implement. The result was that the May 1965 edition of *Instructions for Sea Staff* contained the following section:

ALCOHOLISM

1 In a shipboard community the opportunity to increase drinking habits beyond the accepted social norm is always present; factors contributing to this are: (a) the cheapness and availability of drink on board; (b) prolonged absence abroad; (c) lack of recreational facilities; (d) boredom.

2 Excessive drinking can lead to alcoholism, an illness which about 10 per cent of the population is capable of contracting as a result of the chemical make-up of their bodies. Alcoholism can be defined as any drinking which is continually affecting a man's work performance. If alcoholism is not treated, progressive physical deterioration takes place accompanied by mental disturbance which ends in premature and extremely unpleasant death.

3 The Company has enlisted the assistance of the Glasgow Council on Alcoholism, 68 Gordon Street, Glasgow C1 to diminish the risks of contracting alcoholism by a process of education. i.e. defining the problem,

getting it talked about, and discouraging other than moderate drinking in company, that is, 'social drinking'.

4 If a man nevertheless contracts this illness, the Company engages to attempt, with the help of the Glasgow Council on Alcoholism, to rehabilitate him rather than to dismiss him summarily, provided that in the Company's opinion there are no additional circumstances which make summary dismissal the right course in the interests of the Company.

5 If rehabilitation is achieved–and this involves permanent total abstinence from drinking alcohol–then the Company is prepared to re-employ that man in the rank which the Company considers to be appropriate.

6 Be on your guard against excessive drinking.

All deck and engineer officers had to read this, and the rest of the *Instructions for Sea Staff*, and sign and date a statement that they had done so and fully understood them.

The educational part of this programme was carried out by Mr John Gray, himself a reformed alcoholic, who was on the staff of the Glasgow Council on Alcoholism until he parted company with it and set up his own consultancy, after which we employed him at an annual fee. He interviewed all masters, chief officers, chief and 2nd engineers, visited ships and did a number of coastal passages on board.

To encourage 'social drinking', bars were installed for both officers and ratings at which draught beer was served. Spirits were permitted in the officers' bars but we resisted pressure from the National Union of Seamen to extend this to ratings' bars. An officer was made responsible for seeing that the bar was opened and closed at the appointed times and for the orderly running of it.

The new policy was generally welcomed, but it did not entirely eradicate the problem. A number of men were treated by Mr Gray in collaboration with the patient's own doctor, and some were offered re-employment in a lower rank, which was usually accepted. Two former masters were eventually reinstated in that rank, but after a time both reverted to their old habits. This was not only a sad disappointment but considerably alarming, because a drunken master might hazard his ship. We derived some comfort from the knowledge that our problems were no worse than those of other shipping companies, that 'prevention is better than cure' and that we were doing our best to prevent the human wastage and tragic consequences of the abuse of alcohol.

At least during this period we did not have to contend with a drugs problem, at any rate as regards having addicts among the crew. Smuggling, particularly of heroin, by a Chinese crew was always a possibility but the only case I recollect concerned a young Scottish cadet in whose cabin the Thai customs found a consignment of heroin. He spent some time in gaol before it could be proved that the parcel had been planted.

At each port of call duty free stores were sealed and the entire accommodation had to be opened to search by customs officers. Care had to be taken not to offend the local susceptibilities. European customs were indifferent to 'fornography', as the South Korean customs described it, but blatant pin-up photographs and 'girlie magazines' were liable to confiscation (and perhaps re-sale) in Singapore, Taiwan and Chinese ports.

v

The company tried to encourage more wholesome reading matter by paying an annual subscription to the Seafarers' Education Service in return for which a portable library was placed on board in London at the beginning of a voyage, and replaced by a fresh selection of assorted fiction, biography and general literature in hard covers when the ship returned to London. In addition the ship gradually accumulated its own stock of books, mainly paperbacks, donated by members of the crew and by passengers.

The company also hired sufficient films to allow the showing of a different one each week. The same film was given two or three showings to allow everyone on board a chance to see it. The projector (usually in the charge of and operated by the electrician) and screen belonged to the ship, paid for out of canteen profits. The films which had been shown were exchanged in Singapore for those on a homeward-bound Ben. Films, particularly 'Westerns' were much enjoyed by Chinese crew, even if they could not understand the dialogue, but their favourite pastime was evident from the clatter of Mah-Jong tiles coming from their accommodation, often far into the night.

Model-making ranged from assembling ready-make kits to more

individual creations in wood, and the traditional ship-in-a-bottle where the hull is just slim enough to be slipped through the neck with its rigged masts horizontal, which are then pulled into a vertical position by a single thread.

Some masters kept caged birds, parrots, minah birds, Javanese finches, budgerigars and canaries, but the choice of pets was limited by circumstances and quarantine restrictions.

Officers and passengers played deck golf round the boat deck and deck tennis could be played on a hatch cover. A swimming pool about twenty feet long, fourteen feet wide and six feet lowest depth was built into *Bengloe* IV (1961) and her near sisters *Benvalla* I and *Benarmin*.

Only one ship, *Benalbanach* II,[10] could raise a cricket team, but most ships fielded a soccer team. On the Far East run the opposing side was usually the crew of another ship that happened to be in port at the same time. The Missions to Seamen padres at Port Swetten-ham (Port Kelang) and at Singapore recognised that their work in the cure of souls included the function of arranging such matches. So, many supporters of Hibs and Hearts, Celtic and Rangers found themselves pitted against those of Liverpool and Manchester United from Blue Funnel ships, with much the same fanatical partisanship as would have been engendered if their heroes had met profes-sionally. These matches were usually played in a sporting spirit, but could often result in an injury which temporarily deprived the ship of a crew member.

The design of the containerships resulted in the creation of quite a lot of enclosed space which could not be used for any weight-bear-ing purpose. It was thus possible to incorporate a 'hobbies room' equipped with a lathe and basic woodworking tools, but this was seldom used. One of these void spaces on each of the three big containerships was sufficiently large to accommodate a golf range where the ball could be driven against a loosely draped tarpaulin and this was used by the few golfing enthusiasts to keep their eye in. One master[11] wished to keep his eye in for a different purpose and had his own clay pigeon trap and shotgun.

Pastimes on board ship are just as prone to 'crazes' and fashion as

10 *Benalbanach* II was commanded by Captain A. Sinclair.
11 Captain K. H. Hardie.

they are on shore, though ships were not then able to pick up television at sea which they are currently able to do through satellite transmission. A 'craze' which hit the crews of the big containerships was the joint purchase of giant jigsaw puzzles which were slowly pieced together and once completed were framed and hung in the mess room as a monument to mutual endeavour. There are certainly many more mischievous activities.

Under Mr Ted's chairmanship no wives were permitted to stay on board. After he retired in 1966 this rule was gradually relaxed; officers were able to take their wives, on a rotational basis, for a complete round voyage free of charge in return for keeping the couple's cabin clean and tidy. When the containerships came into service this concession was extended to senior ratings. It was generally felt that the presence of women on board had a civilising effect on the whole ship's company and if it resulted in any misbehaviour the owners never heard of it since it was made known that this could result in the concession being rescinded.

6

Development of the Shore-Side Organisation

circa 1950 – 1970

In 1950 the partnership consisted of Mr Ted, Sir Douglas, James Grieve and Ian Miller, and I became a partner in November that year. The only other change during that decade was the admission to the partnership in November 1959 of Roderick MacLeod, a Cambridge graduate with suitable Scottish connections, who, in the six years since I had recruited him in my capacity as partner in charge of staff, had proved himself an able, tough and energetic administrator.

Nothing resembling a regular partners' meeting took place prior to 1950. Then I persuaded Sir Douglas to have a working lunch with the other partners (except Mr Ted) once a week on Mondays. The chairman did not take this innovation amiss because he knew that it was not aimed at bypassing or undermining him. He chose not to change his routine of coming into the office only on Tuesdays and Fridays. On Tuesdays Sir Douglas usually attended a board meeting at the Bank of Scotland followed by lunch. On Wednesdays and Thursdays one or more partners were often away in London or elsewhere, and on Fridays masters came to the office for interview, so Monday became the chosen day. Until about the end of the sixties these lunch-time meetings, which served a very useful purpose, took place in the Café Royal, five minutes' walk across St Andrew Square from the office.

When we ran out of space at 10 North Saint David Street in the fifties we bought the adjoining premises at 2 Queen Street and connected the two buildings by passages through the walls. This new acquisition allowed us the luxury of a small private dining-room – but no kitchen. So on Fridays we had a simple meal sent in by

L'Apéritif, for many years the best restaurant in Edinburgh, owned by Donald Ross,[1] whose head waiter was a former Ben Line chief steward.

Hitherto a visiting master saw each partner individually to discuss the voyage just completed, plans for the next one, his portage bill, complicated or disputed damage claims from shippers, how he, his ship and crew were faring, but these conversations were one to one, and there had hitherto been no opportunity for joint talks. Now, however, Mr Ted was persuaded to forego his home-made sandwiches and preside at a working lunch attended by the other partners, a marine superintendent and the visiting master. Apart from visits to ships there had been no contact with chief engineers until the Friday lunches were extended to them and the engineer superintendent on a rotational basis, so partners were able to meet them about one voyage in three or four.

In 1963 William Thomson, Mr Ted's nephew and heir, and David Thomson, Sir Douglas's elder son, were simultaneously admitted to the partnership, the former having qualified as a chartered accountant and the latter having graduated from Oxford. The senior partners told me and Roderick MacLeod that the partnership was to be expanded in this way and asked us if we would mind the names of the new partners appearing above ours on the letterheads. They were, I think, pleasantly surprised when we both replied that we would have no objection. We were glad that the family succession was to be assured for another generation, and counted the continued independence and prosperity of the company above the supposed humiliation of being seen as junior partners to these younger men. In the event the senior partners decided not to impose this condition, so from November 1963 the partnership consisted of Mr Ted, Sir Douglas, James Grieve, Ian Miller, myself, Roderick MacLeod, William Thomson and David Thomson.

Having outgrown the space provided by 10 North Saint David Street and the connected annexe at 2 Queen Street, we moved two departments into rented accommodation across the road on the other side of North Saint David Street. Meantime Scottish Life Assurance Co. had acquired the adjoining premises previously

1 A good pen-portrait of him occurs on p.290 of Eric Linklater's novel *Laxdale Hall*, London, 1951, which is dedicated to him and his wife.

occupied by Edinburgh Stock Exchange and were building a new office block on the site which would more than satisfy our space requirements. Scottish Life offered to buy our Head Office to enable them to extend the new block and offered to rehouse us when stage one had been completed. We debated whether we should not be redeveloping our own site but concluded that we knew nothing about that business and had better stick to shipping. So the partnership to whom Head Office belonged decided to accept an offer of £48,000 and to rent space in stage one.

The deal was completed in 1964 but the new premises were not ready for occupation until 1967. For a while all went well and we were delighted to have all the staff reunited under one roof. We did notice some cracks appearing in the structure and then discovered that a marble laid on a supposedly normal floor would roll diagonally across it. We drew our landlords' attention to these phenomena more than once and were assured that there was nothing to worry about. Then in the November of 1971, when there was much activity in the run up to the inauguration of the container service, a facing slab fell off the front of the building into the street. The City Engineer declared the building to be unsafe and its occupants were required to evacuate it within seven days.

By a stroke of fortune Christian Salvesen had moved to new offices a few weeks earlier. Their former Leith Office at 29 Bernard Street was available, our apologetic landlords bought it and rented it to us for six shillings a foot. We were able to squeeze most of the staff into it and rented premises across the road at 28 Bernard Street from the Bank of Scotland for one department and the Board Room. These rented premises were those occupied by Wm Thomson & Co. from about 1890 to 1943. We had been given seven days but achieved the move in five, without a break in operational efficiency apart from twenty minutes while the telex was transferred. With its steep stairways, narrow passages and small rooms we were back in the nineteenth century. The building was described by a visiting German as a 'veritable mouse-oleum'. Mausoleum it was not: more like a beehive. We operated from it until we moved to new premises at 33 Saint Mary's Street in 1977. Meantime the company had returned to its origins and was so near the sea that whenever there was a high tide the basement flooded and had to be pumped out.

[79]

In 1964 James Grieve had a heart attack from which he seemed at first to be recovering, but shortly afterwards he died in Edinburgh Royal Infirmary.[2] Ian Miller's relationship with Sir Douglas had not improved and he found more frequent excuses to be in London rather than in Edinburgh. These absences were extended by the onset of a wasting illness.

Meantime it was generally agreed that the partnership structure with its uncertainties as regards income and unlimited liability had become outmoded, so at the end of October 1964 the partnership was wound up. Ian Miller retired to live in England[3] and with Mr Ted as chairman and Sir Douglas as vice chairman all the other partners became joint managing directors of The Ben Line Steamers Limited, though still managed under the trade name of Wm Thomson & Co., a title retained on the letterheads and elsewhere. All cheques continued to be signed in that style.

Having seen the next Thomson generation firmly, and apparently harmoniously, established, Mr Ted retired in April 1966, but at Sir Douglas's instigation was persuaded to accept the newly created honorary title of president in recognition of his exceptional services to the company over a period of fifty-five years.[4] Sir Douglas's persuasive powers did not stop there: most of the Head Office staff, some members of Sir Douglas's family, the directors' wives, and Percy Rogers representing Killick Martin, made a grand day outing by special train and bus to Mr Ted's Island of Eriska in Argyll. We arrived in time for lunch, after which he was presented with an album of photographs of the Ben Line fleet past and present, and he made the first and last speech I ever heard from him – and did it very well. In the afternoon those athletically inclined could try their skill at water skiing, then a relatively new sport, but much admired by Mr Ted, who had all the right equipment ready for use. The less energetic could explore the island; we have to this day wild yellow iris brought back from Eriska, doing well in the harsher climate of our home in Tweeddale.

Sir Douglas, who now took the chair, had a short reign. As already

2 13 July 1964.
3 Ian Miller died 10 February 1979. At his family's request I read the lesson at his funeral.
4 Mr Ted became a partner in 1911 and was 77 when he became president.

recorded, he became seriously ill in 1968, finally retired from the chairmanship in 1970, but remained a director until he died in 1972.

Meantime Hon. Norman Galbraith joined the board in October 1968 and Mr A.C. Hill retired from it at the end of that year. Even after the partnership was wound up in 1964 board meetings were far less formal than in most companies. We continued to have a working lunch on Mondays followed by a round table discussion when that was needed, as it usually was, to complete the agenda. The agenda was arrived at by circulating a small notebook during the week in which each director wrote the subject that he wished to be discussed. The subject might or might not be supported by papers. The chairman's job was to pre-edit the items listed and then take them in the order most conducive to arriving at a decision with minimal waste of time. No formal minutes were produced, but at the next Monday's meeting individual directors might report on the progress made in implementing the decision which had been reached, or the progress made in a particular area where it had been decided that consultation with third parties and/or the production of further papers was needed.

If this seems to be a remarkably off-hand and amateurish way of conducting business I can only say that it worked well in practice throughout the time that I was chairman.[5] It was founded on complete mutual trust between the directors and it enabled us to take and implement decisions with a minimum of bureaucratic formality, and more quickly than our competitors.

II

The marine superintendent, Captain J. P. Drummond, died in service in 1951 and the senior partners chose Captain John Smith to succeed him. Smith had served as a master in the fleet at sea during the war; he was a charming man of limited vision. The junior partners were not surprised that he found Drummond a difficult man to follow, though he was given Captain Alex Paterson and Captain Ian Liston as assistants. In 1954 Smith was moved to the new post of superintendent in charge of new building and was succeeded by Paterson and Liston, who remained marine superintendents for the rest of their active careers until they retired. They formed an extremely

5 I took the chair informally 1968-70 and officially 1970-82.

effective, harmonious team and the company was indeed fortunate to be able to rely on their outstanding dedication and ability for such a long and eventful period.

On the engineering side Andy Hill was succeeded as chief engineer superintendent by Cecil Hutton. Tall, thin, pale, quietly spoken, very experienced and hard-working, Hutton was a man you were always glad to have on **your** side. While still in his teens he had abandoned his engineering apprenticeship to fight as a soldier in the First World War in the Royal Engineers, and had been awarded the Distinguished Conduct Medal, the highest award for those who were not commissioned officers next to the Victoria Cross, for bravery in action. After the war he completed his apprenticeship with Ramage and Ferguson of Leith and in 1923 joined the Ben Line as an engineer officer. In 1940 he was serving as chief engineer of *Benarty* III when she was captured in the Indian Ocean by a German raider. He and the rest of the crew spent six months as prisoners in Italian Somaliland before being liberated by British forces. When he was repatriated he was posted to the merchant aircraft carrier *Empire McKendrick* and then to *Benlawers* IV, the first turbine ship built for the Ben Line. At the end of the war he was awarded the OBE and in 1946 came ashore as senior assistant engineer superintendent. He succeeded Andy Hill as chief engineer superintendent in 1964, but survived for only three months. On 23 May he went to Head Office in North Saint David Street and left himself only five minutes to run with a heavy bag to the air terminal several hundred yards away in George Street. His wife was waiting for him there, and he died of a heart attack in her arms.

So with unexpected suddenness, the increasingly onerous duties of chief engineer superintendent fell on the shoulders of Hutton's assistant, Henry Paton, who continued in that appointment until his retiral in August 1986. Paton had served his apprenticeship with David Rowan in Glasgow and had joined the Ben Line as a junior engineer officer in 1946. Here again the company benefited enormously from the services of this man of outstanding ability, who had to command the respect of an increasing number of assistant engineer superintendents and specialists, over a long period of rapid change during which second-hand ships were bought, and new classes of purpose-built vessels were added, with a wide range of differing main engines and auxiliary machinery. When a second-hand ship was acquired her inventory of existing spares was brought up to 'Ben Line Standard', an insurance policy which received the full backing of the directors, even when it meant Paton making a trip to Los Angeles where he bought complete HP and LP turbines from the American mothball fleet then being broken up, suitable for *Bennevis* III or *Benrinnes* IV, which had started their careers as escort aircraft carriers and continued in Ben Line service until 1973. The problem of keeping such a diverse fleet equipped with spare parts became increasingly complex, but under Henry Paton's management I cannot recollect a single instance where a ship was unnecessarily delayed.

The main stock of engineering spares was held in a warehouse near the company's London loading berth in Royal Victoria Dock, but spare propellers, tailshafts and other heavy items were held in Hamburg at Howaldtswerke Deutsche Werft, where Ben Line ships usually drydocked at the European end of the route. When the containerships came into service engineering spares for them were held in the Kawasaki Heavy Industries dockyard at Kobe as well as in Hamburg.

Paton was awarded a thoroughly well-earned OBE. It was not at all easy to gain an honour for Ben Line staff. Citations carefully compiled by the chairman, in strictest confidence so as not to raise false hopes, could be submitted either to the Chamber of Shipping or to the responsible Ministry. Both were tried, some nominations being repeated for years in succession until the candidate retired, after which, we were told, there was no chance of an award being made. These recommendations occasionally resulted in the award of a British Empire Medal, more rarely a MBE, very rarely an OBE. That the Ben Line was known to be rather proud of not being part of the shipping 'establishment' probably did not help. Until the 1980s no Thomson, so far as I know, was ever asked to stand for election as president of the Chamber of Shipping (or General Council of British Shipping as it later became). Any such approach would almost certainly have been turned down. The president-designate served for one year as vice-president before assuming office. He then became the formal mouthpiece for the British shipping industry and stood a fair chance of being knighted. I had no hesitation in turning down more than one proposal that I should stand for election, knowing that two years spent more in London than in Edinburgh, preoccupied with many issues in which the company was not immediately concerned, would be incompatible with properly minding the eggs in the Ben Line basket. As a member for some years of the institution's General Policy Committee I saw, or thought I saw, how satisfaction of personal ambition to become president led to neglect of the incumbent's own business. Outside the shipping industry many of the higher awards seemed to go to those whose previous, and subsequent, conduct could not be reconciled with that of a 'Christian gentleman' (a definition of character and nothing to do with social class). This was not really surprising since many of those honoured could not lay claim to being both, or either. Overall, however, the British honours system was useful. Every award to a member of the Ben Line was thoroughly merited, and highly prized. It was not for want of trying that other equally, or even more deserving candidates, were unsuccessful.

In the fifties and sixties the pivotal port in Europe for the Far East run was London, and the Ben Line loaded and discharged more cargo there than at any other port. To consolidate the London base we leased from the Port of London Authority (PLA) exclusive rights to load at C Shed, Royal Victoria Dock. Adjacent to this berth the Ben Line Dock Office was constructed to the company's design and at its expense, though leased from PLA. This was a substantial brick building on two floors, which initially housed a London-based cargo superintendent and assistant engineer superintendent,[6] a representative of Killick Martin and a staff of clerks and typists. Before the Dock Office was ready in 1951 this team worked in difficult conditions from huts and caravans. In 1954 it was decided to set up the company's own stevedoring organisation[7] and this was likewise based in the Dock Office, while a direct representative from Head Office divided his time between there and Edinburgh.[8]

The Ben Line discharged in London in the West India Dock at one

6 Initially Captain W. S. Campbell and C. G. Hutton, OBE, DCM.
7 The stevedores were run by two ex-Ben Line officers, Captain R. Griffiths and Captain J. E. Mackenzie.
8 J. E. Taylor, MBE.

or other of the available berths until PLA were persuaded to build for us a splendid three-storey warehouse at M Shed SW India Dock, which became our permanent berth.

Killick Martin & Co. had been the Ben Line's London brokers continuously since 1883[9] and had survived the Second World War quite well. The partnership was headed by Walter Godin, who saw the beginnings of the Ben Line's post-war expansion before handing over to his son Denys in 1951. Denys took after his father in being mild, equable and, like his remote Huguenot ancestors, devout in his religious observances. He had thought seriously of going into the Church, but had been persuaded to carry on the family business. During his nineteen years first as senior partner and then from 1953 as chairman of the limited company into which the partnership was converted, he ensured that Killick's not only kept pace with the growth of the Ben Line but added to their existing agency interests in the trades with West Africa and took on entirely new agencies, notably Geest and Lykes Lines. Killick's staff numbered 30 in 1945, 160 in 1950, 260 in 1960, 380 in 1970 and reached a peak of 530 in 1974.[10]

Denys Godin's quiet tact was an admirable foil to Percy Rogers's rumbustious enthusiasm. Percy Rogers died in service in 1966. The other directors with whom we regularly dealt during the fifties and sixties were Ronald Dick, who retired in 1962, David Gravell and Peter Bowlby, who were appointed to Killick's board in 1954 and 1961 respectively.

Before the Second World War Killick's prime functions were the recruitment of eastbound cargo with a team of specialist canvassers, and acting as ship agents for the eastbound sailings from London. They also exercised a supervisory role in respect of the Ben Line's agents at other UK and North Continental loading ports, since they coordinated the documentation and prepared the final manifest for each eastbound sailing. All these activities continued after the war, but in addition Killick's began marketing the westbound services. Staff were attached for extended periods to Ben Line agents and offices in the Far East so that they could learn about the 'homeward'

9 *Ben Bulletin*, 1983.
10 David R. MacGregor, *op.cit.*, p.180.

trade at first hand.[11] This was not a one-sided exchange since Ben Line staff from Edinburgh, and from the Far East, trained and worked with Killick's. Bonds between the two companies became even closer when Arthur Kinnear (about whom more later) retired as Ben Line's general manager Far East and became a director of Killick's in 1964. He retired from Killick's in 1975, and five years later George Allan, who had started as a Ben Line trainee in Edinburgh and had subsequently served in its Far East offices, returned to UK and joined Killick's board in 1979.

In the fifties we tried to resuscitate a regular service to and from Leith, but were unable to attract business from Glasgow, where Holt's were well established in a virtual monopoly position. Then P & O sprang a surprise by starting a service to and from Grangemouth, only a few miles up the Firth of Forth, but more accessible than Leith to the central industrial belt of Scotland. The P & O service proved successful and we mounted competitive sailings, which soon resulted in a suggestion from P & O that we should run a joint service. This lasted for a time until P & O withdrew, but we continued serving Grangemouth until almost the end of the cargo liner era. The port was also regularly used from the seventies onwards by the company's chemical tankers, whose development is described in chapter 15.

Companies assume the character of the people who have charge of them. There was a contrast between the team spirit and somewhat puritanical aura of Killick's and the debonair, even raffish, atmosphere of Galbraith Pembroke & Co. Ltd, who were not only the Ben Line's London agents for inward-bound vessels, but also our chartering brokers, sale and purchase brokers, and insurance brokers. The chairman, Sir Gibson Graham, knighted for his war services, presided over a board of virtuosi specialists in these various activities. The agency business was looked after by R.D. Francis, an owlish, patriarchal figure of immense experience, with a great affection for the Ben Line, who continued in business until he was well over eighty, assisted by L.C. Portsmouth, who later became a director. Sir Gibson Graham and his younger brother George were in charge of chartering, in due course succeeded by Sir Gibson's son,

11 David Gravell was the first to be seconded in 1950-51. He became chairman of Killick's in 1975.

John, and Dudley Sinnott. Vernon Fullforth must have been among the best informed, most resourceful sale and purchase brokers in the world at that time. He was assisted by F.J. Burnell, who succeeded him when he retired. The insurance side was directed by Cyril Leigh-Hunt, who talked sound sense, delivered in the manner of a character from P.G. Wodehouse.

III

London was not the only port at which the Ben Line had dual agents: at Hull Oughtred & Harrison outwards, Porter & Henderson inwards; in Bangkok Steel Bros outwards and Anglo Thai Corporation inwards. There were usually good reasons for the dichotomy; Anglo Thai held the agencies for a number of European importers while Steel Bros had good connections with the sources of Thai produce. Similarly Oughtreds were well connected with Yorkshire exporters, while Porter & Henderson had performed efficiently for inward-bound ships since the days of coal bumkers, which had been one of their specialities.

The Ben Line business alone was not sufficient to support an agent, who had to have a number of other strings to his bow. These might be the representation of other lines, who were not in competition with the Ben Line, and/or export and import business as a merchant in his own right. Exceptionally for many years we shared agents, Meyer & Co., with Alfred Holt & Co. at Amsterdam and Rotterdam, who saw to it that we drew minimal quantities of cargo from the Netherlands. We finally parted company in 1965 and appointed D. Burger & Zoon at Rotterdam and Vereeinigd Cargadoorskantor (VCK) in Amsterdam.

Rotterdam, largely razed by German bombing during the Second World War and hideously rebuilt after it, became increasingly important, attracting cargo from West Germany, even from Czechoslovakia. Rotterdam had the advantage of relatively easy access to and from the sea whereas, in order to discharge or load at its competitor, Antwerp, a ship had to navigate up and down the Scheldt in fast-flowing water with little room for manoeuvre, and undergo the further expense and hazards of locking in and locking out of the Antwerp dock system since the few berths directly on the river were rarely available. We did in fact briefly acquire priority use of one of these coveted river berths, but that coincided with an upsurge in the importation of manioc from Thailand. The housewives of Antwerp successfully complained that the manioc dust polluted their washing when it was hung out to dry, so we had to move.

These disadvantages were compensated by having active agents, Aug. Bulcke & Co., largely owned by two brothers Van der Weyghaert, though we dealt principally with a genial, extrovert, much-decorated veteran of the First World War, Martin Lamberigts and his younger partner Robert Crighton, a member of the large community of British origin in business there who had adopted Belgian nationality. Another advantage of Antwerp was the extremely efficient dock labour, who worked quite as hard and fast as their counterparts in Rotterdam, and Hamburg when the latter had recovered from the Second World War. By contrast the dock labour at all UK ports was riddled with Communist-inspired disaffection, restrictive practices, unofficial strikes, and thieving – and went from bad to worse.

At Hamburg we were represented by Menzell & Co. – and had been since before the Second World War. The head of this company, Mr Ehrhardt, became inactive soon after the end of the war and when he died left the business, which included a trade in tobacco and spices, as well as ship agencies and a travel agency, to his adopted son, Ehrhardt Renken, who had been a submariner in the German Navy during the latter part of the Second World War. 'Teddy' Renken was an interesting character, a keen racing yachtsman, keen on alcohol and nicotine too, which may have contributed to his premature demise from a heart attack. But he was keenest of all on building up Menzell to keep pace with the economic expansion of West Germany and in seeing that his firm served the Ben Line to the best of its ability – this despite the fact that Menzell also held the agency of Alfred Holt & Co.'s wholly-owned subsidiary, the Glen Line, (thus reflecting in reverse the role which Meyer & Co. played in Rotterdam and Amsterdam).

As the Ben Line's principal agents in West Germany, Menzell & Co. controlled a network of sub-agents, most importantly in Düsseldorf, Frankfurt and Stuttgart, but also in Bremen, Berlin, Hanover and Munich.

'Teddy' Renken was always refreshingly frank, he was a good

ABOVE Benlomond V , *managed as* Ocean Valentine *1942-46, owned 1946-56.*
BELOW Bencleuch VI *(1949-72) in Singapore with* Benveg I *(1950-51).*

Benlomond VI (*1957-77*).

Benloyal II (*1959-78*), *the first 20-knot ship.*

Benstac *(1968-82), the last cargo liner to be disposed of, 1982.*

Bengloe IV *(1961-78),* Bencruachan III *(1968-80) and* Benvalla I *(1962-72) at Ocean Terminal, Hong Kong, 1969.*

ABOVE Bengloe IV *(1961-78) entering the Clyde from Charles Connell's yard at Scotstoun, 17 April 1961* BELOW, *Masters in their dayrooms:* LEFT *Captain W. D. Cowie, Benlawers V, built 1970; and* RIGHT *Captain E. D. Copeman, Benavon III, built 1949.*

ABOVE *Launch of* Benavon III *(1949-70) from Joseph L. Thompson's yard at Sunderland, 1 November 1948. L to r front row: Sir Douglas Thomson, J. O. Grieve, P. F. Rogers, CBE, Lady Thomson, Mrs Walter Godin (sponsor), S. W. Godin* BELOW *Passengers' lounge,* Bencruachan III *(1968-80).*

ABOVE *Double cabin, and* BELOW *dining room* on Benlawers V (*1970-78*).

ABOVE *Swimming pool*, Benledi VI *(1965-72)* BELOW *Passengers' cocktail bar*, Bencruachan III *(1968-80) – A. M. Peill, Ben Line public relations officer, second from right.*

RIGHT *Removing to Leith, November 1971. The BLC flag, ensign and Ben Line house flag flying from 29 Bernard Street* BELOW *The ill-fated Scottish Life building, 10 North Saint David Street and 2 Queen Street, Edinburgh.*

leader, and had great courage. He knew for some years that he had a weak heart, but this did not prevent him from throwing himself unreservedly into business life. Besides Renken we dealt primarily with Peter Andersen, Paul Sengpiel (who became Renken's successor) and Jorg Lunau. The crunch came when the container service was introduced. Our immediate British competitor, Overseas Containers Ltd, had to pick the agents which would most effectively serve them; for Germany they picked Menzell, relying on the Glen Line connection. They were dismayed, and we were correspondingly delighted, when Renken and his partners said that they wished to represent the far smaller Ben Line Containers Limited because they preferred our style of doing business.

IV

Our principal British competitors had their own, or closely connected, companies which represented them in the Far East. P & O owned an interest in Islay Kerr in Singapore and in Mackinnon Mackenzie who represented them in Hong Kong and Japan. Alfred Holt & Co. owned Mansfield in Singapore and a controlling interest in Straits Steamship Co., which ran coasters up and down Malaysia and across to Indonesia, where Holt's Dutch subsidiary 'Oceaan', managed by Meyer & Co. in Amsterdam had a large share of the trade with Europe. Holt's had been represented in Hong Kong and Japan for many years by Butterfield and Swire, who were substantial Holt shareholders. Wm Thomson & Co. noted all this and compared it with their own situation of being represented in the Far East by merchant agents, who placed the Ben Line's interests second, third or fourth to their other sources of revenue. This gave birth to the daring idea of setting up our own Ben Line offices in the principal Far East ports. The idea owed much to the expansionist aims of Sir Douglas, abetted by Percy Rogers, but the main architect of the changes which took place in the 1950s was Ian Miller.

Just as London was the pivotal port in Europe, so Singapore occupied that role in the Far East during the fifties and early sixties, since trade north of Hong Kong and Taiwan was relatively small. In March 1951 Captain W. O. Atkinson[12] was brought ashore and

12 Captain Atkinson served in Singapore 1951-57 and was succeeded by Captain A.C. McMaster 1957-74.

appointed resident marine superintendent. At the same time some staff both British and local were transferred to the Ben Line from the previous agents, Paterson Simons & Co. Ltd, who remained as factors of the office on their floor of Union Building, overlooking the anchorage from above Clifford Pier. To head the new venture Mr A. S. Kinnear was recruited. Arthur Kinnear had served during the thirties with the Irrawaddy Flotilla Company and with the Army during the Burma campaign. A good leader and organiser, he became a potent influence on Ben Line affairs as the first manager in Singapore, subsequently as the first general manager Far East, and finally as a director of Killick's.

Between 1953 and 1958 further Ben Line offices were established at Port Swettenham, Kuala Lumpur, Hong Kong and Bangkok. In each case some of the staff, both European and local, of the previous agents were given employment, and these were progressively augmented by British staff recruited by Head Office in Edinburgh, and trained partly there and partly by Killick's.

At Port Swettenham the Ben Line office took over from Paterson Simons, but cargo was mainly controlled from Kuala Lumpur so a Ben Line office was established there too. In Hong Kong the Ben Line had for many years been represented by W. R. Loxley & Co. Ltd, import and export merchants, controlled from London by their parent Blyth Greene Jourdain. On my first visit to Hong Kong in 1952 I was able to confer considerable 'face' on Loxley's, and on the Ben Line (though this was not planned and I only became aware of it in retrospect) by staying with the Governor and Commander-in-Chief, Lieutenant-General Sir Terence Airey, for whom I had worked during part of the Second World War. A government launch met me at Kai Tak airport and transported me to Flagstaff House, which lay on the island near the waterfront. There with unobtrusive, noiseless efficiency a Chinese valet unpacked, pressed, and had laundered my meagre suitcase of clothes and attended to every want before I had thought of asking.

Having bought two Austin Reed ready-made tropical suits for 14 guineas apiece in London, my wardrobe had been augmented at even keener prices in Singapore with white duck trousers (usual office wear), a white 'shark-skin' jacket and tropical weight black trousers (obligatory dress for dinner parties) all tailor made in forty-eight hours. I had flown to Singapore in a BOAC Argonaut, the civilian version of the Lancaster bomber. We left London on schedule at 2359 hours on 23 October (my thirty-third birthday) and disembarked while the aircraft refuelled at Rome, Nicosia, Basra, Karachi, Bombay and Colombo, where we arrived in the early afternoon of Saturday 25 October. At Colombo there was a scheduled overnight stop at the Mount Lavinia Hotel. The final stage to Singapore was completed in one hop, leaving at 0730 hours and arriving at 1725 hours local time on 26 October. If I had departed on a different date I could have flown more quickly but with even more intermediate stops in the BOAC Comet service which had just been inaugurated with twice-weekly flights in September 1952. I did indeed subsequently enjoy several Comet flights, and one flight in Concorde, while that aircraft briefly served Singapore: six hours' flying time with a single stop at Bahrein. Having spent the best part of three days to reach Singapore in 1952, nobody thought that an absence of six weeks in the Far East was excessive. Twenty years later – or even earlier – it was not thought unreasonable to flip out and back to San Francisco or Tokyo for a meeting, during an absence of three or four days.

To revert to Hong Kong in 1952, the head of Wang Kee, our shipchandlers, stevedores and Chinese crew suppliers, was a venerable, rich Chinese usually known as 'Uncle' because his niece, May, was married to Wang Kee's managing director, Y. Y. Yeung. Both 'YY' and May were ever helpful and popular in Ben Line circles. 'Uncle' held a banquet at his home – about a dozen courses and the best champagne – attended by the Aireys, the seniors in Loxley's and me. On that first visit I also made the acquaintance of George Marden, chairman of Wheelock Marden & Co. Ltd, who owned Cornes & Co., our agents in Japan. He was a collector of porcelain and ivory, and arranged for his Chinese dealer to assemble about fifty delectable pieces of undoubted authenticity for my inspection. In those days treasures could be purchased very cheaply and I should have bought the lot. Instead I matched my purchases to my pocket and came away with a Ming vase and a seventeenth-century ivory Goddess of Mercy.

The break in the weather between summer and autumn came rather early that year and after a sudden overnight drop of 28 degrees the British troops had to shiver in their tropical uniforms for three days until the quartermasters issued their winter kit. Before and after the Second World War until air-conditioning was introduced, the British heads of businesses lived on the Peak, the higher up the more exalted the status. In summer the altitude ensured a refreshing coolness, but in spring and winter the Peak was often shrouded in damp cloud. When the Ben Line office was established we followed the fashion, so its head and his family had to put up with their clothes going mouldy in the wardrobes and mildew forming on their furniture.

We had had to decide in 1947 between trying to keep our links with China or pinning our hopes on a development of trade between Taiwan and Europe: the political situation made it very difficult to trade with both China and Taiwan. Perhaps more by luck than judgement we chose Taiwan, and over the ensuing years we were richly rewarded. Here our agents were an old-established British merchant firm, Tait & Co. Ltd, headed by Dennis Poltock, whose energies were divided into three parts: coaching Taiwanese swimmers up to international standards – an altruistic but major preoccupation; secondly, looking after Tait's traditional business as exporters of tea, and thirdly, the Ben Line agency, which progressively grew in importance. When Poltock reluctantly retired he was succeeded by an ex-Gurkha officer, taller by half than his erstwhile troops – W.G. Everard, a man of great integrity, with a quiet sense of humour, who recognised and responded to the Ben Line's new role as a major carrier between Europe and Taiwan. Tait's staff included a high-principled English spinster lady, Celia Temple, who, apart from her primary role as Tait's efficient bookkeeper, acted as mother confessor, aunt and nanny to the staff, and to anyone else in the small Christian community in Taipei, the capital, who needed comforting and spiritual advice. Tait's head office was in Taipei, which ships could reach in the days of sail, but now the nearest ocean port was Keelung about twenty-five miles to the north east. The south of the island was served by Kaohsiung, which became increasingly important not only for the export and import of cargo, and in due course as a container port, but also as a world centre for shipbreaking.

A number of adjoining berths at Kaohsiung were reserved for the shipbreakers, most of whom were small family firms. When cargo liners were displaced by containerships in the late sixties and early seventies these berths were filled with ships in various stages of dismemberment. Much of the work with oxy-acetylene cutters was done by women assisted by quite young children. Chunks of steel plate were hoisted ashore by improvised derricks to be re-processed at the steelworks nearby; furniture, doors, panelling, wire ropes, bits of machinery were stacked on the berth to be re-sold: nothing was wasted. The whole ship gradually disappeared where she lay afloat, until the keel could be grappled with wire ropes while it too was progressively demolished. Every ship came to the breaking berths under her own steam. Some were in excellent condition, but when a Ben Line vessel was to be broken up we took off all stores and spares we could make use of before she was handed over, and made sure that painting was kept to a minimum during the last weeks of her life. It was a melancholy business.

In the Philippines we had been represented in the thirties by Hanson, Orth & Stevenson, whose primary interest was the export of hemp. After the war they sold out to Conrad & Co., whom we retained as agents in Cebu, but Dodwell & Co., merchants with broader interests, became our principal agents in Manila. In 1960 Dodwell told us that they had decided to withdraw from the Philippines, so we needed to find new agents. Sir Douglas visited the Philippines and was impressed by the acumen of two brothers Delgado, who had fingers in many pies and thought they would like to add a ship agency, which would be a new venture for them. In the event one of the brothers, Francisco (Paco), and his wife Cita set up a company, named Citadel because it was to be the particular interest of Mrs Delgado, an astute businesswoman in her own right. Citadel took over from Dodwell on 1 April 1961.

The Delgados had a large family, including a glamorous daughter, Isobel, who became a successful cargo canvasser until she got married. She – indeed the whole family – combined commercial activity with moving in high Filipino society. Politically they were in opposition to Marcos and were much disappointed when he was elected President, but they were already rich enough not to need the plums which the latter dispensed to his family and friends. The Delgados took so much to Sir Douglas and his family that they decided to send two of their sons to school at Gordonstoun and a younger daughter to a Roman Catholic school in Kent. All three survived their ordeals, which must have been particularly sharp for the boys, who had to exchange the tropical climate of their homeland for the east winds of Morayshire.

The Delgados' other main interest was the Roman Catholic Church. Paco's father had been Filipino Ambassador to the Vatican and both Paco and Cita were proud of their connections with the Church hierarchy. They paid frequent visits to Europe to visit holy places, to see their children at school and to shop. Shopping was a serious matter and might include the purchase of an expensive motor car, clothes, jewellery, or embellishments for the private chapel attached to their new mansion on the outskirts of Manila. The directors of Killick Martin were quite accustomed to receiving sudden summonses to cope with the results of these expeditions, so they were not on their guard when I concocted a message purporting to come from Cita Delgado that she had located and purchased a massive, ancient, stone shrine at Avicortu in Romania. Would Killick's please advise how it should be transported to connect with a Ben Line ship. No doubt they could arrange for it to be carried freight free to Manila? I allowed half an hour to elapse so that they could consult their atlases and then told them that I had indeed caught them with another April Fools' prank.

Paco and Cita Delgado were charming and generous. At Christmas time extraordinary parcels would arrive for the Ben Line directors – a 'personalised' box of excellent Filipino 'Alhambra' cigars with the recipient's initials carved into the lid, a hardwood rocking-chair inlaid with mother of pearl, 'knocked down', but easily reassembled. The time came when I was chairman that we had to re-enforce rules about the company's servants accepting gifts and for the directors to set an example. This resulted in an edict issued to Ben Line managers in UK and the Far East, all superintendents and masters, with copies for information to our principal agents:

GIFTS

In many countries where we do business, it is not unusual to offer small gifts as a courtesy. It is also a fairly widespread practice among ship-chandlers to offer Christmas presents to customers.

Occasionally someone may attempt to put the Company under an obligation or influence its decision by offering some substantial inducement to
one of the Company's employees. This never has been and never will be
tolerated.

The Board has reviewed the position and has decided on the following
rules which are the same for everybody in the Company.

1 If a gift or entertainment is offered with the obvious intention of putting
the recipient under an obligation to the giver it is to be refused.

2 Calendars, diaries and similar small handouts can be accepted, as can
entertainment which is judged to be in furtherance of the commercial interests of the Company and does not carry the obligation referred to in (1)
above.

3 Any more substantial gift or offer of entertainment should be refused
politely with the explanation that this is strict Company policy. There may
be exceptional circumstances in which gifts cannot readily be refused or
returned – in such cases the matter should be referred to the Director
responsible or to the General Manager Far East (Far East staff) or to the
Marine or Engineer Superintendents (seafaring staff).

A very serious view will be taken of any infringement of these rules.[13]

V

Some entirely new agency connections emerged from the Ben Line's
endeavours to exploit new trades in British North Borneo and
Sarawak during the fifties. These owed something to a friendship
between Sir Douglas and A. L. P. F. Wallace of Candacraig. Sir
Douglas was godfather to 'Dandy' Wallace's son; Mrs Wallace
accepted an invitation to launch a Ben Line ship. When 'Dandy'
Wallace became chairman of Wallace Brothers after the Second
World War he began looking for new areas to replace the firm's
longstanding interests in the extraction of timber from Burma
and Thailand. In both countries these activities had been disrupted by the war and thereafter were progressively taken over
by their respective governments from Bombay Burmah Trading
Corporation Limited (BBTCL) in which Wallace Brothers were
major shareholders. British North Borneo and Sarawak seemed to
offer the best new prospects and in February 1950 North Borneo
Timbers Ltd was set up, owned 50% by BBTCL and Wallace

13 Letter dated 8 December 1976.

Brothers, 50% by North Borneo Trading Co. Ltd, which had been in business at the main centres of the colony for many years. Though BBTCL and Wallace Brothers concentrated their activities mainly in the Tawau area and left the Sandakan area to their trading partners, the relationship was not harmonious, and after a few years BBTCL bought them out.[14] The venture in Sarawak based on Similajau failed to prosper and was terminated after two years, but meantime the Ben Line had become involved in another more successful timber enterprise in Sarawak, undertaken by Colonial Timber Co. Ltd, which is described in chapter 9. However in the early fifties there were optimistic prospects not only from timber but also from hemp, oil palms and cocoa, particularly in the rich alluvial soil around Tawau. In the event these potentially valuable crops succumbed to disease and by 1962, when British North Borneo became Sabah, a state in the Malaysian Federation, most of the timber was moving to Japan, Australia and Korea rather than to Europe.

My first visit to Tawau was on board *Bendoran* III in November 1952. We sailed across from the Philippines having loaded bulk copra at Cebu. On the evening of our arrival the master[15] and I were invited to dinner by the agent, an old Burma hand named Jacques, who lived in a spacious atap hut – there were no brick buildings. After an excellent dinner we were invited to sample our host's favourite black Burma cheroots, which were of extraordinary size and strength. I managed a quarter of mine before departing back to *Bendoran*; she was due to sail at daylight for the log ponds at Wallace Bay on Sebatik Island which BBTCL were developing as their main base. I came up on deck as dawn was breaking to see Jacques's bulky figure advancing towards me with a pipe in his mouth; something protruded from the bowl which glowed in the half dark – the butt end of his pre- breakfast cheroot.

Bombay Burmah employed British managers, many of whom had been expensively educated. A few may have been hungry black sheep from good families, in the East India Company tradition. They all had 'style', and quickly made themselves comfortable in inhospitable jungle surroundings. In 1956 I visited one of their camps

14 A.C. Pointon, *Wallace Brothers*, Oxford, 1974, p.79 *et seq.*
15 Captain Adam Plenderleith.

at Kalabakan, a long hot journey by launch through the mangrove swamps with a Dyak boatman for company, wondering what I should find on my arrival. I was pleasantly surprised. Despite lack of running water, a bath was available. One of the orderly range of atap and timber huts housed the mess which was very adequately furnished with glass, cutlery and linen. We ate and drank well and I remember being astonished by the pure pale beauty of a Burmese princess, who had married one of the British managers.

There were inevitably other instances of mixed marriages. At Sandakan, usually the next port after Tawau, the agent[16] lived in a house on stilts in the water with his common-law wife and growing family of Anglo-Bornean children. He was highly intelligent, well-read, and could spout long passages from Shakespeare. He was also an astute businessman, and later made a fortune.

In the fifties it was possible to fly, as I did, from Tawau to Sandakan, and from there to Jesselton, by twin-engined Rapide biplane which provided an infrequent but scheduled Malayan Airways service, skimming a few hundred feet above the virgin forest and skirting the slopes of the magnificent and allegedly spirit-haunted Mount Kinabalu (13,455 feet) to land on the sandy beach: flights to and from Jesselton (now Kota Kinabalu) were cancelled when the tides were too high. Ben Line ships called at Jesselton, to discharge general cargo and to load small quantities of rubber, copra and other produce. It was a tricky business to berth an ocean-going ship alongside the single small wharf and to bring her off again into open water without going aground. We and Blue Funnel tried to persuade the Colonial Government to improve the port, without much success.

The agent at Jesselton sported a military moustache and club blazer, and drove a somewhat decrepit Lagonda too fast. He had been engaged to a girl in the Home Counties, whose widowed mother, a former model for *Vogue* magazine, had snatched him from under her daughter's nose, and was now trying to make sense of life in her full-blown glory, complaining that Harrods' chintzes faded in the sun and insects gobbled up her dahlias in the garden.

Ben Line ships called at Labuan Island on the north-west coast of

16 K.G. Barrett.

British North Borneo to discharge general cargo which was then coasted to the Seria oilfield in Brunei. I was in the hut which served as a club when the Australian, who was in charge of Labuan's large Second World War Forces Cemetery, came in and ordered 'the usual'. To sustain him in his lonely and harrowing work, a few degrees from the Equator, 'the usual' was a tumbler containing equal parts of brandy and crème de menthe.

VII

In Japan the Ben Line had been represented by Cornes & Co. since 1881. After the Second World War they re-established their head-quarters in Tokyo and their own offices in Yokohama and Kobe, with Japanese sub-agents at Nagoya, Shimizu, Kure, Muroran, Hakodate and Otaru. Cornes, no longer independent, having been bought up by Wheelock Marden & Co. Ltd, dealt in a wide range of British imports, from Rolls-Royce cars to confectionery, and were also Lloyd's agents, but in the years immediately after the war there was very little trade either eastbound or westbound. In the early fifties Ben Line ships visited Japan mainly to discharge large consign-ments of military stores and equipment at Kure, whence they were forwarded to sustain the war in Korea.

When I visited Japan for the first time in December 1952 pathetic groups of crippled soldiers, wearing khaki caps and white robes, begged in the streets. Very few people spoke any European language. Because of the perennial danger from earthquakes one- or two-storey buildings were the norm. The address system in the cities was so inexact that a taxi, if one could be obtained, often had difficulty in finding the desired location.

The industrial revolution which took place in the late fifties and sixties transformed not only Japan's economic standing, but many of its inhabitants' social habits, and the architecture of its cities. The American architect Frank Lloyd Wright's design for the Imperial Hotel in Tokyo, built shortly before the Second World War with oil-based foundations, paved the way for more adventurous struc-tures of many storeys adopted for new office blocks and hotels. Special efforts to increase the currency of the English language and to help foreign visitors were made in preparation for the Olym-pic Games held in Tokyo in 1964. Street names were translated phonetically below the Japanese characters. Notices to the public appeared in English translation, sometimes with surprising results: in the kimono section of a Tokyo department store a notice read 'Ladies have fits upstairs'. My wife and I drove to visit the world-renowned potter Hamada-san at his home in the village of Mashiko about sixty miles north of Tokyo. Deep in the country, a few miles short of our destination, we came to a level-crossing without gates, but even here the warning sign had been translated: 'Beware! the red light flashes thirty seconds after the train has passed.' As I am considerably taller and larger than indigenous Japanese (some sumo wrestlers excepted) the time came when I could not walk down the street without encountering some boy in his black school uniform and cap, who would fearlessly ask: 'Hello, Mister. How tall are you?' No schoolgirl in her equally smart uniform of blue serge skirt and sailor-suit blouse was, of course, ever so forward, though she might be unable to suppress, hand in front of mouth, a titter of wonderment at this foreign giant. Soon, however, respectable Japanese matrons in twos and threes could be seen taking tea together in hotel lounges – in their best kimonos. Except in hotels catering for Western tastes, bread was unobtainable, but by the sixties the Japanese had come to like it: soft whitebread rolls and sandwiches were sold at the kiosks on station platforms in competition with the traditional *bento*. This was a small, flat, compartmented, wooden box containing an individual meal of assorted dried fish, pickled vegetables, fruit, seaweed and rice. Each railway line had its own special mix of ingredients – all seemed to me to be equally delicious.

Some customs, some forms of life, remained immutable. Ronald Freeborn, Cornes's manager in Kobe, had a Japanese wife and an English garden, where he was trying to grow a lawn. Grass as known in UK does not thrive in Japan and the lawn became infested with moss. He asked his wife to get in some help to weed it. While he was away at the office an expert labour force moved in and when he came home every blade of grass had been carefully removed, leaving the moss to flourish in the best Japanese tradition.

When we resumed regular services between Japan and Europe Cornes was headed by Peter Hewitt, who had served with distinction in the Army during the war. He had a deep interest in Japan and the

Japanese, and was well regarded by the British community (he later became President of the British Chamber of Commerce) and by the Japanese exporters. He had no family – apart from black labradors and Pekinese, which miraculously resulted in the only 'Pekador' I have ever seen, a remarkably handsome little dog. Better-planned offspring were produced from breeding pedigree cattle and pigs, mainly from British stock, at his Japanese farm. Hewitt had decided ideas about staffing and staff training: each year he recruited one or two graduates from Japanese universities, some of whom came into the ship agency side of the business. One of these, Masahiro Ogihara, who became a pillar of the Ben Line Office in Tokyo, made the first familiarisation tour of Europe in 1964 during which he visited Edinburgh and stayed in our house. We gave a dinner party for him, and as I knew from my visits to Japan that he was an accomplished performer on the mandolin, which he had brought with him, we promised our guests some Japanese folk songs. After dinner he was persuaded to produce the mandolin and we waited expectantly while he tuned up. He startled us by first playing 'God save the Queen', followed by selections from Bach and Vivaldi and ending with 'Coming through the Rye' – no Japanese folk songs, which he thought would be too ordinary.

In those areas where we had not set up Ben Line offices we often attached a British, Edinburgh-trained, owners' representative to the agent's staff. We followed this procedure in Japan and Manila, and in Jakarta after we were admitted to the Indonesian Conferences in 1960. Later my son Gavin, who had joined the company in 1974 after graduating from Cambridge, transferred from owners' representative in Jeddah to an equally daunting position in South Korea, based on Seoul, where he had to cope with virulent infighting in the agency such as only the Koreans seem capable of.

To coordinate and administer the activities in the Far East we decided to appoint a general manager Far East, based in Singapore. The first incumbent, Arthur Kinnear, was succeeded in 1963 by Richard Thorman, who had joined the company as a trainee ten years previously. When Dick Thorman joined the board in Edinburgh in 1972 he was succeeded by David Smith, who had also spent his entire business life with the company. During the seventies it became increasingly difficult to obtain work permits for British subjects in Singapore. After putting up with much obstruction and harassment we moved the general manager Far East and his small staff from Singapore to Hong Kong in January 1976. Hong Kong was chosen not only because it was a crown colony and no work permits were required, but also because the centre of gravity as regards cargo had moved northwards. Hong Kong itself, Taiwan, and pre-eminently Japan were all developing very rapidly and were soon to be joined by South Korea.

So, at last, in 1970 we took the plunge and set up our own Ben Line offices in Tokyo, Yokohama, Osaka and Kobe. The staff were predominantly Japanese, transferred amicably from Cornes's ship agency department. They proved themselves hardworking and extremely loyal, quite prepared to see the Ben Line get the better of competing lines, whether these were Japanese or of some other nationality. The directors in Edinburgh and the general manager Far East did their best to foster this loyalty by visits during which staff were formally briefed on the latest developments, and informally entertained at lighthearted dinners attended by all, female as well as male, in the particular office being visited. These parties customarily ended with singing: 'Three cras [crows] sat upon a wa' [wall]', accompanied by appropriate gestures, was a particular favourite.

Adequately to describe the Ben Line's agency connexions and all the colourful characters involved in them would need a book on its own. In the era of the cargo liner T. A. Bulmer & Co. Ltd at Middlesbrough, the firm of Henry Tyrer on Blue Funnel's doorstep in Liverpool, James & Hodder in Avonmouth, P. Henderson & Co. and latterly Prentice Service & Henderson in Glasgow, Henri Lecoq in Le Havre and G. Féron E. de Clebsattel in Dunkirk and Paris, Sandilands Buttery in Penang, among many others, served the Ben Line to the best of their diverse abilities.

Vital links between the agents, the stevedores and the ships were the cargo superintendents. These were Ben Line former senior deck officers, or masters such as Captains D. G. Cuthbertson, OBE and E. Massarella. They worked unsocial hours, travelled from port to port, some in the Far East as well as in Europe, and applied their accumulated experience and drive to ensure that the ships were safely and efficiently loaded, and kept to schedule. Theirs was an exacting task, forever coping with differing circumstances, calling for skill, ingenuity, and diplomacy which did not exclude the necessary sharp word when it was needed.

7
Shore-Side Sports and Pastimes

The Scots abroad are even prouder to proclaim their origins than their fellow countrymen at home. The flourishing St Andrew Societies in Singapore, Kuala Lumpur, Bangkok, Hong Kong and elsewhere were well supported by Ben Line staff and regular consignments of haggis were carried in the company's ships for Burns suppers and St Andrew celebrations. By chance and obligation rather than by choice, I attended two of the latter in Bangkok until I learned to plan my itinerary with more forethought. Scottish country dancing is all right in moderation, but one can have too much of a good thing. For some weeks before the Bangkok ball, cosmopolitan groups of Thais and other, mainly European, nationalities were coached to dance eightsomes, The Gay Gordons, Strip the Willow and The Dashing White Sergeant by the male and female *cognoscenti*, not all of whom were Scots. The ball itself took place at the Royal Sports Club and got under way about 10 p.m. During intervals between dances the pipes and drums of Vaijiravudh College (which, I was told, is the Thai equivalent of Eton), dressed in suitably anonymous dark kilts, white tunics and black glengarries, marched up and down the dance floor playing one of the three tunes taught to them by their instructor, a retired member of the Borneo Co. staff.[1] As soon as possible after midnight, when the boys retired to bed, I retired too, but the merry-making continued long after that, and in the middle of the following morning one might encounter somewhat dishevelled revellers, still in more or less full Highland dress.

No manifestation of 'Scottishness' was, indeed is, more bizarre than the annual Jakarta Highland Gathering, initiated by a group of expatriate Scots including the Ben Line owners' representative,[2] in collaboration with the British Embassy, to raise funds for charity.

1 S.S. Marr.
2 R.A.M. Ramsay, MBE.

On this occasion cabers are tossed, shots are put, pipes are blown, races are run, and the whole event is commemorated in a glossy programme incorporating fee paying advertisements and suitably light-hearted editorials.[3]

For the inaugural gathering in 1975 *Benreoch* II carried, freight free, an authentic seventeen feet of Scots pine, six inches diameter at the base. However she was delayed by heavy weather and arrived off Jakarta at midnight only two days before the event. Urged on by the other members of the organising committee - 'Where is the ... caber? The games will be a flop if it isn't there' - Rod Ramsay, the Ben Line representative in Indonesia, realised that exceptional measures were needed. Customs officers tend to be suspicious; the Indonesian Customs, not noted for instant sympathetic flexibility, were unlikely to be impressed if told that this trunk was being imported to see who could chuck it furthest. Ramsay transferred the caber to a launch in the anchorage and, with help and some wading, offloaded it through the surf at a beach well clear of harbour limits where a truck was waiting. So, the caber arrived in time. When the great day came the reputation for stamina of the Scots at home received a boost because nobody proved strong enough to toss it. On subsequent occasions a saw was kept handy as it often is in Scotland.

Ben Line staff, and some of their wives, became members of the Hash House Harriers, though the company cannot claim to have been represented among the founders in 1938, a small group who frequented the Selangor Club in Kuala Lumpur, known as Hash House because of its indifferent culinary reputation. The founders were all British and all bachelors, observing at least one of the commandments laid down by their employers: 'Thou shalt not get married during thy first contract', which in those days usually lasted for three years, without home leave. Another commandment was: 'Neither shalt thou run fast and wild with the local perempuans'. Each Monday they ran a non-competitive hare and hounds paper chase of about five miles, to counteract the activities of the week-end and work up a renewed thirst, which they began to slake with copious drafts of beer immediately after the run. Their activities ceased to astonish the local population during the Japanese

3 Some of the Jakarta Highland Gathering programmes are preserved in the National Library of Scotland.

occupation of 1942-45 and were curtailed, though not stopped, by the Malayan Emergency of 1948-51 with restrictions which lasted for some time thereafter. A second Hash House chapter was founded in Singapore in 1962, followed by Kuching in 1963, Brunei, Kota Kinabalu and Ipoh in 1964. Ten years later when the 1,500th run was held in Kuala Lumpur there were 35 chapters. After that the idea really caught on and by 1988 some 600 Hash House clubs were active in about 75 countries, and in all continents except Antartica.[4]

Several who joined the Ben Line as trainees and went out to man our offices in the Far East came from Scottish schools with a strong Rugby football tradition, and some found places in the teams which flourished in Singapore and Hong Kong. J. F. (Hamish) Muirhead had the distinction of being capped for both Singapore and Malaysia, as well as playing cricket for Singapore, Malaysia and Hong Kong.

Cricket clubs occupied extremely valuable prime sites both in Singapore and Hong Kong. The Singapore Cricket Club also played Rugby football. In 1953 the Ben Line put together a complete XV composed of shore and sea staff which defeated the Singapore 'A' Team 8-5. The Ben Line team maintained its unbeaten record because it never took the field again.

Rugby football was gaining popularity in Japan and Taiwan in the seventies, but in Japan the game which obsessed the business world was golf. Driving ranges appeared on the roofs of city buildings and on vacant plots of ground. The numbers of golf courses increased, but demand far exceeded supply and club membership was extremely expensive. A good deal of business was transacted on the golf course, particularly because the fees could then be allowed as expenses. The ambition of many Japanese businessmen who visited us in Edinburgh was to play at St Andrews. They were astonished to be told how cheap it was for a member of the public to play a round over the excellent Braid Hills municipal course on the outskirts of Edinburgh: the green fee during the fifties was sixpence.

At Head Office there was and is, an annual bogey handicap competition for the Coronation Trophy, presented by Alec Mitchell, to

4 For this information about HHH I am indebted to S.J. Forbes, for long a prominent member, who is also, in his spare time from Ben Line duties, an expert underwater photographer.

[105]

commemorate the crowning of King George VI. This is still played for at Luffness on the shores of the Forth, followed by supper at the club house. When James Grieve died the staff contributed to a Memorial Trophy, which since 1965 has been played for at various courses: Gullane, Dalmahoy and West Linton. The handicapper for both competitions, Harry Cole, playing off a handicap of 9 usually contrived to avoid being the winner, and made sure that no one lifted the cup two years running.

There are marked differences between playing golf in Scotland and in the Far East. These differences are not only climatic; at the Royal Sports Club in Bangkok the course is completely flat and the main hazards are not bunkers but 'klongs', or drainage canals. Each player is provided with a caddy and a 'klong boy'. The latter, clad only in a pair of shorts, stations himself on the bank of the most likely 'klong', having quickly observed whether you tend to slice, or pull, ready to retrieve your ball. 'Klong boys' are apt to go through the motions of wading and searching without apparent success so that they may return later in the day to collect a valuable harvest of second-hand balls. Regular players withhold a tip at the end of the round if reasonable numbers are not immediately recovered.

Golf was very popular in Singapore where Arthur Kinnear's wife Bettina captained the Ladies' Team with distinction. In Hong Kong the only course on the island at Sheko was exclusive and expensive. Another, at Fan Ling in the New Territories, gave birth to an extraordinarily successful club, the Fanlingerers, formed after the Second World War to raise money for the war blinded. The club, to which many serving and former Ben Line staff belong, has a motto (see below) and colours – a yellow Chinese dragon on a maroon background – but no premises. 'The Fanlingerer is a good-tempered friendly animal, originally found in large numbers swinging head down in the vicinity of drinking holes in the New Territories of Hong Kong. Elderly specimens, mostly domesticated, now amble round the links of many lands lingering at times to greet each other with the old traditional cry 'Festina lente, mo kum fai'.[5]

Boating in various forms attracted many staff members both at home and in the Far East. This resulted in one tragedy when a

5 'Make haste slowly' (Latin), 'no go quick' (Cantonese), from *Fanlingerers List of Members*, 1989.

graduate trainee went sailing in the Forth, alone and without a life jacket. The boat was soon washed ashore and some weeks later his body followed. As partner in charge of staff I spared his parents some anguish by identifying him at the little mortuary in North Berwick, which I was able to do without any doubt by the colours of his Oxford college round the neck of his sweater. The waters of the Firth of Forth are treacherous, but can be enjoyed with proper discipline. In the late sixties a few enthusiasts at Head Office founded a Ben Line Sailing Club based at North Queensferry. They bought an old naval whaler for £45 and sold her a few years later when the club was disbanded for £55. In the interim the fifteen to twenty male and female members invested much voluntary labour to make her seaworthy and equip her with a discarded company's outboard motor. Sailing was usually confined to the area between Rosyth and Dalgety Bay for safety reasons.

Benbhui, the company's launch in Hong Kong, was used, when she could be spared from harbour duties between ship and shore, for weekend picnic and bathing parties to which appreciative shippers and receivers might be invited. In the late seventies the company bought a 50-foot junk built in Hong Kong, named *Benveg* (little Ben), which was based in Singapore and performed similar harbour and leisure duties there.

In the early sixties an old ketch, which her owners Richard Thorman and Alec Peill sailed in the waters round Hong Kong, was wrecked in a typhoon. A subsequent private venture, *King Prawn*, owned by David Graham and Captain Douglas Cranna, both then serving on the staff of Far East Management, survived being blown ashore by a typhoon. This second-hand 32-foot junk had a 22 h.p. diesel engine and a dinghy named *Fried Rice*, and gave much pleasure to her owners and to many Ben Line staff and their families.

During the fifties I raised and captained an office cricket team. I have never been much good at cricket, and subscribe to G. K. Chesterton's view that if a game is worth playing it is worth playing badly. Our star performer should have been James Grieve: he ran his own team of friends, the Fireflies, who made a week's annual tour in Yorkshire, but he tended to feel that he would be giving us an unfair advantage by playing for us. Our skills were very limited, and it was not easy to find opponents with comparably low standards, though for several years Edinburgh University Staff fulfilled those conditions admirably. They had one wily bowler, Professor David Abercrombie, and the opposing captain, Dr Dewar, was a sound opening batsman; however the mainspring of their team was Dr Dewar's wife, an enthusiastic Australian who was their organising secretary and scorer. They usually won, but whatever the result we took it in turns to give both teams supper in the Dewars' house or ours. On one occasion a ball from our fastest bowler struck our wicket keeper on the leg, whereupon he burst into flames. After he had been extinguished, received first aid, and the remains of the matches had been removed from his trouser pocket, he gallantly resumed his duties.

One year we were challenged by Pencaitland, a village in East Lothian, which had recently formed a team. The match was to be the first on their new pitch, which on some idiot's recommendation had been specially laid with hill turf. We were due to start play at 6 p.m. – most matches were played in the evening, as far as possible outside office hours – but when we arrived at 5.30 p.m. we found that owing to an administrative oversight the pitch had not been marked out and was covered with two or three inches of grass. There was then some dispute as to who had the key to the shed which housed the mower and other necessaries, such as stumps and whiting. My team mowed the pitch and we went in to field about 7 p.m. Pencaitland's star, and opening batsman, was a miner from Yorkshire who had migrated to work nearby at Tranent. When he was given out lbw for 12 he accepted the verdict with ill grace and immediately returned as an umpire to make sure that no further rash decisions should be made, at his end anyway. Owing to the late start it was agreed that we would play twelve overs each. Pencaitland made 54 for 8, which was quite respectable seeing that the hill turf pitch was spongy as well as bumpy and any ball driven along the ground was quickly halted by the long grass of the outfield, sometimes even by a fielder. The Yorkshire miner opened the bowling from the slightly downhill end and soon had our batsmen in trouble. We were nearly saved by Roderick MacLeod, who had a good eye – he played squash for Scotland and was a mighty hitter – but our last wicket fell in the last over when we were five runs behind. We made a dash to the pub for hot pies and beer before closing time.

From the early fifties onwards the partners gave a party shortly before Christmas. These were first held in the Roxburghe Hotel for staff at Head Office. Then Sir Douglas and Lady Thomson gave one at Holylee, their house in Peeblesshire, attended by two busloads from Edinburgh. In 1954, and for some years afterwards, the party took place in the Adam Rooms at the George Hotel just round the corner from Head Office. Dinner was followed by a speech outlining the Ben Line's achievements during the past year and its aspirations for that coming. Mr Ted was prepared to propose the loyal toast, but both he and Sir Douglas were extraordinarily reticent about speaking in public and delegated this to one or other of their partners. A senior member of staff was appointed to reply on behalf of the guests and this was followed by dancing and silly games, organised for many years by Captain Ian Liston as Master of Ceremonies.

The partners thought it might be enough to hold a party every other year, but the staff thought otherwise and in 1955 organised their own event, to which the partners were invited. I remember attending this and taking part with Andy Hill and others in a race, lying prostrate on the floor, to suck dry a baby's bottle filled with lemonade. We soon outgrew the Adam Rooms and moved to the Assembly Rooms in George Street. The guest list was progressively extended to include retired masters and chief engineers, masters, chief engineers and Ben Line Far East staff who were home on leave, and Ben Line London Dock Office staff, plus their wives. When I became chairman I delegated the speechifying to my fellow directors in turn. In the late seventies, when staff from Atlantic Drilling and their wives were added, the total numbers came to some 450 and we moved from the Assembly Rooms to Prestonfield House at the foot of Arthur's Seat. The considerable administrative burden of issuing invitations, arranging seating plans and designing amusing menu cards was taken on by Alec Peill. The company met the ever-increasing financial outlay, not least in providing travelling expenses and free hotel accommodation for those based outside Edinburgh.

I suppose all this was worthwhile, to celebrate achievement, to tell some of those who had contributed to our success that they were not forgotten in retirement, and to help weld together a large group of increasingly diverse skills under the Ben Line flag.

8

Advertising and Public Relations

Soon after I became a partner in 1950 I found myself in charge of advertising and maintained a close interest in that, and in public relations generally, until I retired. The inherited responsibilities were not onerous since hitherto no money had been specifically allocated for the purpose and our main marketing thrust came from our London brokers Killick Martin, together with our agents in Europe and the Far East.

Sailing cards, giving the forward programme of ships' ports of call with dates, were and remained the most important form of advertisement in order to book cargo. We never lost sight of the need to issue these regularly, and to ensure that they included the essential information needed by a shipper. Sailing cards were sent through the post, but many were also delivered by canvassers, who hoped to book some cargo, or at least to exchange information and promote good relations, by personal visits.

Canvassers needed some inexpensive but useful gift, prominently displaying the Ben Line name, which they could leave on a client's desk in addition to the latest sailing card. Matches were one of the most successful articles to meet this requirement. Our first supply featured a Benmacdhui class ship and a Chinese junk, adapted from a painting by the marine artist Harold Ing. The boxes contained fifty wooden matches of excellent quality which were sought after for ordinary use, and were also prized by collectors.[1] In Japan, where vast numbers of different match-boxes are continually being produced and there are many keen collectors, this first design was accorded special prominence in a book about match-boxes, whose author gave it and the Ben Line useful free publicity on television.

1 The first Ben Line matches were produced by Svenska Tändsticks Aktibolaget; Jyuzo Itami's book was published in 1975; in 1987 Japanese collectors were offering Yen 30,000 (about £116.00) for a thirty-year-old Ben Line match-box – but it had to be full of the original matches.

By the end of the sixties that first design had been superseded by others, but examples in good condition commanded high prices from Japanese connoisseurs. One of the new designs was a flop. When we got to employing advertising agents, who were also public relations consultants, they persuaded us to let them produce a new box. This was quickly withdrawn from circulation in the Far East when it was pointed out that the colours would undoubtedly be interpreted by many of our customers as representing a ship of death on a funeral sea.

Many consultants in this line of business seem more interested in imposing their own style than in reinforcing features which have become familiar and accepted. Changes must of course be made to reflect new developments, but there are great merits in preserving the same themes year after year to symbolise stability and reliability. Our consultants would have liked to change our logo, or trademark, which was already well established, based on the splendidly striking house flag with a bold and basically unchanging type face for 'Ben Line'. I chose this type face in the early fifties and it has been used with minor modification ever since, despite initial criticism from Killick Martin who thought that it lacked elegance. The house flag had been in use since the days of sail, and it was something of a surprise when in 1989 Lord Lyon King of Arms insisted that it should be matriculated. So the Ben Line became an armiger, and Lord Lyon's fee took into account that no research was required to prescribe the design.

The company possessed very few pictures or other artefacts so we took trouble to search out pictures of the sailing ships and early steamers. There were two original sources: one a Ben Line sailing ship master, Captain Alexander Cromarty, who served with the company at sea from 1863 to 1892,[2] and who possessed a natural gift for painting. Secondly there were the anonymous Hong Kong Chinese painters, who specialised in portraying visiting ships and selling their work to the crews. Such pictures as we acquired, besides adorning the Edinburgh office and being lent for exhibition in other offices connected with the Ben Line, were drawn upon to produce a series of high-quality colour reproductions. These were printed on paper which replicated canvas and could be released one by one to

2 Blake, *op.cit.*, p.37.

shippers as an inducement to book more cargo with us so as to make their set more complete.

In the sixties Commander Leonard Moffat, who was an instructor at Leith Nautical College, executed a number of large water-colours of Ben Line ships, which were remarkable for the high standard and technical accuracy of his draughtsmanship, and in the following decade I discovered the work of Colin Verity, an outstandingly able marine artist, who carried out a number of commissions for us ranging from *Benalbanach* I in wartime to *Ben Ocean Lancer* drilling for oil in Arctic waters.

We collected photographs of as many individual ships as we could. Many of these were reproduced in the World Ship Society's *Ben Line Fleet List and Short History*, first published in 1967.[3] From our collection of photographs we issued postcards which were widely distributed and were also sold in ships' canteens.

Splendid professionally built models, usually to a scale of 1:100, were made of many of the new ships as they were added to the fleet. These were expensive, and bulky, but were sought after as showpieces in our agents' offices and we soon had enough models to rotate them between those who could exhibit them to advantage. It was possible to go into mass production when a long-serving Ben Line master mariner, James Hastie, devised a cardboard cut out model of the 21-knot *Benledi* VI (1965) on a scale of 1:561,[4] and we were flattered when Revel, the international manufacturers and distributors of scale model kits, chose the same ship to add to their range of Classic Ships and Aircraft. They produced 150,000 kits of which we took 5,000 to give away to our customers, and found it quite difficult to satisfy demand.

Other popular promotional gifts were playing cards manufactured to our own design by De la Rue, good-quality plastic Chinese chopsticks, beermats and ashtrays. When the British, and other, governments realised the revenue potential of frequent new issues of postage stamps we bought stocks of franked first-day covers addressed to the company: these satisfied our requirements of novelty combined with low cost. It was surprising how many shippers had a philatelist in the family.

3 A revised edition was published in 1980 and a Supplement in 1985.
4 Published by Oxley Studios, Edinburgh, February 1966.

In the fifties we resisted suggestions that we should go in for so-called 'prestige advertising', apart from producing some posters on the theme 'Fast to the Far East'. During the sixties and seventies we were somewhat less restrictive and mounted a series of advertising campaigns in the British national press and the North European shipping trade magazines. These advertisements appeared in single column format with eye-catching line drawings, some of a humorous nature, and the slogan 'Better ship Ben Line', always using the same bold type face for 'Ben Line' and introducing a representation of the house- flag.

At least once a year we met our advertising agents, Interlink, in London to brief them on our recent activities and on our plans for the future. They then put up suggestions for the next advertising campaign in conjunction with Killick Martin.

David Gravell, who became chairman of Killick Martin in 1975, those of his directors particularly concerned with the Ben Line side of Killick's business – Peter Bowlby, R. H. (Bob) Tookey, George Allan – and their staff were a mainstay, as their predecessors had been, in the recruitment of cargo and maintaining good relations with our customers.

Killick's played an important part in planning and manning Ben Line stands at trade fairs such as the Export Services Exhibition at Olympia and international trade fairs held in Bangkok and Japan. These functions were a strain on our sales staff, but were an effective way of promoting our services measured by the great numbers of customers who visited our stands. By the mid seventies, however, we decided that the time, effort and cost involved in this form of promotion was no longer worthwhile.

There remained a need to offer our supporters some imaginative form of entertainment, if only to keep up with the activities of our competitors, and we adopted a proposal that we should sponsor the annual Tatton Park Driving Event. Killick's public relations officer, Dennis Goodchild, and his wife, both equine enthusiasts, worked indefatigably to ensure the success of this venture, which became very popular with customers, their wives and families, particularly those based in the Midlands and Northern England.

Another annual event organised by Killick's was a Ben Line dinner for the increasing number of Japanese firms established in the

London area. These dinners were held in historic locations such as the Tower of London, Guildhall, Lincoln's Inn and the Victoria and Albert Museum. The Ben Line chairman was expected to make a speech on these occasions. I arranged for the member of the company's staff in Japan, who was attached to Killick's on a rotational basis, to translate and tape record what I wanted to say so that I could then try to emulate Eliza Doolittle.

In the late fifties Messrs Cockburn, the Leith wine merchants with whom William Thomson I had served his apprenticeship, discovered in their cellars several bottles of sherry. Each bottle was embossed with the name of a Ben Line ship and the year in which its contents had been carried in cask on a Far East round voyage. Cockburn's very generously presented us with several full bottles, one of which we opened and found the sherry still excellent. In the early years of the twentieth century the partners had shipped an occasional cask, apparently for their personal consumption. Why should not the custom be revived and put to wider promotional use? During a holiday in Spain I visited the bodegas of Wilson and Valdespino in Jerez who expressed interest in supplying us with their 'Solera del 1847', a rich dark Oloroso. The first cask was shipped and we set about designing labels, arranging with a Leith firm to have the sherry bottled, and writing a leaflet exploring and updating the history of Old East India Sherry.

A tasting was arranged on board *Benmacdhui* III in London Docks attended by the Lord Mayor, Sir Dennis Truscott, who was also Master of the Vintners Company, and André Simon, the wine and food expert. The tasting consisted of three wines: the Wilson & Valdespino Oloroso before it had made the voyage, the same sherry after it had travelled and 'Benlarig 1909' one of the precious bottles found in Cockburn's cellars. Preparatory arrangements did not go entirely according to plan, so it was only on the eve of this event that I was able to taste the travelled sherry against the untravelled. What if the former could not be differentiated from the latter? Supposing, even worse, that the voyage had resulted in a deterioration? I was relieved to find that there was indeed an improvement, and even more relieved to have that opinion confirmed the following day by the experts who also found 'Benlarig 1909' still in perfect condition.

Ben Line Old East India Sherry earned us a lot of free press coverage over the years. It was a curiosity, blending ancient sailing-ship practice with novelty. Nobody tried to copy us. We sold some, but most was given away in bottles, half-bottles and even quarter-bottles. The presentation was quite as important as the contents; we took great trouble in designing the labels – a large rectangle including a map of the voyage, on the opposite side an oval extolling the contents, and a neck label bearing the name of the ship and the year in which the cask had travelled.

My experiments with labels had an unexpected sequel. On Fridays a master, who was on leave after completing a voyage, visited the office to discuss the results and receive instructions for the next voyage, after which he lunched with the partners and marine super-intendent. Lunch was deliberately kept very simple: soup, cold meat and cheese, to remind masters how lucky they were to enjoy ship's fare – and to demonstrate that the partners did not lush themselves up! Before taking our places at table the assembled company drank sherry. On this occasion we waited until Mr Ted raised his glass and then all drank together. Spluttering, gasps and exclamations showed that we had experienced an unpleasant surprise. Rapid detective work on the offending bottle enabled me to explain that some months previously I had been trying out various label designs and, having no sherry, had used tea brewed to the appropriate hue as a substitute. I also protested that this was not a practical joke and that I had no idea how that bottle had found its way into the drinks cupboard. Some, perhaps, believed me.

After two or three experiments we settled on a basic design for a Ben Line calendar consisting of twelve coloured photographs of Scottish scenes, selected to reflect the appropriate season, with a good spread of geographical locations. The cover could be removed to provide a wall calendar showing twelve months at a glance on the back of which was the current fleet list and a map showing the locations of the mountains after which the ships were named. Below each photograph the dates of the current month in bold type were flanked by those of the previous and subsequent months in less assertive, but still easily readable, type.

These calendars proved very popular and we had no difficulty in usefully distributing 40,000 copies every year. As our activities increased in Japan a special version in the same format was produced

[115]

with the date portion in Japanese. The calendars could be encountered in remote places around the world, and many recipients cut out and framed favourite pictures to decorate their living rooms.

I insisted on making the final choice of photographs personally, but the main work of organising the production and distribution was carried out by Alec Peill, who joined Head Office as public relations officer in 1966, having previously served with the Ben Line in Singapore, Hong Kong and Tokyo. In his spare time in Hong Kong he made a name for himself on television as 'Uncle Alec'; playing the guitar and singing in 'Children's Hour'.

Our other annual product was a red pocket diary distributed in about the same quantities as the calendars. Here again we tried to keep the format constant year after year, though as an economy measure fewer had leather rather than plastic bindings.

Learning how popular our calendars were, the Glen Line thought they would go one better by producing a book of photographs featuring the Glens after which many of their ships were named. We were amused to find captions such as 'Glen . . . looked down on by Ben . . .' Wm Thomson & Co. certainly didn't despise these keen competitors, but had no objection to others giving the wording a metaphorical interpretation.

Glen had amalgamated with Shire Line in 1920 and some of their ships still bore the names of Welsh counties. Even so confusions of identity between Glen and Ben occasionally arose. When a new Ben ship came into service we usually held a press reception on board in London Docks. At one such reception a politician,[5] who had been a distinguished officer in the Royal Navy, accepted an invitation to make an address. He began by saying that he retained a very high regard for the company 'because of the heroic part played during the siege of Malta in 1942 by the *Breconshire* . . .'. Sir Douglas, standing at his side, interrupted in an irate, audible whisper: 'You've got the wrong bloody company!'

Mr Ted enjoyed films; he never went to a cinema, but regularly watched television. He responded favourably to the idea of making a film about the Ben Line's services between Europe and the Far East. The prospective professional film-maker, Mr Patrick Young of

5 Vice-Admiral John Hughes Hallett, CB, DSO (1901-72), Parliamentary Secretary to the Minister of Transport, 1961-64.

Connaught Films, came to the office to show us a promotional film which he had recently completed. The screen and projector were set up in the board room and I went upstairs to tell Mr Ted that everything was ready. 'Right,' he said, 'where is this board room of yours?' We decided to engage Mr Young and it was agreed that though the aim would be to publicise the fleet as a whole, and this was reflected in the title *Eastern Sisters*, the star of the film would be *Benloyal* II, the first 20-knot ship of any nationality on the Far East Run, whose master, Captain G. M. McGill, was an imposing, photogenic figure with an unmistakable deep voice.

Mr Young and his film crew embarked on *Benloyal* in London and began shooting thousands of feet of 35 mm film. Roderick MacLeod was the partner who had the difficult job of controlling from Edinburgh the eccentricities of Mr Young who, we were told, was no more unpredictable than most other film directors. Captain McGill and his crew stoically put up with the sudden changes of plan, occasional non-appearance, and his potentially dangerous habit of falling asleep while standing up.

Eastern Sisters was a great success, shown to many invited audiences in Europe and the Far East and loaned out to film clubs. It was also shown on every ship in the fleet. The first showing in Hong Kong was, at the request of the Missions to Seamen chaplain, to the inmates of Stanley Prison. The response from Head Office for approval of this request was that it would be useful to try out the film on a captive audience.

A few years later we commissioned another film, *The Bens 1944-1968*, intended to nourish the morale of our own staff as well as to impress our shippers. This 20-minute coloured film illustrated the development of the fleet, which at the end of the Second World War had only six surviving ships with an average speed of 12 knots and a total carrying capacity of about 2½ million cubic feet. 'Today the Ben Line fleet of over thirty cargo liners includes eight ships with a speed of 20 knots or more, and has a total carrying capacity of about 23 million cubic feet.'[6] The film was shot by several cameramen, amateur as well as professional, and showed the different classes of ship at work in Far Eastern ports. It also included shots of activities

6 Advertisement for the film, which was compiled and produced by Campbell Harper Films, Edinburgh; script by Robert Kemp, spoken by Victor Carin.

at Edinburgh Head Office. It was shown on board all the ships, also to shore-based staff, and at various promotional functions for customers.

We used audio-visual promotion again, though not in the form of a film, immediately prior to the introduction of the container service in the early seventies. As described in chapter 13, the Trio Service began in December 1971, but our first containership was not delivered until October 1972. We did have our own containers and the principle of the Trio consortium was that each member line carried other members' containers as well as its own. We had to accustom our shippers to this novel idea, and to persuade them that we could offer a thoroughly efficient service even though we had no containership. This was achieved by many showings to invited audiences of an ingenious, multiple projection presentation, quite novel at that time, consisting of still photographs connected by a recorded narrative. One of the directors of Hall Advertising, the Edinburgh-based company which put this presentation together, was a young MP, David Steel, later to become Leader of his party, who offered to arrange a showing at the Houses of Parliament. This proposal was greeted with enthusiasm. The unusual venue would attract many of our customers and would surely help to demonstrate that we were on solid foundations. Alas, the plan was scuppered at short notice by another MP who successfully argued that Parliament should not be the scene of a commercial promotion. That MP was my old friend Enoch Powell with whom I had served in the Army. He did not consult me on the matter, but we remain friends, though not always agreeing with each other's views.

Communication with one's own staff is a very important aspect of public relations, not only to promote morale but also because all members of the company, and their families, project its corporate image in one way or another. While the entire fleet consisted of cargo liners engaged in the trade between Europe and the Far East, liaison between our offices, agents and ships' crews was maintained by the marine, engineer and cargo superintendents and managers going about their duties, and through visits by directors. A periodical typewritten news sheet was issued from Edinburgh to help keep the 'galley wireless' up to its usual high standard of reliability.

During the seventies the scenario altered radically. The containerships spent very little time in port; the chemical tankers, bulk carriers, managed ships, those of the surviving cargo liners which were on charter, and the oil-drilling rigs were operating in novel trades, often in far-flung parts of the world. Various measures were taken to present the corporate identity which we so much wished to preserve. An annual *Chairman's Review* was given a wide circulation throughout the organisation, though we kept its contents from the attention of our competitors and the general public, and never made it available to the press. We instituted regular meetings between directors and managers: 'We rely on managers to pass on information to their departments just as we rely on Masters and Chief Engineers to keep their crews informed. Effective communication is two-way; it is important to listen as well as to talk.'[7] Thirdly, and importantly, *Ben Bulletin* replaced the typewritten news sheet in 1974.

Dick Thorman was put in charge of controlling its budget, directing its format, content and publication, and Alec Peill became its general editor. The format, that of a tabloid newspaper with black and white, and later coloured, illustrations, has remained substantially unchanged ever since its first issue.

Ben Bulletin's objectives were to inform, to entertain and to record. The quite frequent references to it in this book bear witness to its value as a source of historical information, and it has always had the merit of being a great deal more reliable, as well as being in better taste, than most other tabloids.[8]

In the seventies there were over 1,000 seafarers in the company and each issue of *Ben Bulletin* listed them by name, showing in which unit of the fleet they had been serving on a given date with separate lists of those on leave or on courses ashore. A map showed the worldwide location of each unit on that particular date.

Many contributions in the form of articles, news items and photographs came from readers ashore and afloat; the contents included profiles of offices and the people who served in them, the profiles of ships and rigs. It proved a useful vehicle for transmitting information about the new venture into offshore drilling, which was to provide so many Ben Line staff with an alternative means of livelihood.

7 *Chairman's Review* 25 November 1976.
8 A set of *Ben Bulletin* issues is held in the National Library of Scotland.

In 1975 I resisted proposals that we should use our 150th anniversary as a promotional theme. We did however mark the occasion by giving a commemorative present to all serving and retired members of the seagoing and shore staff. The men received a pair of cufflinks and the women a pendant. To go beyond this, deliberately to draw public attention to our longevity, seem to me to be tempting fortune, particularly when our Labour government appeared to regard private companies as an unpleasant anachronism, which should be deterred and if possible destroyed.

At the end of 1975 I said:

We have, over the years, derived great benefit from being a compact, hard working, family business. The growth of that business has resulted in increased numbers of staff, but I like to think that this will never mean the introduction of impersonal, bureaucratic, management procedures. Our staff, male and female, ashore and afloat, at home and overseas are the life blood of the Company. It is in great measure thanks to them and their predecessors, that though the Company traces its origin back over 150 years to 1825, it is today quite as strong and vigorous as it has ever been.[9]

9 *Chairman's Review* 18 December 1975.

9

Cargoes

1945 – circa 1970

In the immediate postwar years the company resumed its role as the carrier of low-paying, predominantly weight cargo. German and Japanese competition was, for the time being, eliminated, but the Ben Line continued to be the poor relation compared with P & O and Alfred Holt's Blue Funnel and Glen Lines. Eastbound cargo was scarce, westbound even scarcer. Ships in the Ben Line fleet for which no employment could be found on the liner berth were time chartered to other companies including P & O, Prince Line and City Line, or were fixed for voyage charters such as bulk salt from Port Said to Calcutta, bulk phosphate from Kosseir on the Egyptian coast of the Red Sea to Australia and bagged oats or bulk sugar from Australia to Europe. This scenario continued until the delivery of five purpose-built 16-knot ships[1] in 1948-49 began to give the company a competitive edge.

Anyone who thinks that the British armed forces enjoyed years of peace after 1945 needs to be reminded of the Emergency in Malaya (1948-51); the Korean War (1950-53); unrest, stimulated by the Chinese, in Hong Kong in the sixties; Indonesia's 'confrontation' in North Borneo and Sarawak which began in 1961. All these needed armaments, ammunition, land vehicles, aircraft, spares and stores. The Ben Line made a speciality of catering for these varied cargoes. Killick Martin, particularly Percy Rogers, did their best to foster good relations with the Services. Percy Rogers was paying us a visit in Edinburgh when I told him that we had just received a telephone call from the War Office; Sir Richard Hannay wished to speak to him as soon as possible. 'Hannay? – ah yes, important chap, I know him. I'll get on to him right away.' He telephoned the War Office and asked to be put through to Sir Richard Hannay. After a pause the

1 *Benmacdhui* III, *Benvenue* IV, *Bencleuch* VI, *Benavon* III, *Benalder* V.

operator said 'That's funny. I know the name well enough, but I can't seem to find him in our directory.' At this point I thought it wise to remind Percy that April Fool's Day had come round once again and that Sir Richard existed only in John Buchan's imagination.

Carrying military cargo was a two-way trade because the armed forces shipped home BLR (beyond local repair) vehicles and even the empty packing cases which had contained eastbound stores and equipment. A BLR jeep paid freight and so did an empty packing case, but several of both could be stowed inside a BLR 3-ton army truck. Our superintendent in Singapore, Captain W. O. Atkinson, exercised much ingenuity in such ways of economising in space and maximising the return to the ship. He taught many ships' officers how this might be done, but sometimes such cleverness received a setback. We were offered a squadron of armoured cars from Southampton urgently needed in Malaya. These would have suited the next sailing admirably, but they were half an inch too high to be stowed in the tweendecks. We were about to decline them when it was pointed out that there was really no problem because their tyres could be deflated sufficiently to reduce the height. Only when they were presented for shipment did we find out that they had solid tyres. It was no consolation to discover that the military themselves were sufficiently unaware of this innovation to go to the length of including a tyre pressure gauge in the vehicles' toolkits.

Later, when Atkinson was serving in London the first Buccaneer aircraft was entrusted to the company for carriage to Singapore where it was to undergo tropical trials. For security reasons it had to be shipped below deck and there were few ships in the trade, apart from the Ben Line's heavy-lift ships, with hatches long enough to accommodate the aircraft in its cradle, which Atkinson designed and the Ministry of Defence adopted as standard. The Buccaneer, still on the secret list, could not be photographed, but the company's archives contain many spectacular pictures of very large pieces of plant and machinery, locomotives, railway carriages, tugs, barges and motor torpedo boats all successfully carried by the heavy-lift ships. On one occasion Chinese painters working overside on the hull of *Benarty* VI in Hong Kong were tipped off their staging when the whole ship canted over with the weight of the minesweeper she was discharging. Some could not swim, but fortunately none suffered worse than a fright and a ducking.

Explosives, both military and commercial, were a particular speciality of the Ben Line. These were mainly loaded in the explosives anchorage at Holehaven and later Chapman Anchorage, both in the Thames, immediately before sailing outward bound. They could not be brought into the Ben Line regular outward berth at C Shed Royal Victoria Dock. Magazines made of timber were specially constructed for each shipment and were necessary to comply with safety regulations. What they contributed to safety apart from deterring pilferage, is open to question.

Pilferage was a perennial problem both in Europe and at Far East destinations. In UK shipments of bottled whisky and consignments of cigarettes were particularly prone to broaching. We shipped large quantities of Brand's Chicken Essence; this was often pilfered at destination, even after the manufacturers ceased to name the contents on the packing cases: the Chinese prized it as an aphrodisiac.

A large share of the market for civilian motor cars was shipped from London, principally Austin, Morris, and Ford from its plant at Dagenham. These were at first shipped 'unpacked', which was wasteful of ships' space and attended by frequent claims for damage or pilferage. Ford pioneered CKD (completely knocked down) cars delivered to the ship in standard cases which could be stowed one on top of another and assembled at Ford installations in the East. During the sixties unions and management combined to ruin the British car industry, and Mercedes-Benz emerged as a major exporter to the hitherto British-dominated markets. In May 1965 the company discharged in London some of the first Japanese cars to be marketed in volume in UK. These, with the somewhat unlikely name of Compagno Berlinas, were manufactured by Daihatsu of Osaka. Later the same year *Benledi* VI carried four Toyota Coronas, which were exhibited at the London Motor Show. This trickle of Japanese exports developed into a flood so large that the liner companies were unable to deal with it and most of this traffic was left to specialised car carriers, notably the Finnish company Wallenius and Hoegh of Norway.

During the fifties, sixties and seventies there were spectacular developments in the westbound trades from the Far East to Europe.

A principal reason for setting up the forerunner of the Far Eastern Freight Conference in 1879 had been the imbalance between the eastbound and westbound trades. In those days the eastbound trade was far greater, as it was between the two World Wars and on into the fifties. Thereafter the pendulum swung the other way, so that by 1972 the volume westbound was more than double that moving from Europe. Six years later the ratio of east to west was about 3 to 5, i.e. less than double.[2]

Hong Kong, primarily an importer, apart from being an entrepot for Chinese exports such as wood oil, ginger, duck feathers for eiderdowns and pig bristles for paint brushes, became a major exporter of goods manufactured in the colony. Taiwan (Formosa), newly independent after fifty years of Japanese domination, switched much of its agricultural produce to Europe, and then extended its exports to cheap textiles and many other manufactured items competing with Hong Kong. When I first visited Japan in 1952 its people were still in a state of shock from the war. There was little sign of industrial activity, the roads were appalling, the telephone system chaotic, and I remember thinking it must be about even chances whether the country would revert to its pre-1868 isolation and medieval traditions, or become Westernised on the American model, set by the occupying forces. The transformation of Japanese industry, which had hitherto been based largely on cheap imitations of Western products, to one of great variety, rich in original design, and usually of excellent quality, was awesome in its rapidity and thrust. By 1978 cargo carried in conference vessels from Japan to Europe had reached 3 million freight tons a year compared with 1.4 million from Hong Kong and 1.2 million from Taiwan.[3] The upsurge of South Korea was also astonishing. During the sixties and seventies the inhabitants rebuilt their war ravaged country with amazing vigour, and massive foreign aid. They imported the best practitioners, including British, to teach them how to make cars, build ships and establish heavy engineering. This challenge to their Japanese neighbours (not to mention their European teachers and competitors) was developed in a wide range of manufactured goods with a relish born of traditional animosity. A Korean regards every

2 Eric Jennings, *Cargoes*, 1980, p.5.
3 *Ibid.*, p.11.

Japanese as a ruthless oppressor, and to a Japanese all Koreans are crafty thugs.

Wm Thomson & Co. eventually rid themselves of the concept that every ship should ideally be full and down to her marks for as much of her voyage as possible. There was, however, no disadvantage in filling the same space more than once, if the ship could spare the time. So-called 'wayport cargo' loaded and discharged at intermediate ports on her itinerary could improve the voyage result substantially. Dried cuttlefish from Muroran on Hokkaido destined for Hong Kong might be replaced by tubs of live fish on deck from Hong Kong to Singapore. These fish must have been very valuable because they were accompanied by attendants equipped with paddles to aerate the water. Much of a ship's deck space between Hong Kong and Singapore was often occupied by large baskets of fresh vegetables. Junks came alongside shortly before a ship sailed, the shippers loaded their cargo themselves, paid the freight and received a parcel receipt stating that so many catties[4] of vegetables had been received 'freight prepaid, on deck at shipper's risk'. Usually more than one shipper and several consignees were involved. Nobody accompanied this cargo, yet on arrival in Singapore the consignees came aboard immediately, knew precisely what they were looking for, and where it was. There were never any complaints or disputes, but just how all this was achieved remained known only to the Chinese.

Another instance of Chinese ingenuity concerned the Royal Navy's drydock in Hong Kong. After the war the Admiralty decided that they no longer needed it, so it was sold by tender and acquired for a low sum by a Chinese, who did not want a drydock either. He knew however that Hong Kong citizens had difficulty in disposing of their waste. By making a charge for every load of rubbish tipped into it he more than recouped the purchase price, and when the drydock had been filled he was left with a valuable building site in a prime location.

Trincomalee, the British naval base that was progressively run down after the Second World War, before being handed over to

4 One catty = about 1.3 lb or about 600 grammes.

newly independent Sri Lanka, has a vast, natural, deep-water harbour, where the Ben Line loaded tea. I paid a courtesy call on the Sri Lankan naval officer in charge, who occupied one room in the former British flag officer's headquarters, but he was not an admiral, just a depressed commander without a ship. Tropical vegetation had encroached on the deserted, stone-built living quarters, stores, magazines and repair shops. That day there was not a single active ship in the great harbour, and where battleships, cruisers and destroyers had lain at anchor there were two laid up, rusting merchantmen.

The Ben Line occasionally called at Galle, and more frequently at Colombo, for tea, coconut oil, desiccated coconut, coir fibre and spices. These calls were for cargo bound to the United Kingdom only, because the Ben Line had no conference rights either to Continental European ports, or from Europe to Ceylon (Sri Lanka).

Wayport trades were particularly important on the westbound voyage in the years immediately after the Second World War, before the producers of primary produce had recovered from the war and before Hong Kong, Japan and Taiwan became major producers of manufactured goods.

The Ben Line carried large numbers of bulldozers and earth- grading machines from the Philippines to Dar es Salaam. These were United States surplus war material destined for the British Government's ill-fated groundnut scheme. After Dar-es-Salaam the ships went to Mombasa to load stores and a deck cargo of petrol in cans for Mahé, capital of the Seychelles Islands, which was then a British colony. At Mahé they picked up a parcel of up to 1,000 tons of bagged copra. The Ben Line pioneered this service from Mahé in 1946, but it lasted only a few years because Seychelles copra found a market outside Europe and the colony's other exports, such as vanilloes, calipash and calipee (turtle meat from the back and belly respectively) did not warrant a special call.

While the Suez Canal was open all ships called at Aden homeward bound as well as eastbound because oil fuel was cheaper there than anywhere else on our itinerary. We were encouraged by the Aden Protectorate Government to mount a westbound service to the ancient port of Mukalla about 300 miles east of Aden. This would initially be for timber, of which there was a great shortage, and rice, but it was hinted that Mukalla might become a new centre of prosperity if oil discovered in the interior could be exploited. We knew that space taken up by cargo for Mukalla might be refilled with cotton and cottonseed cake, which we had been carrying regularly from Port Sudan since 1946, or with other seasonal crops of potatoes and onions from Port Said.

Accompanied by my wife, I made the initial reconnaissance for the westbound service to Mukalla in February 1959, flying there from Aden in a DC3 (Dakota). Passengers were seated on the port side, while the starboard side was piled with assorted bundles of luggage and cargo, including three goats and several baskets of live fowls. While we were walking from the aircraft to the small tin shed, which served as the terminal, an Arab with a rifle, and a bandolier of cartridges across his chest, fired in the direction of a herdsman with his flock. It was explained that this was the normal method used to keep the runway clear. We stayed with the British Resident, a bachelor Scot named A. J. McIntosh, widely known as 'Touche'. Like many British, he had a deep affinity with Arabs and was very knowledgeable about their ways, while they revered him as a father figure and many came to the Residency to seek his advice. The less important sat cross- legged in the large entrance hall. The seniors were taken up to 'Touche''s chintz drawing-room.

He told us that Mukalla had recently been visited by a British Parliamentary Delegation. In advance of the delegation's arrival he had felt it necessary to warn the Sheikh of Mukalla that the MPs would be extremely displeased if they discovered that he kept eunuch slaves. The sheikh took the point and informed his slaves that they were to be freed. This caused consternation: the slaves said they were well fed, not overworked, and liked living in the sheikh's palace; it would be very cruel to turn them out – how were they to make a living? Eventually a happy solution was found; their some- what effeminate appearance was disguised in a form of military dress, and for the duration of the delegation's visit they were passed off as the sheikh's private household troops.

I did not see the sheikh, but was received by the old, blind head- man who had a finger in every pie. He asked me how many wives I had, how many sons? He also asked me how rich I was – a difficult question, because although I could correctly describe myself as a shipowner, and was fully empowered to negotiate on behalf of the company, my shareholding might not have represented more than the sum total of lavatory seats in the Ben Line fleet.

The service to Mukalla turned out to be one of our less successful pioneering ventures. The development of the Hadhramaut did not take place, and the days of the Aden Protectorate were drawing to a close. In any case while the Suez Canal was again shut by war from 1967 to 1975 ships had to be routed via the Cape of Good Hope, or through the Panama Canal.

When the first closure took place in 1956 the heavy-lift ship *Benledi* V was loading the tanks and vehicles of a British armoured regiment at Akaba, the port of Jordan, to bring them home. She was commanded by Captain Tommy Sutherland, a very popular master, one of the few teetotallers. Starting life as a miner, before going to sea, he had 'come up through the hawse pipe', that is had attained command, having begun as an ordinary seaman. On being told that he would have to sail home via the Cape of Good Hope, Sutherland said he did not have up-to-date charts on board. Captain D. S. ('Danny') Sinclair, who had been sent out to Akaba to superintend the loading, told him: 'Don't worry, just keep on south until your butter stops melting. Then turn right.'

Rubber plantations were established on the Malay peninsula only during the first decade of the present century, but were so successful that by the late twenties worldwide exports were running at over 400,000 tons a year. Each bale in the large trade to Europe was presented for shipment in a tea chest, but after the Second World War the carrier had to cope with naked bales sprinkled with talc. This was supposed to prevent them from sticking together, but did not always have that effect.

The Dunlop Rubber Company invented a process in the twenties, which prevented the sap of the rubber tree from congealing by treating it with ammonia. This liquid rubber – latex – was shipped in drums until in 1933 Blue Funnel carried the first bulk consignment from Singapore to Dunlop's installation in Liverpool's Gladstone Dock. After the war an installation was built at Hull and *Benvenue* IV discharged the first of many shipments there in September 1949.

Tin from Malaysia was a very valuable and much sought after cargo. Some of it paid freight three times over before ending up in somebody's dustbin. Initially shipped in gleaming, glossy ingots sufficiently large and heavy to make them difficult to steal, it was carried back in the form of tinplate and made into cans for the large crops of pineapple exported not only from Malaysia and Singapore but also from Taiwan and the Philippines.

To cope with increasing demand for the carriage of bulk liquids both eastbound and particularly westbound, all the new Ben Line ships after the Second World War were fitted with deeptanks of varying sizes, usually about 200 tons. Different liquids required different preparation of the tank, and latex was the most sensitive. In Singapore Mr Wong, the one-armed contractor – popularly known as 'One Wing Wong' – employed an army of Chinese women, 'Wong's Virgins', who cleaned the surface to bare metal, perched on bamboo scaffolding inside the tank. When it had been inspected by a Lloyd's surveyor they coated it with paraffin wax, applied very hot and very fast by brush. After a further inspection the tank was ready to receive the latex.

Coconut oil from the Philippines, Malaysia and Colombo needed heating which was supplied by removable heating coils in the tank. The same applied to palm oil from Malaysia and Singapore, which became a major export in the sixties when millions of rubber trees were felled and replaced by oil palms, reckoned to give a better return in the face of competition from synthetic rubber. In accordance with Murphy's Law the heating coils would, in all probability, have to be removed from the tank to receive its next booking, which might be DOP or DIOP,[5] chemicals used in the manufacture of plastics, from Germany or UK to Hong Kong or Taiwan. There were also shipments of bulk creosote from Hull to Manila. To reduce the laborious and expensive cleaning and preparation we experimented with various forms of bitumastic coating and some of the last cargo liners were fitted with stainless steel tanks.

Other commodities regularly carried in bulk were parcels of scrap and re-rollable steel, chrome ore from Masinloc in the Philippines and ilmenite ore from Port Swettenham. Ilmenite, a grey sand used in the manufacture of paint, had to be loaded at the bottom of the hold to allow its high moisture content to drain away. Least popular with crews was bulk copra from the Philippines because it was

5 DOP = di-octyl-phthalate; DIOP = di-iso-octyl-phthalate.

infested with little, black, biting flies. These 'copra bugs' penetrated the accommodation and were a great nuisance until colder weather suppressed them. By contrast, baled hemp from the Philippines was a good, clean cargo, uncomplicated apart from being easily combustible, and paid a good rate.

Maybe the large quantities of second-hand back axles and lorry parts should be included in the bulk cargo category. They were shipped from UK to Singapore and Malaysia where they were used by Chinese transport operators to prolong the life of their vehicles, carrying twice the designed load, until they ground to a halt.

With more frequent sailings and faster ships, which matched and then outpaced our competitors, the Ben Line was able to attract much more high paying general cargo. P & O invoked an old agreement that bullion should be reserved to them, but we disputed this. The movement of gold and silver bullion by sea became increasingly infrequent, though we carried many consignments of coin and bank notes. Much mail had been traditionally carried by P & O but as early as November 1951 *Benavon* III loaded 75 tons of Christmas mail in Singapore for UK. A few years later Ben Line ships were regularly flying the Royal Mail pennant.

III

Timber in various forms was an important component of westbound cargo, and the company did much to help develop the timber trade from British North Borneo and from Sarawak, land of the White Rajah Brooke. We were encouraged to start loading from North Borneo by Wallace Brothers, the very successful managers of the Bombay Burmah Trading Corporation Ltd, which still had a dwindling presence in Burma but had bought new concessions in North Borneo for which they had great hopes. The extraction process was unsophisticated. One man standing on a bamboo platform about twenty feet from the ground felled the giant tree with an axe at the point where its natural buttresses tapered away into the symmetrical trunk, and might take a whole day to complete his task. The trunk was then sawn into lengths of up to twenty feet, dragged to the river by tractors (which replaced elephants imported from Burma), and floated down in rafts to the log ponds at Wallace Bay, some miles up-river from the little port and township of Tawau. At Wallace Bay they were marked and measured to await the ocean carrier, which loaded them direct from the water with her own derricks. These logs were destined for London and other ports, most of them for peeling to make veneers. North of Tawau, at Sandakan with its superb natural harbour, we loaded sawn timber from lighters because the wharf was in such a rotten state that it could not be used.

During the Second World War two Australian servicemen[6] found themselves in the jungles of Sarawak. They both had some knowledge of timber, but had never seen such vast stands of magnificent trees, unexploited, in practical proximity to the Rejang river, which is navigable by ocean-going ships. After the war they invested most of their savings in a second-hand motor fishing vessel and used the rest to fill her with Australian commodities which they knew would command a ready market. Having sailed their craft to Sarawak they sold her and her cargo, thus providing themselves with sufficient funds to buy a forestry concession and set up in business. Most of the trees which they had admired were a little known hardwood species, ramin. When sawn it has a fine grain and uniform white colour, ideal for furniture making, and for staining to imitate other more costly woods. The Australian partners formed a company, Colonial Timber Co. Ltd (CTC), but they still needed to find reliable, regular carriers for their product and to create a market for it in Europe. In both these respects the Ben Line helped, and the whole enterprise was a triumph, which later concessionaires, mainly Chinese, copied.

The Rejang area also yielded illipe nuts, which grew wild but fruited only intermittently. The nuts belonged to the picker, so in those years when they did ripen the local population temporarily abandoned their usual occupation to gather them. Illipe nut butter was considered superior to cocoa butter by European chocolate manufacturers and the nuts paid a good rate of freight, but could spoil and be liable to spontaneous combustion if loaded too wet. A moisture test was carried out when the ship arrived in Singapore and if it was above the limit the consignment had to be discharged and allowed to dry out.

CTC required a factotum at their base on the bank of the Rejang river to coordinate the loading of the ships. Mr Shepherd had

6 John Bartle and Lester Minchin.

knocked around the world, dogged by ill fortune, and was walking down Piccadilly in a mentally and economically depressed state when he spotted a £5 note lying on the pavement. To cut a long story short, this find set him on the road to obtaining employment with CTC. 'Shep' was very popular with the many Ben Line ships which came to load ramin logs, and later sawn timber, in the Rejang river. Eventually when he came home on leave, relatively well off, he dropped a £10 note on the pavement just where his luck had turned, in the hope that someone would pick it up and be as fortunate as he reckoned he had been.

Beech, elm coffin boards and good-quality oak – also dried green peas – came from Hokkaido, the main north island of Japan, which in climate and appearance has much in common with Scotland. It is now connected by a tunnel with Honshu, but in those days it was regarded by the citizens of Tokyo or Osaka as being even more remote than Scotland appeared to a Londoner. I took my wife with me when I visited Hokkaido and told her to pack warm clothes, but nothing smart because by Japanese custom she would be excluded from parties which, our Tokyo agents assured us, were always confined to male guests, fussed over by professional, hired, female attendants. When we arrived at Otaru, the main port, we discovered that Hokkaido etiquette was somewhat different. The Ben Line agent handed us an invitation to a cocktail party in honour of Mrs Strachan which was to take place at 4 p.m. that afternoon. Darkness and the end of the working day fall early in the winter months. Clearly Mrs Strachan was billed as the star attraction, and so it turned out to be. Her appearance in a very workaday brown woollen dress by Marks & Spencer contrasted with the gorgeous silk kimonos of the female attendants, but she was besieged by the male guests many of whom had never before met a European woman, let alone a fair-haired beauty.

The natural hardwood forests of the Malay Peninsula had been well looked after by the colonial administration and had survived neglect during the years of Japanese occupation. Felling had been carefully controlled and natural regeneration encouraged. I visited a concession in the vicinity of Port Kelang (Port Swettenham) owned by a Chinese Malaysian, which was equipped with its own light railway; power saws were used for felling and the workers wore hard helmets. After that hot and thirsty day our host took us to an establishment specialising in toddy, the milky juice of the toddy palm nut. The nuts, picked from the crown of the tree and dropped to the ground by trained monkeys, are split and the milk is drunk from mugs after it has been allowed to ferment for a few hours, by which time it has about the same alcoholic content as a strong ale. I had read about this delectable liquid, well-known for centuries in the East India Company's annals, and it came up to expectations.

The Ben Line loaded enormous quantities of sawn hardwood from Singapore and Port Kelang (Port Swettenham), mainly red and white meranti, but there were attendant difficulties and drawbacks. Shippers were eventually persuaded to present their planks in bundles, but these were not uniform in size and each bundle contained several different lengths. This meant lost space in the ship and the likelihood of claims for split ends and broken planks. The light metal bands securing the bundles tended to break, so one saw the stevedores at destination picking individual planks out of the stow to make up a sling load for discharge.

Over the border in Thailand the natural teak forests had been progressively ruined by improvident husbandry and poaching, winked at by corrupt officials. So we loaded comparatively little timber there. The basic export was rice in bags with small quantities of wet salted buffalo hides, lead ore in bags, bales of gum and increasing amounts of tobacco. Then somebody realised one day that manioc (tapioca), growing wild on many a hillside, could be cheaply converted into cattle fodder. The Ben Line had carried high grade tapioca starch, shipped by the Thai branch of the Bombay Burmah Trading Co., and used as a coating for glossy printing paper, but that had been in relatively small quantities. The export of this newly popular fodder, used as a substitute for barley and destined mainly for Rotterdam and Hamburg, grew so rapidly that the lines could not manage it in parcels and whole ships were chartered to cope with it.

It ill behoves a shipowner to complain about any increase in the amount of cargo offering. His job is to try to adapt to the changing requirements of his customers and to differentiate between long-term trends and short-term fads. In the latter category there were many surprises. How does one account for the temporarily inexhaustible

German appetite for asparagus in glass jars, canned, and later frozen, mushrooms all from Taiwan? Why were the South Koreans successful for a time in exporting to Europe thousands of tons of photograph albums? And who could have predicted the even larger volume of artificial flowers from Hong Kong? This was at first thought to be a passing fashion, but turned out to be a prosperous perennial trade. Our foreman stevedore at Grangemouth said he was convinced that the population of Malaysia lived on a diet of canned milk, Tunnock's Caramel Wafers and Drambuie.

IV

The carriage of animals in both directions was another Ben Line speciality. One shipment of racehorses to Penang was reported in the local paper with the headline 'Ben Line delivers 13 live horses', implying that this was exceptional, but I remember no fatalities, though horses could suffer from seasickness and give cause for concern to their attendant professional groom by going off their feed. In their stalls on deck, so narrow that they could not fall down in rough weather, they were bound to lose condition during the sea passage, but they soon recovered after reaching their destination. We carried many racehorses to Hong Kong where one owner gave Ben names to his entire string.

Probably the largest consignment of animals carried by the company was that loaded in *Bendearg* at Southampton in February 1965, fifty-five pedigree stock to be shown at an International Livestock Exhibition, which opened in Tokyo that April. One of the major awards was the Ben Line Cup for the best overall animal. *Bendearg*'s shipment consisted of 29 Large White pigs, 2 bulls (Hereford and Angus), 6 heifers (Hereford, Angus and Friesian) and 18 sheep, rams and ewes of four breeds (Border Leicester, Romney Marsh, Ryeland and Southdown). They were in charge of an expert stockman assisted by members of the crew.

Animals were popular with the crew; they were an additional interest, and volunteers could earn an honorarium for feeding, mucking out and hosing down animals such as pigs which were not accompanied by a professional. I learned from a very experienced master, Captain J. Cringle, that the sovereign cure for a pig off its feed was to give it a pair of kippers. Pedigree pigs were often shipped after

[134]

they had been served, with the intention that they would produce a litter soon after their arrival at destination. Occasionally the timing went wrong and then there might be casualties among the piglets. The extra trouble caused was compensated by the fact that every live piglet paid additional freight. Nowadays pigs *do* fly – and every racehorse temporarily becomes a Pegasus. Père David's deer, named after the missionary who saw and described them, had become extinct in their native China, but had thrived in captivity in England. In the fifties we carried out two pairs with which it was hoped to re-establish the breed.

Strong attachments to horses and dogs were characteristic of the officers (and wives) of British cavalry regiments long after their principal business had been conducted in armoured vehicles. The Ben Line carried from UK to Malaya not only the tanks of such a regiment but a number of their dogs. When the dogs arrived off Port Swettenham (Port Kelang) on board *Benmacdhui* III the Malay customs announced that, although they were healthy, they would not be allowed to land and any that did so would be destroyed. *Benmacdhui* lay in the anchorage awaiting a berth. The master, Captain J. C. Harvey, was in a quandary. Neither he nor their owners wanted the dogs to be transported round the Far East and then back home, while the alternative of delivering them to their death was unthinkable. That night a launch came alongside, took off the dogs and landed them at a secluded beach. The following evening, when *Benmacdhui* was berthed at the quay, the regiment's commanding officer and his brigadier came aboard to thank Harvey for his co-operation. After drinking to the regiment, and the dogs, and the ship, and the Ben Line, Harvey saw them to the gangway amidst much mutual goodwill, slapping them both somewhat familiarly on the back. The brigadier and the colonel discovered later that Harvey had concealed a rubber stamp in his hand and that their white dress jackets bore the imprint SHIP BY BEN.

Harvey was a very able and popular shipmaster, genial, corpulent, with a military moustache and an endless repertoire of jokes and stories, some very funny, others very blue, which he took great pleasure in recounting. His natural histrionic ability was exploited, after he had retired, in one of a series of BBC colour documentary programmes shown on television in 1972 entitled 'The British

Empire – Echoes of Britannia's Rule'. In Harvey's programme, made with the full cooperation of the company, he starred as the captain of a Ben Line ship trading in Far Eastern ports and waters. He was another instance of a master being identified with a particular ship – in this case *Benmacdhui*. He liked passengers – not all masters did – and some passengers stipulated that they wished to travel only on Harvey's ship. One of his regulars was a Mr Frost of London Zoo who went East each year to collect tropical fish. He brought these home in glass tanks, suspended from the bulkhead, so that they should not become seasick – at least that was Harvey's story, but he was an expert puller of legs. When George Blake was writing his Ben Line history Harvey told him about an uncannily intelligent, black and white pawed ship's cat called Psyche, which gave birth to twin kittens in a lifeboat on *Benreoch*. Psyche went ashore in London, failed to rejoin *Benreoch*, but boarded *Benvorlich* for the voyage to the Far East, transferred to *Benvenue* for the homeward passage to London, and when *Benreoch* arrived there she was waiting on the quay side to be reunited with her family.[7] It was only after Blake's book had been published that Harvey admitted Psyche was a fiction.

Shipments of Alsatian guard dogs, fifteen or twenty at a time, with one or sometimes two handlers from the RAF Regiment, usually provided no problems; but one such consignment carried, as it happened, by Captain Harvey in *Bendoran* IV was troublesome. Soon after the ship left her berth in London all the dogs began to howl and kept up a piercing lament day and night. The handlers were nonplussed and nothing they could do would quieten their charges until suddenly the howling ceased. It was then discovered that this coincided with the breakdown of an experimental 'barnacle buster', an electric circuit round the hull which emitted an ultrasonic bleep intended to deter barnacles from adhering to the ship's side, thus economising on scraping and painting. We concluded that the bleep did not discourage the barnacles, but it certainly distressed the dogs.

Because the Ben Line often went out of its way to help Edinburgh Zoo I was invited to join its Management Committee. The Zoo's head gardener was an enthusiast who had constructed a Japanese garden round a small pond near the Fellows' House. When some Japanese scientists attended a seminar at Edinburgh University they

7 Blake, *op.cit.* p.78.

visited the Zoo and were brought to view the Japanese garden. They were accompanied by an interpreter, since in those days almost as few Japanese spoke English as vice versa. The director, head gardener and one or two members of the Management Committee greeted the guests and the director asked what they thought of the garden. After some moments of consultation the interpreter announced: 'They say it is wonderful. They say in Japan we have *nothing* like this.'

10

Mainly about Money

As I said in the introduction this does not pretend to be an economic history. During the narrative some costs have been quoted when these seemed significant and were readily available, but all the figures are as they were at the time and it is necessary to relate them to the purchasing power of the pound sterling. This remained almost constant not only during the transition from sail to steam in the 1860s to 1890s but right on to the outbreak of the First World War. In the twenty-five years between 1914 and 1939 a depreciation of one third took place, so in 1939 the pound was then worth the equivalent of 66 new pence. By the end of the Second World War in 1945 that value had fallen to 32 new pence and by 1966 it was down to 22 new pence. Thereafter inflation really took off (under both Labour and Conservative governments), so that by 1976 the 1914 pound's purchasing power had fallen to 7 new pence and went on declining.[1]

The problems of conducting an international business against that dismal background were to a large extent caused and certainly compounded by the accompanying social upheavals. During the First World War a generation of Britain's male leaders was decimated. During the Second World War the United States' economy became dominant, and after it Britain's will to govern its empire disintegrated. The reckless immigration policy pursued during the fifties and subsequently (without reference to the electorate) might well have led to bloody revolution by a less tolerant nation, but perhaps no deterioration was more damaging than that which took place in the sixties and seventies when successive British administrations failed to curb unprecedented inflation, kept taxation at penal levels, and allowed excessive power to the trade unions. As the cut-off date for this book is 1982 the further dire consequences of the British government's abandonment

1 Cf. Malcolm Fellows, *The Blue Funnel Legend*, Basingstoke, 1990, p.xiv.

of fiscal policies helpful to shipping, and the impact of European Community legislation fall outside its scope.

II

When The Ben Line Steamers Limited was formed in 1919 the authorised capital was £750,000, of which only £545,590 was issued in £10 shares. In 1942 the par value was halved and shareholders received £5 per share held. In 1982, and beyond, the authorised capital was still £750,000 and the number of issued shares was still 54,559, held predominantly by the Thomson family. This extraordinary achievement was the result of successive Thomsons, and their trusted colleagues, putting the continued prosperous independence of the company before personal gain. Profits were either ploughed back into improving the fleet, or put to reserve and until the container revolution external borrowing was kept to a minimum.

No dividend was paid between 1930 and 1937. From 1938 to 1940 there was a dividend of 3% free of tax and from 1941 to 1951 6% less tax. From 1952 to 1982 the dividend was held at 10% and the annual cost to the company remained minimal.

The Ben Line Board maintained a power of veto on share transfers. When these occurred the price might have to be agreed with the Estate Duty Office. That was not necessary when in 1949 I was offered and, with some penny-pinching, purchased 50 shares at £7. But the alarm bells rang when the Mitchell family announced that they wished to sell their holding, which amounted to about 20%. After protracted and at times heated negotiations Mr Ted bought the Mitchell shares for £22.10s each in 1953, which increased his holding to 45%. In the following year Mr Ted formed E. G. Thomson (Shipping) Ltd (EGTS) and transferred almost all his shares to it so that it became the major shareholder. EGTS also owned at any one time up to three ships, which were chartered to the Ben Line.

As an exempt private company the Ben Line was able to exclude from its audited accounts details of turnover, fixed assets, profit, depreciation and transfers to and from reserves. It seemed possible that when the Companies Act 1967[2] became law we would need to disclose much more information, unless we were able to use the already existing Shipping Companies Exemption Order which

2 Companies Act 1967, 2nd schedule, para 25.

recognised that it was in the national interest that shipping companies should not be compelled to disclose valuable information to their foreign competitors.

We argued that for a company of our size (at that time twenty-three cargo liners) we were in an unique position in that all our interests were concentrated in the trade between Europe and the Far East. No other company in this trade, British or foreign, was in that position; they were all engaged in more than one trade and could avoid giving precise information about the relative merits of one trade as compared with another. Details of our turnover, profit and depreciation would be valuable not only to our existing competitors, Dutch, French, German, Japanese and Scandinavian but also future potential competitors in China, Malaysia, the Philippines, Singapore, South Korea, Taiwan and Thailand. We said that the Ben Line had been able to take its full share of the expansion in the Far East trade partly because of its willingness to defend itself against competition, e.g. in the freight war against Mitsui, and that in any dispute there was an advantage in one's own financial strength being concealed from one's adversary.

The Ben Line Steamers Ltd had an agreement with Wm Thomson & Co. that the partnership, in return for managing the fleet, should receive 2% of the gross freight in commission. Each year a figure for commission was struck as at 31 October. From this figure deductions were made, the main ones being the salaries of office staff and trade charges which covered numerous headings. Thereafter the balance was distributed in varying proportions to the partners. Mr Ted received the equal highest proportion from 1920 to 1931 and the highest from 1931 to 1945 but thereafter voluntarily declined to accept anything at all. This put him in a strong position to override the agreement between The Ben Line Steamers Ltd and Wm Thomson & Co. by reducing the latter's commission to what he considered an appropriate figure whenever the Ben Line had a particularly good year. These adjustments, if not deliberately concealed from the junior partners, were certainly not discussed with them. I as a junior partner was reasonably satisfied with my share. When I became a partner in November 1950 I was informed that my monthly salary would cease but that I could overdraw up to £1,200 on the partnership account. For the ensuing year my share was one fourteenth which amounted to £1,399.11s.1d. By 1964 my share had risen to twenty eightieths or £8,815.5s.6d, on which it was possible to raise and educate our four children and to allow my wife and me to live in reasonable comfort. There was even room for a few luxuries – books and wine in my case.

In addition to the partnership share, which became a salary fixed for a year at a time after the partnership was wound up, there was the opportunity of obtaining a profit from Sir Douglas's syndicates (operated after Sir Douglas became ill by his son David) through the ownership of one or more 64th shares in individual ships or, in the case of William Thomson IV (who was not included in the syndicates) from participation in EGTS. To finance the purchase of 64th shares it was possible, and for most of us necessary, to draw on a 'Loans on ships account' funded by the company. The syndicates, Sir Douglas Thomson & Partners and Sir Douglas Thomson & Others, owned between them up to three ships at any one time which, like the EGTS ships, were chartered to the Ben Line. The owners of course had to bear the risks of all the manifold misfortunes which may, and sometimes did befall a ship. So one could never be sure what the financial result would be, nevertheless losses could be set against tax – if one had the income.

Some of us were fortunate enough to benefit from both the syndicates and EGTS. In 1970 Mr Ted decided to give shares in EGTS to Hugh McMichael, his confidant who was a director of EGTS, Sylvia Thomson the wife of William Thomson IV, and the three Ben Line directors who were not members of the Thomson family, i.e. myself, Roderick MacLeod and Norman Galbraith. On my recommendation, and with the approval of William Thomson IV, Mr Ted's heir presumptive, the number of shares to the three Ben Line directors was scaled down in order to give shares to two long-serving members of staff.[3]

III

Alongside the development in ship design and the means of transporting cargo there was a parallel revolution in the processing of information.

Until the partnership was wound up in 1964 a senior partner wrote

3 J. E. Taylor and J. P. Young.

out in his own hand in a 'day book' (still preserved) on 31 October each year the figure for commission earned, the deductions, and how the balance of profit was distributed between the partners. Until 1951 he also wrote out in his own hand the partnership's trial balance in the same ledger. In the fifties we were still transcribing manifests by hand, converting piculs and catties to tons, hundredweights, quarters and pounds, and Hong Kong dollars into sterling at one shilling $3^{3}/_{16}$ pence – with the help of tables. In the early fifties the Head Office Accounts Department possessed one manually operated 'Facit' calculator, and in Singapore and Hong Kong they still relied on the abacus.

Perhaps the first break into the new era came when we installed a telex link between Head Office and the Cable and Wireless Office a few hundred yards away in Edinburgh. In the following year, 1955, we were linked by telex to Killick Martin's Office in London and to some of our agents on the Continent. Thereafter this new vehicle gathered rapid momentum until it became the principal means of typewritten communication with all our trading areas.

The Bank of Scotland, of which Sir Douglas was a director, was one of the first institutions to install its own main-frame computer and I think it was Sir Douglas who persuaded Percy Rogers, before he died in 1966, to persuade his board to do the same. At all events in 1967 Killick Martin became the first shipbroker in the United Kingdom to install a main-frame computer and the first in this country to use it for shipping documentation.[4]

In 1966 all the Edinburgh Head Office accounting was transferred to the Bank of Scotland computer. Fortunately we continued to run the old system in parallel because numerous technical difficulties were encountered. These eventually led to moving the accounting processes back to Head Office in stages. There followed a period when everything was carried out by Ben Line staff using accounting machines. At length full scale computerisation was successfully introduced, using our own ICL machine, in 1979.

Mr Ted and Sir Douglas kept a close eye on financial affairs while they were still active. After James Grieve's death William Thomson IV became primarily responsible for the running of the Head Office Accounts Department with the assistance of Mr T. R. (Tommy)

4 David R. MacGregor, *The China Bird*, 1986 edn, p.181.

Park, who like William Thomson IV was a qualified chartered accountant. When Park retired, David Walker, an experienced and qualified accountant was recruited, and in 1975 was appointed to the board as financial director. The other changes in the composition of the board during that decade were the appointment of Dick Thorman and Hamish Muirhead in 1971 and Sir Douglas's youngest child, W. A. C. (Bill) Thomson, in 1978.

In general Mr Ted and Sir Douglas distrusted so-called expert, professional advisers. We had lawyers, Boyd Jameson and Young of Leith, but seldom needed to call upon their services. We had auditors, A. & J. Robertson, with whom Mr Ted had served his apprenticeship, and with whom William Thomson IV had started his apprenticeship before they merged in 1960 to become Robertson & Maxtone Graham. One of the partners in this firm, Hugh McMichael, was both the Ben Line's auditor and the trusted confidant of Mr Ted, who as already related, made him a director of EGTS and gave him shares in that company. In those days when professional integrity was undoubted and had not been infected by transatlantic fashions such a relationship was regarded as entirely above board. When Robertson & Maxtone Graham lost its identity by merging with Thomson McLintock in 1975 the climate had changed and McMichael had to relinquish his directorship and sell his EGTS shares.

While external borrowing remained minimal the Ben Line's bankers, National Commercial Bank of Scotland (subsequently amalgamated with The Royal Bank of Scotland), were kept at arm's length and merchant bankers were an unrecognised species. There had to be a change of policy in order to finance the large investment in containerisation and the subsequent complex transactions connected with diversification. The Royal Bank lent willingly on favourable terms. We needed lawyers well versed in shipping, corporate finance and English law, and were well served by Norton Rose, Botterell & Roche. We also needed advice and reassurance that we were taking no greater risks than those which seemed unavoidable and chose J. Henry Schroder Wagg as merchant bankers.

One exception to the reluctance, prior to 1970, to seek external advice had been the commissioning of management consultants. These consultants were unusual for those days because the firm was run by a woman. The Anne Shaw Organization had done an investigation for Killick Martin and came to us with their recommendation. We decided to let them loose on the partners and the work of Head Office first before trying them in other areas. The consultants' aim was to identify spare fat which could be pared off with a saving to the company that would justify their fee. The investigation took place in 1962 and we were by no means displeased when their detailed analysis failed to find any evidence of overstaffing and gave general approval to the existing structure.

The consultants next did an investigation into our London Dock Office followed by one on housekeeping on board ship. We knew that savings were possible, particularly in the latter area because we had tried to conduct our own economy campaign five years earlier in 1959. As we had said then, 'It is easy to keep a ship in tip-top condition with unlimited expenditure. The measure of the Masters' and Chief Engineers' problem is to maintain present standards on less resources.'[5] We felt it necessary to repeat this when advising masters and chief engineers of the consultants findings:

In the liner service between Europe and the Far East all lines charge the same rates of freight on the same commodities, thus, a line competing with us would, in theory, earn approximately the same freight and make the same profit as we do for a similar voyage carrying similar cargo. But if we are to keep ahead of our competitors we must aim at earning more than they do and having more to re-invest in the business. We derive a substantial advantage in this respect through not being a public company and not having large numbers of shareholders. This enables us to re- invest all but a tiny fraction of the annual profits in new ships or in other fleet improvements. But this in itself is not sufficient to enable us to retain, let alone improve, the position we have achieved in the trade. This is why we must aim to be more efficient than our competitors: more efficient in management and more efficient in operation . . . A comparison of the maintenance costs between different ships in the fleet reveals that there is a wide variation in expenditure and some of the ships on which less is spent are just as well maintained as those on which more is spent.[6]

As a result of the consultants' report we introduced a Planned Maintenance Scheme to eliminate the excessive maintenance which was being carried out by some masters, particularly in painting

5 Circular dated 1 May 1959.
6 Circular dated 20 May 1964.

instead of washing down with good non-caustic detergents; we reiterated an instruction that as far as possible all brass work was to be painted over; masters and chief engineers were provided

with more comprehensive price lists: 'It is always easy to spend money when it is not coming our of one's own pocket and there is some excuse for extravagance and waste when one has no idea of the value of the items ordered.'[7] The carrying of excessive victualling and canteen stores was reduced – and so on.

We next employed the Anne Shaw Organization in 1970 to look afresh at the work of the directors. We were running the conventional fleet and setting up Ben Line Containers Ltd simultaneously. This presented us with obvious organisational problems; we needed, and were given, reassurance from the consultants that we were not attempting the impossible.

These investigations were time consuming for all the participants, but were worthwhile as much for the reinforcement of our own ideas as for the innovations which they produced. The latter came, or the consultants cleverly made them appear to come, mainly from within the company. Some solutions became obviously apparent as a result of the consultants' painstaking analyses which nobody in the company had time to compile.

V

During 1970 there was an unprecedented increase in costs which were outside the company's control. In order to justify to Shippers' Councils a very large increase in rates the Far Eastern Freight Conference commissioned an independent firm of chartered accountants to analyse those costs which were common to all member lines. Their findings showed that in the fifteen months to the end of March 1971 bunker fuel had increased by 107.5%, repairs by 21.0%, stevedoring westbound by 18.8% and eastbound by 15.6%. Total costs had increased during this short period by 23.666%. This resulted in the largest increase in FEFC rates ever introduced: 17½% in two stages, the first in February 1972 and the second in August that year.

That, however, was only the beginning. After 1968, when the conference tariffs for the trades between Europe and the Far East were

7 *Ibid.*

quoted in US dollars instead of sterling, the value of the US dollar fluctuated wildly against that of the other currencies in which the lines earned and paid. These other currencies, about fifteen or sixteen of them, were simultaneously fluctuating against each other. William Thomson IV was closely involved in devising the concept of a Currency Adjustment Factor (CAF), expressed as a percentage, which could be added or subtracted from any given rate and could be varied from month to month. There were separate CAFs for each major territory, one for UK, another for North Continent, another for Japan, and so on. The CAFs were arrived at by measuring the value of the US dollar against a basket of currencies appropriate to each territory and were calculated by an independent firm of chartered accountants.

It was possible to persuade the member lines and the Shippers' Councils that CAFs represented an equitable solution and they were introduced in 1973.

At the end of that year the *Chairman's Review* stated:

We earn our freight and pay our disbursements in at least fifteen different currencies all of which have been frequently altering in relation to sterling and to each other. Thanks to the inauguration of Currency Adjustment Factors (on the invention of which the Company took a leading part and which have since come to be widely adopted outside our own trades) we have been to a considerable extent protected from the ill effects of floating currencies, but the expenditure of managerial and administrative time has been very large.[8]

Towards the end of 1973 there was a sudden contraction in the availability of oil fuel and in 1974 its price increased by a further 400%. To meet this the CAF concept and mechanism were adopted to formulate a Bunker Adjustment Factor (BAF). So from 1974 onwards the freight rate on any given commodity was subject to a CAF and a BAF which might vary at monthly intervals.

On the domestic scene most of our outstanding foreign indebtedness had been converted to sterling loans by the end of 1976, but the problems caused by the fluctuations in exchange rates remained.

All our business is international in character to the extent that much of our revenue and expenditure are in currencies other than sterling. We

8 *Chairman's Review* 24 December 1973.

are regularly earning and spending in some sixteen different currencies throughout the world. In recent years we have seen the value of sterling decline by more than half in relation to the German mark and the Japanese yen, while in the last few weeks sterling has fluctuated markedly and unpredictably against the US dollar, in which most of our freight tariffs and many of our fixtures [of chartered ships] are now quoted. These violent movements add a new dimension of risk to our transactions, but it is and will remain the company's policy not to gamble on making a profit out of exchange fluctuations; within Government regulations and so far as our means permit, we aim to neutralise this risk so that we end up as neither the gainers nor the losers. This policy is easy to enunciate, but more difficult to carry out.[9]

Trying to carry it out resulted in transferring most of the company's indebtedness into US dollars in 1979, since this was the basic currency for income from ships and rigs and the acquisition or disposal of assets.

Funny stuff is money – and seldom ha ha!

9 *Chairman's Review* 7 November 1978.

11

Perils of the Sea

When I was a little boy and met with some mishap my dear Nanny would comfort me: 'There, there, worse things happen at sea!' And in church we sang the hymn 'For those in peril on the sea':

> From rock and tempest, fire and foe
> Protect them wheresoe'er they go.

To that abbreviated list there is much to be added: collision, stranding, freak waves, abnormal tides and currents, and machinery failures. Ben Line ships experienced all these. Fog is a perennial hazard; ice too, though not encountered on the company's usual routes.

From the end of the Second World War up to the time of writing the Ben Line suffered a single total loss. *Benledi* IV, commanded by Captain J. Liston, was outward bound, fully laden, off Malta when in the early hours of 24 February 1950 fire caused by a ruptured oil fuel settling tank broke out in the engine room. Despite immediate action by the crew, the fire spread rapidly. HM destroyer *Childers* and a British merchant vessel responded at once to SOS messages. Two Admiralty rescue vessels with powerful hoses arrived from Malta and *Benarty* IV, homeward bound, came to stand by. On the evening of 26 February, after two and a half days of continuous firefighting, rough seas defeated any further efforts. The ship did not sink, but was towed into a Maltese bay where she was declared to be a constructive total loss.[1] *Benledi* IV had been built for the company in 1930; her luck had held throughout the war, and in March 1948, commanded at that time by Captain A. P. Paterson, she had survived a serious fire in her cargo while she was discharging in Genoa. This was thought to have been caused by feckless shore labour attempting to pilfer cargo.

Another fire believed to have been started by shore labour occurred

1 The episode is described in greater detail by George Blake *op.cit.*, pp.176-7.

in *Benvorlich* III while she was discharging Thai jute in Dundee early in 1963. The crew took appropriate action by releasing the ship's own stock of CO_2 into the hold and making the hatch airtight. This might well have been effective, but the law stated that, if a fire occurred while a ship was alongside the wharf, the city's fire brigade must become responsible for fighting it. The local firemaster had not had a nice jute fire to deal with for some time and seemed determined to make the most of it. He immediately had the hatch opened, whereupon the cargo burst into flame again. Tons of water were poured in, together with fresh supplies of CO_2. This procedure continued for some days, despite remonstrances including mine; the hatch was opened at intervals to see how things were going. Ultimately the fire was declared to have been put out. There had been no injuries, but there was some structural damage to the ship, and a large bill from the fire brigade. Such episodes involved the shipowner in various kinds of irrecoverable loss. There was disruption to the schedule of sailings; if a general average were declared this caused resentment by the cargo owners whose goodwill one wished to retain; every claim whether general or particular average was taken into account by the underwriters, who annually reviewed the insurance premiums. We did indeed consider copying Alfred Holt & Co. who, probably alone among shipowners, carried their own hull and cargo insurance but the Ben Line's generally excellent record kept the premiums down and we decided that it was more prudent to avoid tempting Fate.

Fate struck *Bencruachan* III, commanded by Captain D. S. 'Danny' Sinclair, in the early hours of 3 May 1973 as she headed into a moderate south-westerly gale about sixty nautical miles south of Durban. In the darkness, as the ship surmounted one rise and began plunging down a long deep trough, she was struck by a gigantic freak wave, probably about seventy-five feet high, which crashed down on her forecastle and No.1 hatch, fracturing her hull and tearing open No.1 hold. A less strongly built ship would have perished. Five years previously a 46,000-ton tanker had sunk with the loss of all but nine of her crew after a similar encounter in the same area. No lives were lost on *Bencruachan*; all the passengers, including an elderly lady with a plastic hip, were safely winched off by helicopter, an experience which they no doubt dined out on for the rest of their lives. The wave left the ship crippled with an 8-degree droop on her forward section, which was down by 12 to 15 feet from normal. She was towed stern first to Durban for temporary repairs. Permanent repairs, involving removal and replacement of the bow section, were carried out in Rotterdam as by this time British yards had priced themselves out of the market. Thanks to meticulous measurements made in Durban the new bow section was prefabricated and fitted unmodified with minimum delay. *Bencruachan* continued to serve on the liner berth for another seven years before being broken up in Taiwan – the last British flag Far East steam turbine cargo liner.

Typhoons in the China Sea are a perennial hazard, but improved weather forecasting and communications meant that the relatively slow, though by no means entirely predictable, movement of the eye of the typhoon could be plotted and broadcast at frequent intervals, enabling vessels at sea to steer clear of serious trouble. It was a different matter if a ship was caught in port. In May 1960 *Benhiant* I, commanded by Captain Charles Donnelly, was working normally in the anchorage of Hong Kong harbour, but when a typhoon appeared to be approaching dangerously near she was moved to a specially strengthened typhoon buoy, where she continued working. Then the full fury of the typhoon struck from the east. At about 2 a.m. she parted her cable and, despite exerting maximum engine power, she was sent on a terrifying tour of the western end of the harbour. To the danger of going ashore was added that of colliding with other ships, which had been moored at adjacent typhoon buoys and had broken adrift at the same time. About 9 a.m. the wind went round to the west. By this time *Benhiant* had managed to get two anchors down, but the force of the storm was still so great that with engines full ahead she was driven astern, dragging her anchors for about four miles through the anchorage, ending up, when the typhoon abated at last, off the end of the new runway at Kaitak.

The Director of Civil Aviation telephoned the Director of Marine asking him to get *Benhiant* moved so that the airport could recommence operations. The Director of Marine, though cooperative, was not too sympathetic: 'If you will put your bloody runway in the middle of my harbour this is what you can expect.'

Captain Donnelly and his crew had managed to save *Benhiant* from the fate of some ocean-going ships and many smaller craft, which were driven ashore, but she was involuntarily responsible for more expensive damage than a delay to the resumption of air traffic. Her anchors had clawed up and destroyed a new telephone cable laid between Victoria Island and Kowloon on the mainland. This cable had earned the company a handsome freight, carried from UK expertly coiled in the hold of a Ben Line ship. I thought I remembered that its equally remunerative replacement was again entrusted to the Ben Line, thereby affirming that it is an ill wind which blows nobody any good, but am told that owing to the urgency of the situation the new cable came from Japan and was carried by a competitor.

A typhoon struck Kaohsiung in Taiwan in August 1977. No Ben Line vessel was in port, but the gantry cranes at Pier 64, where we and other Trio containerships loaded, were toppled and crumpled as though they had been made of cardboard, and stacks of loaded containers were overturned.

The Taiwanese were avid consumers of polythene, that new commodity, and careless about how they disposed of it. Until the dangers of waste polythene were recognised a ship could be suddenly immobilised in confined waters due to the underwater shipside grating attached to the seawater inlet chest becoming clogged, thus starving the coolers and condensers. We had some instances of this happening in the approaches to Bangkok as well as Taiwan, but fortunately escaped accident.

The machinery failure which I most vividly remember occurred in October 1965. I was in Japan, where I had attended a British Exhibition, for which *Bengloe* IV had carried out a 1909 Rolls-Royce Silver Ghost, some paintings by Sir Winston Churchill and a modern double-decker bus. The bus, a curiosity for the Japanese, not least because it was manned by specially picked, jovial British drivers, had been chartered to run a shuttle service between the Seibu Department Store and the exhibition. These and other exhibits were to be returned in *Benreoch* II. Morning tea and an English-language Japanese newspaper were brought to my hotel room. On opening the paper I saw a front-page photograph of *Benreoch* with her bow embedded twenty-five feet into the wharf at Yokohama. While approaching her berth she had gone full ahead instead of full astern, due to human error compounded by the malfunctioning, or inadvertent switching off, of a 'wrong way alarm' in the engine room. There were no casualties and it was more expensive to repair the wharf than the ship, but we could have done without the publicity, which was not confined to the English language press.

Benedin suffered a breakdown of her main engine in 1969 off the west coast of Africa. *Benrinnes* IV happened to be in the vicinity and towed her in to Monrovia for repairs. *Benrinnes* then resumed her voyage but within a few hours came across a disabled Greek ship which she towed to Dakar. These two operations in quick succession earned her crew some worthwhile salvage money.

Another serious incident, for which the ship and her master could in no way be blamed, took place in August 1978 when *Bencruachan* III was in the southbound convoy through the Suez Canal and was passing from the Great Bitter Lake into the Little Bitter Lake. Captain O. ('Ossie') Tucker reported to Edinburgh:

After the anchor had been weighed at 1544 hours on 7 August I remained on the bridge until the pilot had swung the ship's head towards the main channel... As all appeared to be in order I handed over command of the bridge to the Chief Officer, Mr J. Steel, and informed him that I would be typing in my day room. At 1622 hours the Chief Officer phoned me that due to ship No.13 breaking down ahead of us, causing all vessels astern of her to take the best possible stopping action they could, the pilot was turning us short round to port . . . and there was sufficient water for us to make the turn. [The alternative would have been to anchor, but that was unsafe because *Bencruachan* was likely to collide with a dredger.] I completed my typing, then answered the call of nature, and while so doing, or just about! was called again on the telephone by the Chief Officer who informed me that the pilot was having doubts as to the depth of water. I immediately returned to the bridge, but I suspected I felt the vessel's progress being marred as I ascended the ladder to the bridge. . . . At 1631 hours the vessel grounded, and in so doing developed a slight list to port.

Refloating was attempted by using the main engines but this proved ineffective, as were the efforts of Suez Canal Authority tugs. Following survey, and soundings made round the vessel, it was decided to discharge some 1,700 tons of bunkers, 750 tons of salt water ballast and about 1,200 tons of general cargo into barges. The supply of barges for cargo was erratic, but meantime Captain A. M. ('Archie') Watters, Marine Superintendent, had arrived from Edinburgh and made the Suez Canal Authority and our agents sit up and take more notice. Captain Tucker reported: 'Our agents, Messrs

ABOVE, LEFT *H. Paton, OBE, chief engineer superintendent 1964-86, director Ben Line Offshore Contractors, 1982-86* ABOVE, RIGHT *Bosun William Walker, joined 1944, retired 1973, known affectionately as 'The Beast' (because of his physique, not his nature), presented with the BEM by 'Mr Ted' on Benarty VI , 11 July 1963* BELOW, LEFT *A. S. Kinnear, manager Ben Line Singapore office, 1951, then general manager Far East until 1963; director Killick Martin 1964-75* BELOW, RIGHT *Captain A. P. Paterson, senior marine superintendent 1954-82.*

ABOVE *Ben Line Dock Office, C Shed, Royal Victoria Dock, London. The company carried many fire engines.* BELOW *Maritime Building, Collyer Quay, Singapore. The Ben Line office was on the eighth floor.*

BEN LINE

Old East India Sherry

A BACKGROUND HISTORY

LEFT, ABOVE AND BELOW *Ben Line matchbox* ABOVE *Cover of* Old East India Sherry: A Background History.

BELOW *Ben Line Old East India Sherry tasting, London 1958. L to r: Sir Denis Truscott, GBE, TD, Lord Mayor of London and former Master of the Vintners Company; M. F. Strachan, MBE; Captain J. C. Harvey, OBE.*

	London	Liver-pool	Grange-mouth	Middles-brough	Hull	Ham-burg	Rotter-dam	Antwerp	Havre
BENVANNOCH	....	....	11 May	18 May	....	7 May	3 May	....	....
R **BENWYVIS**	....	....	....	1 May	....	....	....	....	....
BENRINNES	....	29 Apr	....	....	....	15 May	11 May	25 May	....
BENCLEUCH	....	....	....	....	28 Apr	....	4 May	7 May	....
BENHIANT	....	....	2 Jun	....	....	13 May	22 May	25 May	18 May
R **BENARMIN**	....	....	....	....	....	5 May	....	....	....
R **BENLOYAL**	4 May	....	17 May	....	....	29 Apr	9 May	....	....
R **BENMHOR**	16 May	....	....	17 Jun	28 May	8 Jun	4 Jun	....	....
BENLAWERS	....	23 May	....	....	....	9 Jun	....	15 Jun	4 Jun

LEFT AND BELOW
From Ben Line home-ward sailing card, 1967.

Principal European Agencies

Principal Eastern Agencies

LONDON
Killick Martin & Company Limited

SINGAPORE
The Ben Line Steamers Limited

Amsterdam	Vereenigd Cargadoorskantoor
Antwerp	Aug. Bulcke & Co. Succrs. Ltd
Avonmouth	James & Hodder
Basle	Keller Shipping Ltd
Birmingham	A. H. Seale & Co. Ltd
Bradford	R. Thomas & Co. (Bradford) Ltd
Bremen	Gebrüder Specht
Cardiff	John Cory & Sons, Ltd
Copenhagen	Nordisk Express AS
Dublin	George Bell & Co. Ltd
Genoa	Gastaldi & Co
Glasgow	Prentice, Service & Henderson Ltd
Gothenburg	Nordisk Express A.B.
Grangemouth	Buchan & Hogg Ltd
Hamburg	Menzell & Co. Schiffsmakler
Havre	Francois Lecoq
Helsinki	Oy Enroth Ab.
Hull	Porter & Henderson
Immingham	John Sutcliffe & Son (Grimsby) Ltd
Liverpool	Henry Tyrer & Co. Ltd
Malmo	G. Almqvist & Co
Manchester	Henry Tyrer & Co. Ltd
Middlesbrough	T. A. Bulmer & Co. Ltd.
Marseilles	G. Feron E. de Clebsattel & Cie
Newcastle	W. A. Souter & Co. Ltd
Oslo	Berg Hansen & Co
Paris	G. Feron E. de Clebsattel & Cie
Rotterdam	D. Burger & Zoon
Southampton	Killick Martin (Southampton) Ltd
Stockholm	Nordisk Express A.B.
Vienna	Oesterreichisches Seefrachtenkontor, G.m.b.H·
New York	Simpson Spence & Young

Tokyo	Cornes & Co. Ltd
Yokohama	Cornes & Co. Ltd
Osaka	Cornes & Co. Ltd
Kobe	Cornes & Co. Ltd
Pusan	Hyopsung Shipping Corporation
Hsinkang	China Ocean Shipping Agency
Taku Bar	China Ocean Shipping Agency
Shanghai	China Ocean Shipping Agency
Canton	China Ocean Shipping Agency
Hong Kong	The Ben Line Steamers Ltd
Taiwan	Tait & Co. Ltd, Taipei
Manila	Delgado Shipping Agencies Inc.
Jesselton	Harper Gilfillan (Borneo) Ltd
Labuan	Harper Gilfillan (Borneo) Ltd
Sandakan	Harper Gilfillan (Borneo) Ltd
Tawau	Harper Gilfillan (Borneo) Ltd
Wallace Bay	Bombay Burmah Trading Corporation Ltd
Kunak	Mostyn Estates Ltd
Rejang River	C.T.C. Ltd, Sarikei
Bangkok	The Ben Line Steamers Ltd
Haadyai	Diethelm & Co., Ltd
Surabaya	P.N. Djakarta Lloyd
Semarang	P.N. Djakarta Lloyd
Djakarta	P.N. Djakarta Lloyd
Belawan and other Indonesian Ports	P.N. Djakarta Lloyd
Kuala Lumpur	The Ben Line Steamers Ltd
Port Swettenham	The Ben Line Steamers Ltd
Penang	Sandilands Buttery & Co. Ltd
Colombo	Aitken Spence & Co. Ltd
Djibouti	Mitchell Cotts & Co. (Ethiopia) Ltd
Aden	Luke Thomas & Co. (Aden Shipping) Ltd
Port Sudan	Contomichalos Sons & Co. Ltd
Khartoum	Contomichalos Sons & Co. Ltd
Jeddah	Mohamed Fazil Abdulla Arab
Suez	Assiut Shipping Agency
Port Said	Assiut Shipping Agency

Heavy lifts LEFT Benalbanach II *(1947-65) discharging 48-ton locomotive at Port Swettenham, 1948* BELOW *Seaward defence craft for Singapore being loaded on to* Benwyvis II *(1955-63)* BOTTOM, LEFT *Lighter being loaded on to* Benledi V *(1951-63)* BOTTOM, RIGHT *Centurion tank being loaded on to* Benarty V *(1956-62), June 1959.*

ABOVE, LEFT Benledi V (1951-63), commandeered and temporarily renamed HMS Ivy during the Suez Crisis, 1956, carrying military vehicles ABOVE, RIGHT Bencleuch VI (1949-72) loading Morris Minor and Oxford cars in London in the fifties BELOW Pigs loaded on Benlarig III (1961-69) in Southampton for Kobe, Japan. During the six-week voyage the two cadets looking after twelve pigs will feed them 4,800 lb of pigmeal and 300 lb of mangels, and will use 3,000 lb of straw.

Benledi IV *(1930-50) on fire 130 miles east of Malta, February 1950.*

Bencruachan III *(1968-80) disabled by freak wave, 74 miles SE of Durban, May 1973.*

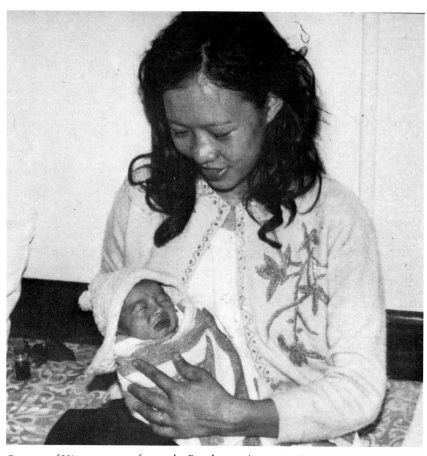

Rescue of Vietnamese refugees by Bendearg, *August 1980.*

Assiut Shipping Agency, have performed well, although things take a little longer in Egypt.' On the afternoon of 21 August the vessel was refloated with the assistance of tugs, and the reloading of cargo was completed in the Great Bitter Lake on 25 August.

On that day Captain Tucker reported:

I regret this costly incident, but am pleased that the vessel suffered no damage. I do not wish you to think that I am, in any way, passing the responsibility, or part of it, off on to the Chief Officer. I do wish to put on record how hard he has worked, and assisted me with the paper work required to ascertain eventually how much bunkers, cargo, water, etc were required to be discharged in order to refloat the vessel. The other Deck Officers and Cadets have worked very willingly in a variety of occupations from charting the area upon which we were grounded, and its approaches for the eventual refloating of the vessel, to tallying cargo and shifting barges, in addition to their normal duties.

Bencruachan carried a passenger, exceptionally at that date after suspension of the passenger service, and he was 'press-ganged' into becoming a tally clerk, and performed excellently and willingly. The seamen were used in a multiplicity of ways, including guarding cargo in the hatches being worked, and gave an excellent account of themselves.

Water rationing had to be introduced but the Catering Department, despite water shortages, managed to keep us supplied with three square meals a day, and served many additional meals to the multitude of persons who kept calling on the vessel... At the present moment we are anchored in Suez Roads awaiting bunkers, stores, fresh water and trust there will be no delay.

That, however, was not quite the end of the story. Immediately prior to the ship's departure from Singapore seven crew members (five engine room and two catering) were taken ill. The cause of the sickness was not readily ascertainable but inhalation of toxic fumes from a consignment of toluene di-isocyanate, destined for Jakarta, which had formed part of the cargo discharged and reloaded in the Suez Canal was suspected, and confirmed by a surveyor who was specially flown out from Holland. Fortunately none of the crew were permanently affected and the drums of chemicals were safely discharged at Jakarta by stevedores wearing gas masks and protective clothing.

Perils were not confined to salt waters. The bulk carrier *Benledi VIII* loaded slightly over 37,000 tons of iron ore at Puerto Ordaz some 120 miles up the Orinoco river, where the navigable channel keeps shifting and marker buoys are not always reliable. With a pilot on board she sailed on 2 March 1981. At 2131 hours that evening when she was about 40 miles down river from Puerto Ordaz the helmsman reported that she was not answering the helm and it was realised that the vessel was aground. Attempts to refloat her at high water with four local tugs and the ship's main engines were unsuccessful on 3 and 4 March. That day we signed a Lloyd's salvage agreement, no cure – no pay, with Messrs Smit of Rotterdam and Terminales Maracaibo CA as joint salvors. Smit had extremely powerful salvage tugs stationed round the world and would send the two nearest, meanwhile Terminales Maracaibo would discharge some bunkers and cargo to barges. *Smit London* and *Smit Salvor* arrived on 10 March but repeated attempts throughout the following week were unavailing. At last, after 1,200 tons of bunkers and 5,300 tons of cargo had been discharged, the tugs assisted by *Benledi's* main engines, refloated her on the morning of 19 March. Having ascertained that the main engine and rudder appeared to be undamaged and all compartments were watertight, the bunkers and cargo were reloaded at a safe anchorage. The iron ore was destined for Immingham so before making the Atlantic passage a diver examined the hull at Trinidad. Fortunately he found no structural damage. The whole operation was expensive enough without that.

If Ben Line ships did not need overmuch rescuing themselves, they performed many successful rescues of others. The containership *City of Edinburgh* was involved in an exceptional sequence of such operations. In 1977, outward bound in the Indian Ocean Captain Seaton Murray reported:

We were alerted by our Auto Alarm in the early hours of 18 August that we had a vessel in distress in our vicinity. On investigation, it was found that the MV *Lira* (ex-British) was on fire and the crew were abandoning her. We were the nearest vessel and the only one answering the call. I advised *Lira* that we were on our way to her aid. When we arrived at the given position there was no sign of her and we decided to search on a five mile square of the position. On one of the legs we sighted two red flares. We headed for them and later saw two more flares and finally picked her up on our radar.

By now it was daylight and by the time we arrived at the *Lira* we could see that the ship was on fire from forward to No.4 hold. The bridge, accommodation and engine room were ablaze. The ship was listing to starboard and well down in the water. We heard a small explosion as we approached. Her crew were away in one motor boat and three life rafts. We took *City of Edinburgh* in as close as seemed safe, bearing in mind the danger of further explosions. There was a slight to moderate south-westerly sea with a moderate swell running. We safely embarked all twenty five of the crew which consisted of Filippinos, Burmese, Indonesians and Maldive Islanders. All departments gave valuable assistance in the rescue operation.

From the Captain I was given to understand that there had been an explosion in No.2 hold which had quickly ignited the other holds and the engine room. The cargo consisted of timber, rubber, tin, and cocoa beans and the vessel was on voyage from Malaysia to Rotterdam. When the crew were safely aboard, we punctured the rafts and pulled the plug out of the life boat. The distress message was cancelled and a navigation warning was sent out to all ships giving an accurate position of the stricken ship from our Satellite Navigator.[2]

A few weeks later, homeward bound on the same voyage *City of Edinburgh* rescued nine Vietnamese refugees, who at the request of the United Nations High Commissioner for Refugees, were carried on to Suez, where they were safely disembarked. They had gone through the ordeal of being rescued by a South Korean ship and then abandoned when their identity was discovered. Such callousness was not an isolated instance, and it seems that some foreign owners instructed their masters to turn a blind eye to Vietnamese refugees because of the expense of looking after them and possible difficulties in landing them. By the Maritime Convention Act, 1911, Section 6, the master of a British ship must, so far as he can do so without serious danger to his own ship and crew, render assistance to every person who is found at sea in danger of being lost, and if he fails to do so he is guilty of a misdemeanour.

City of Edinburgh's next rescue took place two years later. Captain John Pritchard reported:

On 7 October [1979] at 1345 hours we received a message on the radio from a US search and rescue plane that a boat containing Vietnamese refugees was fifty miles from us. . . . We altered course for the boat. The Satellite

2 *Ben Bulletin*, no. 11, October 1977, slightly abbreviated.

Navigator was invaluable, as we had to steam between the Prince Consort and Vanguard Banks. At 1608 hours we sighted the boat. She was flying a white flag carrying SOS in red and on the canvas covering the cabin we could see the words NO FOOD ENGINE BROKEN.... There were 47 people in the 45 ft boat, 34 men, 6 women and 7 children ranging in age from 1 to 9. One of the women was six months pregnant. No food and only a few gallons of stagnant water were on board. We took the people aboard and opened the sea cocks of the boat, estimating that she would sink in an hour or so. We gave food and water to the refugees and then the Chief Officer and I took all their temperatures. With the help of Mrs Mary Thom, the carpenter's wife, we examined them physically and found that, apart from some ulcers on the children's legs, they were all in reasonable health, but in very obvious need of nourishment. The people had left Saigon on 26 September and had been at sea for twelve days.

The men were bedded down in the gymnasium and the women and children in the Suez Canal Boatmen Cabin. The pregnant woman was having some difficulty in breathing, owing to the excitement and relief of being rescued. We gave her some oxygen and moved her to the conference room to give her a little more space. I would like to pay tribute to the way in which the ship's company rallied round in great fashion. Within an hour of the refugees boarding the ship, for example, a collection of clothes had been made, blankets issued and many offers of help made. Mrs Thom deserves a very special mention as she took the women and children into her care from the start and looked after them right up to the time they left the ship. We arrived at Tokyo and made directly for the Quarantine Anchorage. Officers there were very quick and efficient and issued clearance in under an hour.

Immigration Officers came aboard and by 1830 hours had completed questioning the rescued people. As it was now too late for the Minister of Justice to issue landing permission, the Vietnamese stayed aboard over the weekend [at the Company's expense] and were eventually landed in the care of the Japanese Red Cross at 1230 hours Monday 15 October.

Another instance of spontaneous response from a Ben Line ship's company to those in need occurred when *Bendearg*, one of the last surviving conventional ships, came across a craft carrying Vietnamese refugees on 9 August 1980. Captain Joseph Schofield reported:

While on passage from Hong Kong to Singapore in position 9° 35' N 109° 41' E ... we sighted a small assault craft displaying what appeared to be signals of distress. Because the craft possessed two machine gun turrets, we first made a full-speed run past it, in case it contained pirates. It was obvious from the number of women and children in evidence that they were refugees from Vietnam, so we returned to pick them up.

We commenced embarking them at 1732 hours and by 1840 hours they were all on board... The craft was cast adrift and a general warning was broadcast to all ships and to Singapore Radio that it was a danger to navigation. The refugees had been afloat for 16 days... They had started off from Saigon, where with the connivance of dockyard personnel, they 'acquired' a naval landing craft which was in dock for repairs. The food and water situation was fairly desperate when they were rescued. The craft ran out of fuel after three days, and they began to drift back towards Vietnam, their only means of propulsion was an army parachute fastened to a jury mast. It was this flapping parachute which attracted the attention of Mr Wyatt, Chief Officer.

In one incident they were surrounded by fishing vessels who were about to attack them. By sticking pieces of wood through the empty gun turrets, and training them on the boats they were able to bluff the fishermen into thinking they possessed machine guns, and they swiftly retired from the area. About 30 ships had steamed straight past them before *Bendearg* stopped and picked them up.

There were 30 males, 29 females, 17 children, and one infant born on the landing craft two days before. A feeding bottle for the infant was quickly fashioned by a ship's fitter from items in the Chief Engineer's boiler water testing chemistry set! With the exception of the nursing mother, all the refugees seemed in reasonably good health, although some of the children were suffering badly from salt water sores. The mother's condition improved somewhat with good food and rest, and she was taken to hospital by United Nations Personnel as soon as we berthed alongside at Singapore. We arrived at Singapore Quarantine Anchorage at 0713 hours on 11 August, and the Quarantine Officer, and Immigration Officer boarded almost immediately. They spared no effort to clear the ship for berthing, and we were alongside Godown 33/34 at 1030 hours.

United Nations Officials boarded as soon as we were alongside, and with the help of interpreters, did what they could for the refugees. Until the British High Commission accepts responsibility for the refugees they must remain on board under guard. We have just learned that responsibility has been accepted, and after all documentation has been completed we expect to disembark them tomorrow.

The ship's crew are to be complimented on their actions both during the rescue, and afterwards to ensure the wellbeing of the refugees. The Deck Ratings spare no effort to keep them comfortable and happy, and the children amused. The Catering Staff have coped magnificently in catering for 76 extra meals three times daily, and both departments have cheerfully given up their mess rooms and share their wash rooms with them. The sum of £382 has been collected by the ship's company to buy clothes, etc for them. This will be presented to the United Nations Representative when they leave the ship.[3]

Not all rescue operations involved refugees. On 16 April 1978 at 1440 hours *Benmhor* on passage from Kobe to Singapore and to the south east of Kyushu (30° 30′ N 132° 05′E) sighted a life raft with occupants waving to attract attention. *Benmhor* VII took aboard sixteen Japanese men and the life raft, survivors from a fishing vessel, *Miyazaki Shinoumaru*, which had capsized at 0430 hours the same day with the loss of one man. Radio contact was established with the Japanese Tenth Regional Maritime Safety Headquarters, who requested that the men be transferred to a Japanese patrol vessel off Okinawa, and this was successfully effected.[4]

City of Edinburgh and Captain Pritchard rescued another boat load of refugees in 1982. Since then the company has received a Christmas card each year: the latest from an address in Middlesex reads: 'With love and gratitude from Tan Duong and family, and 34 Vietnamese refugees rescued by the *City of Edinburgh* in June 1982.' In the following year Captain Pritchard married Miss June Imrie, Sir David Thomson's secretary, whom he had met at the Ben Line dinner and dance. Now the Christmas cards are forwarded to his widow as he died suddenly at sea in 1986.

3 *Ben Bulletin*, no. 20, December 1980 – slightly abbreviated.
4 *Ben Bulletin*. no. 13, July 1978. Captain O. Henderson was Master of *Benmhor* VII.

12

The Freight Conferences

The Conference system covering the complex of many trades between Europe and the Far East had developed extensively since the first 'Agreement for the Working of the China and Japan Trade Outwards and Homewards' signed in August 1879 by five British lines, including Wm Thomson & Co. That agreement developed into the Far Eastern Freight Conference (FEFC) which at the outbreak of the Second World War had eighteen member lines of which six were British. To the surviving founder members P & O, Blue Funnel, its wholly owned subsidiary Glen, and Wm Thomson & Co.'s Ben Line had been added Ellerman & Bucknall and Blue Star, who had joined in 1915 and 1930 respectively. There were two Japanese lines but all the rest were European: the French, Germans and Dutch were each represented by two lines and there was one each from Denmark, Norway, Sweden and Italy.[1] All member lines accepted some limitation on their territorial rights, i.e. where they might load and discharge, and on the tonnage they might carry at agreed rates of freight. But some, including the more recently joined British lines, had to be content with meagre rights compared with those of the founder members.

The Ben Line's position since before the Second World War was that we could load from ports on the East Coast of UK (defined as those between Cape Wrath and Portland Bill), but the entire west coast was a Blue Funnel preserve. On the Continent we could load limited amounts of cargo from northern France, Belgium, Holland and Germany, but had no rights from Scandinavia, nor from Mediterranean ports which were controlled by a separate Conference. In the homeward direction, however, the Ben Line had

1 Eric Jennings, *Cargoes – A Centenary History of the Far Eastern Freight Conference*, Singapore 1980, p.48, gives a somewhat larger membership, perhaps partly accounted for by counting Blue Funnel (Ocean and China Mutual) and Glen (Glen and Shire) as four.

unlimited rights from all areas to all destinations. Building on these foundations the Ben Line were by 1970 mounting the second largest number of sailings after Blue Funnel of any member line in the FEFC and its allied conferences.[2]

From its earliest days the Conference Secretariat was based in London, and the periodical owners' meetings were also invariably held there. These were often stormy; Mr Ted, who represented the Ben Line during the thirties, was on generally bad terms with the Conference chairman, Mr A. D. Lang of P & O. After the Second World War Sir Douglas took the lead in representing the Ben Line and I became his No. 2, even before I had been admitted to the partnership. In those days a mutually agreed convention prescribed that member lines should be represented at owners' meetings by not more than two delegates, one of whom should be either the head of his company or have the authority to commit it to a binding decision.

In June 1949 a double precedent was created by holding an owners' meeting not in London but in Oslo, to which delegates' wives were invited in the hope that they would be an antidote to business rivalries and animosities. The British delegates and their wives (excluding mine who was shortly due to give birth to our first child) travelled from Newcastle to Bergen on a scheduled service run by a fast, uncomfortable ship, the *Venus* whose gyrations during a rather rough crossing made many of them seasick. At Bergen we were ushered aboard coaches from the Norwegian royal train and taken up over the mountains via Finse, where they were still skiing in the long midsummer days, and down into Oslo.

Our hosts were Wilh. Wilhelmsen (WW), a privately owned company which had joined the Conference in 1926 and, like the Ben Line, had a series of ships built by Charles Connell. The senior partner, Captain Wilhelmsen, was an expert shipowner and earned additional respect by being a qualified master mariner. He was so short that his legs did not touch the floor when he sat at the

---

2 In those days there were no comprehensive statistics of lines' carryings. Conference expenses were funded by dividing the total expenditure between lines according to their number of sailings. In 1970 the five lines which contributed most were Blue Funnel £77,000, Ben Line £67,000, NYK £44,000, Hapag £34,000, East Asiatic Co. £32,000.

conference table. What he lacked in physique was amply compensated by the towering figure of Mrs Wilhelmsen. Until he retired and handed over to his son Tom he regularly attended owners' meetings, but seldom spoke, leaving that to his No. 2, who on this occasion was his partner, Mr Niels Werring. I was a bit shy at being placed next to Werring at lunch, but he soon put me at my ease. To the inevitable question 'Have you been in Norway before?', I told him that the last time was a very brief visit some eight years previously when I had taken part in the Commando raid on the Lofoten Islands. 'You know', he said 'what every Norwegian mother prays? – make my son a shipowner.' There was every evidence in his own magnificent house, and in our entertainment, that *his* mother's prayers had been answered most bountifully.

In 1949 the member lines formed quite a small gathering. The British and French had resumed operations immediately after the war and the Scandinavians and Dutch recommenced their services in 1948, but there were no Germans and no Japanese. Hamburg Amerika Linie (Hapag) and Norddeutscher Lloyd were readmitted in 1952, but deprived of rights to load in UK. In the same year Nippon Yusen Kaisha (NYK), the leading Japanese member, was also readmitted followed in 1953 by Osaka Shosen Kaisha (OSK), the other Japanese prewar member, both with curtailed rights.

Seating arrangements at owners' meetings had to be changed to accommodate readmitted or entirely new members, but some placings remained constant. The chairman occupied the central position on one long side of a rectangular table with the Conference secretary on his right and next to him a P & O delegate. On the chairman's left were the Blue Funnel delegates and next to them the Ben Line. In 1949 the chairman was Mr D. F. Anderson of P & O, later knighted and appointed chairman of his company. The Blue Funnel representatives were Mr R. H. Thornton and Sir John Nicholson. Roland Thornton was the author of a book[3] which I later made required reading for Ben Line trainees.

If he found himself in a tight corner at the conference table he would deliberately cloud the issue by putting his hands in front of his face while continuing to expound his argument in the hope that

3 R.H. Thornton, *British Shipping*, Cambridge 1939, revised 2nd edition, 1959.

the opposition would lose the thread. Obfuscation was also characteristic of the utterances of Mr Anduze-Faris, who led for Messageries Maritimes, but in his case it resulted from his unique pronunciation of English. In contrast Mr J. C. Aschengreen the bald, bespectacled and usually benign spokesman for the East Asiatic Company was a model of accuracy and enunciated his views so clearly that he was able to impart profundity to quite simple statements, and was always listened to with respect. Prince Axel of Denmark, a director of East Asiatic Company attended regularly but left the talking to his colleague. Outside the meeting he was a large, jovial and sociable figure, fond of good food, good drink and beautiful women.

The Oslo meeting was considered a great success and it became the established practice for member lines individually, or in collaboration with members of the same nationality, to act as hosts for a June owners' meeting to which wives were invited. It was agreed that the British should organise the 1951 meeting, but there was considerable surprise when Sir Douglas proposed that it should be held in Scotland, and that the Ben Line would be primarily responsible for the arrangements. There was some further hesitation on the part of our British colleagues when we proposed that the meeting should take place in the small East Coast resort, North Berwick. However this was ultimately agreed and proved to be an inspired choice. P & O appointed one of their directors Mr (later Sir Frederic) Harmer and one of their passenger specialists, Mr Morris, to act as advisers and watchdogs, and I, to whom the detailed arrangements had been delegated, got on very well with both of them. Planning and organising the meeting had to be fitted in on top of my other responsibilities and, apart from Sir Douglas's support and encouragement, I had only the part-time assistance of one newly joined, somewhat erratic trainee. Not for the first or last time I was grateful for my wartime training under Enoch Powell and at the Staff College in Haifa. The former taught me what could be achieved by individual effort and at the latter I learned how to produce detailed accurate results under pressure. The organisational problems were compounded by the decision to make this a joint meeting of three large, separate Conferences, the Far Eastern Freight Conference, the Australian

Tonnage Committee and the India Pakistan Conference. P & O was a member of all three, and many lines were members of two, whereas the Ben Line was involved only in the Far East trade.

The manager of the Marine Hotel, Mr Hiller (brother of Dame Wendy Hiller), threw himself into the preparations with great enthusiasm. These took the best part of a year because he had to decline all bookings for a week in June. The problem of what to do with a few permanent residents was solved by inviting them to participate in some of the entertainments.

Flagpoles were erected along the hotel frontage (which faced inland) to display the houseflags of all the participating lines. In the foyer the GPO installed a temporary Post Office which could transmit and receive cables. The main lounge facing on to the Firth of Forth became the meeting room for each of the three Conference meetings, which took place on succeeding days.

Wives and those delegates not involved in meetings were entertained with trips to Edinburgh, and to local monuments such as Tantallon and Dirleton Castles. On one day there was a Borders tour in a fleet of hired cars, which visited a woollen mill, where each lady was presented with a cashmere jersey. This was followed by a sheep dog demonstration at Sir Douglas's home, Holylee near Walkerburn, and tea at Peebles Hydro Hotel. Evening entertainments included a display of Scottish country dancing and a conjuring performance during which members of the audience had their pockets picked and discreet items of clothing magically removed.

I met a number of prominent shipowners including the chairman of a leading transatlantic passenger line, who surprised me by saying that he had never visited New York – and never wanted to. I was not altogether surprised when it subsequently transpired that his Paris office employed a thousand people to transact business requiring only a fraction of that number.

When the formal meetings had been completed those who could spare the time were taken on a two-day Highland Tour. The participants were each provided with an illustrated and annotated map of the route: 'In this brief note we have not attempted to describe the scenery which, provided the weather is fine, can safely be left to speak for itself. If the historical allusions refer mainly to bloodshed and revolt, this is perhaps a true reflection of the stubbornly pugnacious

[163]

elements in the national character.' The Ben Line's competitors maybe recognised the appropriateness of the last remark.

The North Berwick meeting undoubtedly 'raised the Ben Line image', as they say nowadays, in the eyes of the international shipping community. It also set standards which subsequent host lines sought to emulate with varying degrees of success. Increasing membership ruled out further joint meetings with other Conferences but the Far Eastern Freight Conference persisted with an annual summer meeting to which wives were invited. We felt that the Ben Line had earned a season ticket at North Berwick and did not again volunteer to be the principal organiser, but we collaborated fully with our British colleagues as co-hosts in Torquay, Hong Kong and Bath. Other summer meetings were held in Copenhagen, Kyoto, Paris, the Portuguese Algarve, Scheveningen, Singapore, Stockholm, Venice and Vienna.

Apart from these summer occasions there were regular owners' meetings in February and October which took place in London. For some years these were held at the Baltic Exchange whose conference room was dominated by its arms, displayed on a large wall plaque, with the proud motto 'Our Word Our Bond' – a motto which in those days the member lines lived up to.

Adam Smith observed 'People of the same trade seldom meet together, even for merriment and diversion, but the conversation ends in a conspiracy against the public, or in some contrivance to raise prices'.[4] I venture to disagree with the great man in regard to the FEFC; its activities were not against 'the public' – its customers, whose goodwill and support were vital in realising the objective of promoting prosperous trade at stable rates of freight. Uncontrolled competition may be attractive to theorists; in practice the USA decimated their mercantile marine after the Second World War by adhering to that concept, while at the same time exporting to other parts of the world sharp business practices which had been largely unknown while world seaborne trade was dominated by the British. The transatlantic trades, in which the Ben Line took no part, seemed to be in almost perpetual chaos. As regards the second part of Adam Smith's comment, there was certainly plenty of discussion

4 Adam Smith, *Wealth of Nations*, Glasgow edn., p.145.

about rates of freight, but by no means always as to how they might be raised. Active outside competition often involved reductions, and if rates were too high this could impede or even kill trade which member lines wished to encourage.

Rates of freight were only one strand in the fabric of conference negotiations which fell into three broad categories. The first comprised those between lines who were already members about trade rights, i.e. the amount of cargo a line might carry from specified areas to specified destinations. The Ben Line's prime objectives were to preserve and exploit its unlimited westbound, or homeward, rights from all areas to all destinations; to prevent other members from acquiring eastbound, or outward rights from the East Coast of UK, and to expand its limited rights from North Continental Ports.

All lines serving the Far East were allotted a ceiling quota of eastbound general cargo at Antwerp, Rotterdam/Amsterdam and Hamburg/Bremen. Each national group of lines received a percentage allocation which was then split in agreed proportions between the participants. The British and French lines formed a single national group. The percentage shares were translated into tonnage at two-monthly intervals on the basis of a forecast of the volume of cargo likely to move during that period. This complicated structure ensured a fertile soil for inter-group and inter-line negotiations to adjust the shares of cargo. An important factor in such negotiations was past performance; if one line had consistently undercarried its share there was good reason for that share to be reduced and allotted to another line. If a line overcarried it could be accused of cheating, but might defend itself by claiming that its competitors were offering an inferior service and that turning away cargo solely because a quota had already been filled could bring the conference system into disrepute.

The second category concerned negotiations between existing members and a line seeking membership. The Conference delegated these to a committee of members which was given an agreed mandate to try to reach an agreement. Sometimes all efforts to find a peaceful solution broke down and then there was a freight war, such as that which began in 1953 when the Japanese Mitsui company was refused membership. Two Japanese lines had just been readmitted and were not enthusiastic about the prospect of sharing their rights with a newcomer, and the other members were united in resisting Mitsui, which was in the process of rehabilitating itself as one of the most powerful 'Zaibatsu' (vertically integrated companies) controlling large amounts of cargo. A costly fight raged until 1956 when Mitsui were admitted 'under wing' of NYK. Subsequently in 1961, under the Japanese Government's rationalisation scheme, Mitsui merged with OSK.

Another major freight war erupted in the sixties when the Italian Lauro Line, loading against the existing national line Lloyd Triestino, drew cargo at cut rates from Northern Europe and Italy necessitating expensive reductions in rates on similar cargo from UK and North Continental ports. Lauro was ultimately admitted after a long fight, in 1971, but subsequently collapsed and effectively went out of the cargo liner business.

Until the late sixties Conference membership remained relatively constant and agreements once reached were usually adhered to in good faith. Between 1967 and 1979 fourteen new members were admitted: two from South Korea and one each from Japan, Taiwan, Philippines, Thailand, Singapore, Malaysia, Egypt, Italy, Spain, Belgium, East Germany and Poland. Most of these were newly formed 'national' lines which received the backing of their governments, thus introducing a political dimension into the negotiations. There was little argument that a 'national' line had a right to carry a share of the cargo moving from and to its territory even if the trade was adequately covered by existing Conference services, but there was plenty of opposition to the idea that it should make its operations viable by carrying cargo from and to other areas served by long established member lines and other 'national' lines.

Support for those who wished to create new 'national' lines came from the United Nations Conference on Trade and Development (UNCTAD) established in 1964. All countries were given an equal voice in its deliberations so UNCTAD was dominated by the 'less developed nations' and in 1974 published the United Nations Code of Conduct for Liner Conferences. This recommended the principle of 40:40:20. Thus in the trade between UK and Japan, for example, 40% would be carried by the British lines, 40% by the Japanese lines and 20% by 'cross traders', i.e. all those lines who were neither

British nor Japanese. This arbitrary formula cut across many interests of the established lines and was a fruitful source of dissension.[5]

The third category of negotiations concerned rates of freight. In the earliest days the tariff of rates charged by the member lines could be printed on a single sheet of paper. Seventy years later the eastbound tariff had become an ever-expanding book and the westbound trades had their own tariffs in which the rates had to be correlated with those from other areas so that, for example, canned pineapple from the Philippines could compete on equal terms with the same commodity from Taiwan and Malaysia.

One of the main reasons for introducing the conference system in the Far East had been the imbalance between the eastbound and westbound trades. At the end of the last century and again between the two World Wars the eastbound trade far outweighed the westbound. After the Second World War the pendulum began to swing in the opposite direction with the upsurge of exports from Hong Kong, Japan, Taiwan and later South Korea. By 1972 the total volume of trade carried in conference vessels had risen to 13 million metric tons of which less than half was eastbound. Six years later the total volume had risen to 18 million tons and the ratio of eastbound to westbound was about 3 to 5. Not all the westbound cargo was destined for Europe: there was a rapidly growing movement to Red Sea ports (a one way trade since there was no eastbound cargo from this area) which exceeded 1 million tons during the seventies.[6]

The diversity of commodities was constantly being extended. A committee of brokers, including a representative of Killick Martin, received applications and fixed a rate having regard to value, stowage factor, rates already established for similar commodities, and any other relevant considerations. I asked Killick's to get a rate fixed for swallows' eggs in lead-lined cases from North Borneo, a main source of the Chinese delicacy birds' nest soup, which is made from swallows' nests. The eggs were destined for London and were to be used in a beauty preparation manufactured by Elizabeth

5 See Ronald Hope, *A New History of British Shipping*, London, 1990, which covers the subject from its earliest beginnings to 1988 with scholarship and clarity. The author's description of the factors which contributed to the decline of British shipping is particularly lucid and compelling.
6 Eric Jennings, *op.cit.*, p.5.

Arden, but details of value etc were unknown. This was not an altogether implausible application, seeing that the tariffs contained rates for quail's eggs and shark's fins, likewise mop heads, fog signals and lollipop sticks! Having despatched the message I allowed half an hour to elapse before reminding Killick's that it was April Fool's day, but by that time a canvasser had been despatched to Elizabeth Arden's factory at Willesden. I had to apologise for wasting the time of both Killick's and the celebrated beautician.

All the FEFC tariffs were quoted in sterling until 1968 when it was decided, despite opposition from the Ben Line, to convert them to the US dollar, which was thought to be more stable and less subject to inflation. Going over to the US dollar did not solve the problems of currency fluctuation, nor the sudden fourfold increase in oil fuel in 1974, nor the necessity for more frequent rate increases to keep pace with inflation. Currency fluctuations were met by making rates of freight subject to a currency adjustment factor (CAF) and on top of that a bunker adjustment factor (BAF) was introduced to compensate for the enormously increased cost of oil fuel which was exacerbated during the closure of the Suez Canal (1967-75) by extended voyages via the Cape of Good Hope or the Panama Canal. CAF and BAF and the need for more frequent increases in the basic rates of freight gave rise to the third category of negotiation, that of explaining, justifying, and where necessary modifying the measures which the FEFC proposed to take. The multiformity of shippers and their vast geographical spread made this task very difficult until Shippers' Councils were established. In the mid sixties the FEFC initiated consultations in Europe with those Shippers' Councils which then existed. In the ensuing years Shippers' Councils were established in Japan, Hong Kong, Malaysia, the Philippines, Singapore, South Korea, Taiwan and Thailand.

Two key figures in promoting the orderly functioning of the FEFC were its chairman and its secretary. Mr R. M. Thwaites, who had succeeded Sir Donald Anderson as chairman, died unexpectedly in 1963 and Sir Herbert McDavid, recently retired as chairman of the Glen Line, became the first FEFC chairman who was not from the P & O stable, and the first to fulfil the role full time.

Previously incumbents had combined that with looking after their own business, as his successor Sir Andrew Crichton another P & O director, did from 1966 to 1969, when he became the first chairman of Overseas Containers Limited. Between 1969 and 1976 there were three chairman all with Holt backgrounds,[7] notably Sir John Nicholson (1969-72) whose role in steering the FEFC successfully into the container era is discussed in chapter 13.

Nicholson tried to persuade me to succeed him but I received the full backing of the Ben Line board in declining the invitation. I knew that the job of trying to lead the company through the uncertain, rough waters of the seventies could not be combined with devoting much time to Conference affairs and frequent travelling to London and other parts of the world. Furthermore the Conference chairman's role as arbiter and mediator in an atmosphere of increasing lawlessness and bad faith would have deprived the Ben Line of a degree of manoeuvrability, since it would be difficult to exercise the ultimate sanction of announcing that we no longer felt ourselves bound by agreements which many other parties were disregarding. I did agree to continue to be chairman of the FEFC Public Relations Committee, which sought to explain the Conference's objectives, not only to shippers, receivers and the general public both in Europe and the Far East, but to the staff of recently joined members and their agents.

Reverting to the Conference chairmanship, Nicholson was followed by Mr H. O. Karsten (1972-76), who joined OCL after being chairman of Glen Line, and when I again declined to succeed him Jhr M. F. van Lennep became the first non-British chairman, gallantly assuming the thankless task from 1976 to 1979 after he had retired as chairman of Nedlloyd.

The man who had even more direct and frequent contact with member lines than the Conference chairman was the Conference secretary. The FEFC Secretariat in London was headed by Mr C. R. Hawkins from 1939 to 1964 (with a break for war service). Cyril Hawkins, short, balding, industrious, with a good sense of humour and a great appetite for tea and cigarettes, never allowed his early training with Alfred Holt & Co. to influence his impartiality. This tradition of scrupulous fairness was maintained by his successors Mr J. G. Cotesworth (1964-71), who came from Butterfield & Swire's office in Japan, and Mr R. G. Sutton (1971-79). Miss Jean Sparks, a

7 W. H. McNeill (1969), H. O. Karsten (1972-76).

mainstay of the London Secretariat, very efficient and knowledgeable about the complexities of Conference agreements and Conference lore, and often the only female to appear at London owners'
meetings, became Mrs Ray Sutton.

By 1979 the FEFC had thirty-two member lines from twenty-two
states. We had long outgrown the premises of the Baltic Exchange
– and its motto. Owners' meetings in London were held in the
ballroom of the Dorchester Hotel and microphones were needed.
The convention that at least one delegate from each line should be in
a position to commit his company to a binding decision was still
observed by the British lines, but was disregarded by many of the
others. Competition from the Trans-Siberian Railway and from the
Taiwanese Evergreen Line was serious, and was used as an excuse
by many lines for internal malpractice which became increasingly
destructive. To a network of expensive local secretariats in Europe
and in the Far East was added a Cargo Control organisation, which
attempted to defeat malpractice by both carrier and shipper, backed
by a Neutral Body which imposed fines on member lines found
guilty of infringements. Some malpractice, mainly the offering of
rebates on the agreed tariff rates, was the result of principals being
unable to control their agents, but much occurred because member
lines were prepared as a matter of policy to go back on their word
and break the agreements which they had made with their fellow
members.

By the late seventies it became clear that it was time to review the
workings of the London Secretariat. Mr H. J. Kruse, chairman of
Hapag Lloyd, succeeded Jhr M. F. van Lennep as Conference chairman and it was agreed that Roderick MacLeod with the assistance
of outside consultants should study the Secretariat's functions and
make recommendations. The upshot was that Mr B. L. Allen was
recruited for the new post of director, Ray Sutton remained secretary
in charge of a central division dealing with Conference agreements,
applications for membership, trade shares, public relations, staff administration and accounts. A separate economics and finance division dealt with tariff matters, pricing statistics, trade forecasts and
budgeting. A third commercial division handled relations with shippers and trade bodies, outside competition and cargo control. This
third division was shortly afterwards split off to form a UK Area

Secretariat comparable to those which had existed on the Continent and in the Far East for some years. The FEFC had evolved into a vast bureaucratic organisation.

Outside the FEFC group of conferences the Ben Line were applicants for memberships of the Ceylon Continental Conference which would have enabled us to load from Sri Lanka to destinations other than UK to which we exercised rights as members of the Colombo Homeward Conference. We were never successful with these applications, but in 1960 we were admitted to the Indonesia Europe and Europe Indonesia Conferences. This was despite blocking tactics employed not so much by four newly formed Indonesian 'national' lines, which had their own financial and political problems, but by Holt's Dutch subsidiary Oceaan, and by Hapag which since the Second World War had built up a very successful service.

Norman Galbraith, a director since 1968, headed the Ben Line Conference Department for many years until he retired in 1986 after completing forty years' service with the company. As a matter of policy however all the Ben Line directors took some share in Conference negotiations. They were a fascinating microcosm of international affairs, where of course perceived self-interest predominated, and this could result in alliances which cut across national boundaries. On many issues the Ben Line made common cause with its British colleagues, but sometimes we found ourselves at loggerheads with them. We had strong ties, for example, with the Danish East Asiatic Co. because they and we had a major interest in the trade between Europe and Thailand.

13

The Container Revolution

On 30 December 1971 the first containership in the Far East trade sailed from Japan for Europe.[1] In the course of the next ten years the role of the conventional cargo liner was virtually eliminated in this trade. Why the container revolution occurred at that time, why it took the form that it did, and how the transformation was achieved so rapidly is a fascinating story.

For some British shipping companies it was to mean the end of their existence as recognisable entities. For many seafarers, shore-based staff and labour it was to mean an end to their careers or a drastic change in the way they earned their livelihoods. This and the succeeding chapters show how the Ben Line faced up to these challenges and either mitigated or overcame them.

The concept of carrying goods in containers was not new. Before the First World War van-like containers were carried on British railways and ferried across the Irish Sea. Already in 1933 the International Container Bureau was established as an arm of the International Chamber of Commerce in Paris to promote the greater use of containers. After the Second World War British railways operated lift-van services between UK and the North Continent. During the Korean War (1950-53) supplies for the American forces were carried in 'Dravo-boxes'. The use of containers was further exploited by American shipping companies in the run up to the Vietnam War and during the war itself (1965-73). Malcolm McLean, the founder and first president of Sea-Land, one of the companies principally involved, has been named the father of modern container transport. He described himself as 'a trucker with one foot in the

1 NYK's *Hakone Maru* 1950 TEU (20-foot equivalent units). TEU became the standard measurement of the cargo capacity of a containership; equivalent because most such ships could accommodate one 40-foot container in the place of two 20-footers.

water' and it was he who in 1956 first loaded truck trailer bodies on the deck of a modified oil tanker. In the fifties and early sixties Sea-Land and another American company, Matson, converted ships partially by installing vertical slots, or cells, so that containers could be loaded on top of one another in the holds, as well as on deck. However it was not until 1964 that the world's first purpose-built fully cellular containership came into service, running a weekly service between Fremantle and Melbourne.[2] Then in the spring of 1966 Sea-Land arrived on the Ben Line's doorstep by starting a transatlantic service calling at Rotterdam, Bremen and Grangemouth. Some of us from Edinburgh made the short journey to see the converted ship, which could carry 166 35-foot containers[3] in the holds and another 60 on deck. These were discharged and loaded by the ship's own gear, and Sea-Land's own road transport made the inland journeys. This was all very interesting, but we had no direct involvement in the transatlantic trade and did not feel directly threatened by Sea-Land's operations. By this time, however, others did see themselves endangered and had, unbeknown to us, laid plans which were to turn the British shipping industry upside down and revolutionise the carriage of cargo in many trades besides the Far East.

We certainly appreciated the desirability of improving on the expensive inefficiency of conventional cargo handling. Dock labour was becoming ever more expensive and in some parts of the world, including UK, Australia and USA, increasingly capricious and unreliable. Strikes, unofficial as well as official, go-slow tactics, and other restrictive practices were resulting in cargo liners spending half their time or more in port. Losses by pilferage from relatively easily broached packaging were a worldwide problem.

Many thought that these ills could be at least ameliorated by development of the concept of 'unit-loads', persuading shippers to pack their cargo on pallets or skids, to bundle their sawn timber (hitherto loaded and discharged piece by piece at about three tons per hour). A container is of course a form of unit-load, but in the early sixties, when there was a move in the direction of unit-loads in

2 Associated Steamship Company's *Kooringa*.
3 Sea-Land had the misfortune to base their operations on 35-foot before 20-foot and 40-foot containers were adopted as the international standards.

the Far East trade, the problems of ownership of the container, freighting its contents, getting it loaded with cargo, discharged, and returned full of cargo seemed insurmountable. The FEFC set up a Unit Loads Committee in the early sixties to wrestle with standardising the measurements of pallets and skids and devising freighting rules for them. We were kept closely in touch with developments because Roderick MacLeod was chairman of this committee, which also considered the problems presented by containers. In due course the Unit Loads Committee did the lion's share of the work leading up to the production of the first FEFC container tariff, and in many other ways MacLeod was responsible for making the Ben Line's contribution to the successful containerisation of the Far East trade far greater than it might otherwise have been.

II

The public announcement of the formation of Overseas Containers Limited (OCL) in September 1965 came as a complete surprise to us and to all the other British and foreign cargo liner companies who were not included, but saw themselves threatened by this extremely powerful British consortium.

Information about the genesis of OCL has recently been published. By the beginning of 1965 the Australian government

was considering seriously the prospects of containerising Australia's main trades. Since Australia had no major national line of her own, the possibility was that the Australian government would turn to Sea-Land to inaugurate the service. Since Sea-Land were by this time transporting vast quantities of war supplies westwards across the Pacific to Vietnam, American entry into a major Blue Funnel region seemed an imminent danger.[4]

Two Holt partners, Ronald Swayne and Lindsay Alexander,[5] advocated containerising the trade, and the latter presented a paper recommending the creation of a consortium to reduce the risk of cut-throat competition between individual shipowners. In a confidential letter dated 4 May 1965 Sir John Nicholson, chairman of

4 Malcolm Falkus, *The Blue Funnel Legend*, Basingstoke, 1990, p.362.
5 Alexander succeeded Sir John Nicholson as chairman of Ocean, Swayne succeeded Sir Andrew Crichton as chairman of OCL; both were knighted.

Holt's, told Sir Donald Anderson, chairman of P & O, that Holt's were contemplating the formation of a British consortium to undertake a joint venture in containers. It was natural that Holt's first approach should be to P & O since they were the only other British line with a large stake in both the Australian and Far Eastern trades. Nicholson's letter set out two aims: the operation must, first, 'be conducted on a sufficiently large scale to sustain what may be quite a large investment' and, second, must 'avoid competition in this field between individual Conference members'. To achieve the first objective he envisaged participation by 'at least four if not all six of the largest Groups'. The six would embrace British & Commonwealth Line and Furness Withy, both public companies, both without rights in the Far East trade; Cunard, also without rights in the Far East trade, and Ellerman Lines which had rights in both the Australian and Far East trades. Nicholson clearly envisaged a container venture in both trades, but realised that achievement of his second objective could well be frustrated by Conference members who were excluded from the proposed consortium. He was particularly fearful that the Ben Line in the Far East trade and Blue Star in the Australian trade might be driven to undercut the consortium's rates, and he therefore suggested to Anderson that both might be invited to join.

Anderson replied immediately that P & O were also considering some sort of container consortium and 'if we are to work with anyone else, it is Alfred Holt & Company whom we certainly would choose'. In a discussion which followed Nicholson pressed successfully for the inclusion in the consortium of the British & Commonwealth Line and Furness Withy, and a joint approach to these companies was made. P & O argued persuasively that any larger grouping could run foul of anti-monopoly legislation.

The four companies, which between them controlled two-thirds of the deep-sea general cargo-liner tonnage of the UK, agreed to form Overseas Containers Limited. The four concerns had much in common, for all were public companies with similar responsibilities in terms of dividend performance and accountability. Ben was excluded, against Nicholson's wishes who recalled in a subsequent memorandum that 'I was fearful – unnecessarily as it turned out – of the harm they might do if excluded'.[6]

6 *Ibid.*, pp.364-5.

We, of course, were unaware of all this, but had we been invited to join OCL on the terms accepted by the other four participants, we would have declined. The member companies of OCL were prepared from the outset to submerge their individual identities, to contribute substantial sums of cash and some senior members of staff, who were told to go and play containers. We were determined to preserve our identity and, as far as possible, our independence.

While we were still speculating on the implications of the formation of OCL and the likely repercussions on the Far East trade we received an invitation from Mr A. F. Hull, chairman of Ellerman Lines, to meet him and representatives of what Sir Andrew Crichton, OCL's first chairman, termed in his usual breezy way 'the odds and sods', i.e. all the major British deep-sea cargo-liner companies which had been excluded from OCL. These were, besides Ben and Ellerman, Blue Star, Cunard and T. & J. Harrison. The upshot was the formation by these companies in January 1966 of a rival consortium, Associated Container Transportation Ltd (ACT).

Ellerman, Blue Star and Cunard (through its subsidiary Port Line) had important interests in the Australian trade and therefore felt themselves immediately threatened. Ben was still unconvinced that containerisation would work and believed that in any event some time must elapse before it had any significant impact on the Far East trade, but membership of ACT gave us a valuable opportunity to observe and learn at first hand from others' experience – and mistakes.

Many thought that containerisation would spell the end of the Conference system through the formation of groups such as OCL and ACT, which would cut across the rights of individual lines. There was little doubt that, unless the Australian venture was a disaster, OCL would containerise its share of the Far East trade. But what was its share? What business had British & Commonwealth and Furness Withy in that trade? If lines without existing rights entered the Far East trade there was of course the possibility that the Ben Line might participate in the Australian or other trades.

I and Roderick MacLeod were appointed as Ben's representatives on the ACT Board. He and William Thomson shared my view that if containerisation was a commercial success, and if we failed to meet the challenge, our large share of the Far East trade which had been built up over the years would be usurped by others. Sir Douglas took no active part in ACT. He was not only sceptical about the success of containers but thoroughly disliked the prospect of constraints on our freedom of action which might be placed upon us by cooperating closely with other lines. These views were shared by his son David. Mr Ted was also included to be doubtful. In March 1966, when Sir Douglas was in the Far East and Australia, I discussed with him a paper by Captain Alex Paterson on what might be done to modify the last two Benledi class 21-knot cargo liners, which were due for delivery in 1967 and 1968.[7] Mr Ted considered that making them more adaptable for unitised or containerised cargo would tend to spoil them as conventional cargo liners. He thought it unlikely that containers would represent more than ten per cent of our trade in three years' time and that we would have for a considerably longer period a large volume of trade which required handling in the conventional manner. If containerisation developed more rapidly than expected he thought it might be necessary to get rid of a number of our conventional ships and buy either tankers or bulk carriers which might be converted to containerships. He was not convinced that high speeds would be essential in such ships. Very careful thought would have to be given to what we should build after the Benledi class but we would be more likely to know what we needed when developments in the container sphere were clearer.

In the event we did modify *Bencruachan* III, the last of the Benledi class, and as already related, attempted to hedge our bets with the next new ship, *Benlawers* V, delivered in 1970.

Mr Ted retired in 1966 and became the Ben Line's first and only president. After his retiral I visited him periodically, as did William Thomson, to tell him about the latest developments and what we young lads on the Board were up to. He always listened with interest but, to his great credit, never attempted to interfere.

III

ACT's first step was to set up a working party whose primary remit was to form a company able to provide the member lines, at their individual option, with services such as inland road transport, the

7 *Benalbanach* III, delivered July 1967, and the improved Benledi class 21½-knot *Bencruachan* III.

evaluation of tenders for the construction of containers, and shipping documentation, which might be more efficiently provided on a centralised basis. Roderick MacLeod became the first chairman of this working party so Ben were actively involved from the outset in setting up ACT Services (ACTS). When ACTS had been established and ACT Australia (ACTA) were running up to the inauguration of their container service (their first ship sailed in the spring of 1969) the chairmanship was transferred to J. G. (Jim) Payne of Blue Star. MacLeod took over again during the run up to the start of the Far East service.

There was a difference of approach between the members of ACT. Ben were determined to preserve their identity, and as far as possible, their independence. Ellerman and Port Line (Cunard) felt more inclined to submerge their individual identities, as the members of OCL had done. Blue Star were more in sympathy with Ben's policies. Harrison, who were not involved in either the Australian or Far East trades, were anxious not to undertake financial commitments which would be of no benefit to them. These differences were resolved by negotiation and compromise. However, it was clearly established that the ACT member lines were entitled to determine how the container services that they provided in their respective trades should be marketed and operated. This central principle, on which Ben were particularly keen, was never compromised.

Apart from resolving internal operational issues there was the important question of what attitude ACT should adopt towards OCL, and towards the non-British lines involved. Ellerman and Port Line thought we should try to cooperate closely with OCL and that seeking to make any form of common cause with foreign lines might jeopardise ACT's relations with OCL. Ben, on the other hand, believed that OCL's behaviour so far indicated that they were not really prepared to cooperate, and that seeking to build up and strengthen ACT by arranging close cooperation with other lines would enable us to bargain with OCL from strength, which would make a favourable relationship between ACT and OCL more rather than less likely. A compromise acceptable to Ben was reached in August 1966 just before Mr S. Storm-Jorgensen, the director in charge of the Danish East Asiatic Company's shipping interests, met the ACT representatives in London. I knew Storm-Jorgensen very well and believed that he, and maybe his Scandinavian colleagues, wished to cooperate with ACT. It was agreed that we should tell him about the talks which had already taken place between ACT and OCL in the Australian context and listen to everything he might be induced to say, but that the Scandinavians should not be offered participation just now in ACT. Storm-Jorgensen did not appear to be surprised by this attitude but told me privately after the meeting that East Asiatic would have been prepared to participate then whereas his Scandinavian colleagues, the Norwegian line Wilhelmsen and the Swedes, Brostrom and Transatlantic, felt that it would be dangerous and premature to become involved in either ACT or OCL.[8]

Several Ben approaches to Holt's and P & O about how they viewed the future of the Far East trade were rebuffed or sidestepped, maybe because the OCL camp could not at that stage foresee how matters would develop. As time passed without any sign of cooperation from OCL I became increasingly convinced that Holt's and P & O hoped Ben would not accept the challenge of containerisation and would be squeezed out of the Far East trade. This unfriendly, but perfectly legitimate, commercial objective could, I thought, have been encouraged by Sir Douglas's patent lack of enthusiasm for containerisation and its implications, and might be reinforced by his absence from the scene of active operations, unless we adopted a defiant stance. Our suspicions were further increased when we learned that OCL had talked and come to some form of understanding with the Germans and Japanese, but not with us.

In 1967 we formed, registered and publicised three ACT companies in Hong Kong, Singapore and Kuala Lumpur. These were, in the event, never activated but were designed to let OCL know that we would not be walked over. When there was still no sign of cooperation from OCL we had talks with the Danish East Asiatic Company about the possibility of joining them in a ScanDutch group and made sure that news of these talks reached the ears of OCL.

The crunch came, at last, at the end of 1968. A meeting chaired by Sir John Nicholson was convened on 19 December. Ben was

8 Note on ACT discussion about cooperation with other lines, 25 August 1966, attended by Hull and Alastair Lloyd (Ellerman), Rae (Blue Star), Hollebone (Port/Cunard) and Strachan (Ben).

represented by myself, Roderick MacLeod and William Thomson. The other participants were Dennis Martin-Jenkins and David Lloyd (Ellerman), Lindsay Alexander (Blue Funnel), Henry Karsten (chairman of Glen), Keith Reynolds (P & O) and Sir Andrew Crichton (chairman of OCL).

Alexander told us what a technical man in Holt's had learned about Sea-Land's intentions from someone whom he described as 'a fellow member of the freemasonry of technical men'. Sea-Land had been so successful that they were now in a position to embark on a large-scale shipbuilding programme. In January 1969 they would go out to tender worldwide for eight ships with a speed of more than 27 knots powered by steam turbines manufactured in USA.

Their length would be at least 900 feet, beam 105ft. 9ins. (maximum for the Panama Canal), depth 64 feet, capacity 1,100 35-foot. containers, but adaptable to carry 40-footers. The source of the information said it was Sea-Land's intention to mop up as much world trade as possible. Blue Funnel's technical assessment was that this specification represented the ultimate in containerships and that anything smaller would eventually become uneconomic. They thought that delivery of the ships might be possible in mid 1971.

In OCL's view such a fleet, equivalent to about sixty conventional cargo-liners, made it imperative to press on with containerising the Far East trade. At least that part of it which they regarded as the industrial north, i.e. Japan, Hong Kong, plus perhaps Taiwan and South Korea.

OCL said they wished to know whether ACT would agree to investigate the possibility of not denying participation to any FEFC member line on the basis of its established share of the trade, provided that it was prepared to make the necessary investment. If, say, the Scandinavians or the Dutch (or, unspoken, Ben and Ellerman) were not given this invitation they might well link up with Sea-Land, which would be a pity. Secondly, OCL said they wished to know whether we would agree to talking, as British lines jointly, with the Japanese and Germans. Nicholson said that he was under considerable pressure from the Japanese to have talks with them, also from the Germans who were being repeatedly approached by other European FEFC members to find out what was going on, they having become aware that both the Germans and the Japanese had reached an understanding with OCL that they would keep each other informed of developments.

The OCL camp said they had calculated that if the British, Germans and Japanese were able to agree on a common policy they would command a sufficient share of the trade to run a weekly container service independently of anyone else. They also felt that if these three national groups could find common ground there was a better chance of the other FEFC members falling in with that policy.

After a brief recess to consult with our Ellerman colleagues we replied that we would indeed be prepared to participate in joint British talks with the Germans and Japanese. We decided that this reply should be made without entering into any caveats, which might only have the effect of limiting our own manoeuvrability, and without, at that stage, asking for any further practical details, which could again have the same effect.

We know now that an OCL board minute of the following day, 20 December 1968, recorded that:

Ocean Fleets [Holt's] and the P & O had agreed on the feasibility of containerising this [the Far East] trade and, bearing in mind the threat from Sea-Land, had recognised the urgency to develop in the first instance a container system in the Japan-Hong Kong service. Existing Conference Lines were to be invited to join and an approach had been made to Ben Line which had resulted in their acceptance.[9]

We had for a long time been apprehensive about the harm that OCL might do to us: we were not aware of just how frightened they were of what Ben might do to them.

The proposed British-German-Japanese talks chaired by Nicholson took place in January 1969 in San Francisco, resulting in agreement to build ships only sufficient to carry lines' existing share of the trade, and to invite other FEFC member lines to participate. From these and subsequent talks emerged the three nation group which became known as Trio.

Sir John Nicholson was chairman of the FEFC from 1969 to 1971, in which year he retired from Holt's (or Ocean as they had now become), where he had been the dominant influence since the fifties. He epitomised what has been termed 'the unashamed intellectual

9 M. Falkus, *op.cit.*, p.367.

and social elitism of the Holt system of management'.[10] That the container revolution took the form it did in the Far East trade, and that the transition was effected relatively smoothly, owed a great deal to his efforts and personality. He had a restless appetite for action. He was also ultra-sensitive to political trends. I remember him talking to me about the Chinese-inspired unrest in Hong Kong, where he foresaw the direst consequences, and on another occasion he asked me whether I shared his view that a Marxist revolution in UK was a distinct possibility. To subordinates, including his own staff, who were in no position to defend themselves, he could be inconsiderate and brutal. He was almost invariably very polite to me, but in dealings with other shipowners he was inclined to put backs up by unintentional arrogance and condescension. In negotiations I sometimes felt more comfortable when he and his colleagues were in opposition to us rather than when they and we were trying to fight a joint cause. He struck up a particular rapport with a very able, ambitious and charming Japanese, Yoshia Ariyoshi, chairman of NYK, who was generally regarded as the pre-eminent leader of Japanese shipping. This probably helped to ensure that the Japanese joined Trio, but Ariyoshi cleverly exploited the relationship, sometimes to the detriment of British interests, though that did not prevent him from being awarded an honorary OBE.

After Nicholson had succeeded in laying the foundations of Trio there was an intensive statistical evaluation of carryings to establish the share of the trade to which each line was entitled, and hence how many ships they should build. This necessitated agreement on the approximate capacity and speed of the ships, which in turn was conditioned by the competition they might have to face from Sea-Land. These negotiations were not entirely finalised when at the end of May 1969 OCL announced that they had placed orders for four containerships for the Far East trade.

Four ships was well within the share which OCL could demonstrate they were entitled to. On 2 June Ben responded with a press release:

In a statement issued in Edinburgh, Mr M. F. Strachan, Deputy Chairman of Associated Container Transportation Limited (ACT) and a Joint

10 *Ibid.*, p.11.

[182]

Managing Director of the Ben Line, commenting on the announcement by Overseas Containers Limited (OCL) of their order for 4 container ships for the trade between Europe and the Far East, said:

> The OCL announcement comes as no surprise to ACT since there has been cordial consultation on the subject of the containerisation of the Far East/Europe trade for some time past.
>
> There is a difference in the methods of operation as between OCL and ACT in that the ACT Lines preserve their individual identity and develop the trades in which they are traditionally interested.
>
> Of the five component companies of ACT, Ben Line, Ellerman, and to a small extent Blue Star, have an interest in the Far East trade.
>
> The Ben Line, next to Blue Funnel, are the largest cargo carriers of any nationality in the Europe/Far East trade and it follows that the main onus of developing the ACT containerisation interest in that trade will fall upon the Ben Line.
>
> The Ben Line and its ACT colleagues are fully prepared to meet the challenge and to offer container facilities to shippers at the appropriate time.
>
> While the ACT Lines will preserve their independence from OCL and any other group this will not preclude cooperation between ACT and all other interests who wish to see containerisation introduced in an orderly manner within the framework of the Conference system thereby preserving stable rates and services.

IV

The ACT lines with Australian rights formed ACT Australia Ltd (ACTA) and built three ships with Bremer Vulkan which they named *ACT* I, II and III. They envisaged that the Far East lines would form a parallel company, ACTFE and name their ships *ACT* IV, etc. Ben argued successfully that from a marketing viewpoint it would be madness not to capitalise on the Ben Line's existing excellent reputation with shippers and consignees, so in March 1970 Ben Line Containers Ltd was formed in which Ben held 80 and Ellerman 20 per cent. Blue Star did not participate because they had not exercised their small Far East rights for many years and therefore had no carryings to justify a share.

There were prolonged negotiations between Ben and Ellerman to determine their relative shares based on recent past performance. The figures showed a split of 82.5 and 17.5 per cent, but Ben agreed to adjust this to 80 and 20 per cent in return for a cash compensation of about £275,000. This was quite attractive to Ben since it slightly reduced our share of the enormous capital investment needed for a venture whose success nobody could at that stage predict. As things turned out it proved an advantageous investment for Ellerman.

We got on well with Ellerman, who were usually prepared to be guided or persuaded by Ben. Sir John Ellerman, son of the founder, took no active part in the large group built up by his father. He lived in South Africa and devoted himself mainly to marine biology. The founder had bought up a number of other lines and the group had considerable interests in the trades with India and Pakistan, South Africa and Australia. In the Far East they were relatively weak. Hull, the Ellerman Lines chairman, died after a short illness before ACT really got under way and was succeeded by Dennis Martin-Jenkins, who had two sons in the company. We dealt mainly with Dennis Martin-Jenkins, David Lloyd, his brother Jeremy and their cousin Alastair Lloyd, who was mainly concerned with the Australian trade and took a leading role in the development of ACT and ACT Services.

Negotiations between the Trio lines about how many ships should be built eventually resulted in agreement on a combined fleet of seventeen: OCL five (one more than their initial order), BLC three, Hapag Lloyd (formed in 1970 by a merger between Hamburg Amerika of Hamburg and Norddeutscher Lloyd of Bremen) four, NYK three and Mitsui OSK two. Because each containership was to have such a large capacity for cargo it was difficult to equate the number of ships exactly with individual lines' shares based on past performance. BLC could not justify more than 2½ ships but we argued that we were not prepared to sacrifice half a ship's capacity and be limited to only two ships. The Trio fleet was increased to twenty by subsequent agreements that NYK, Mitsui OSK and Hapag Lloyd should each add an additional ship in 1976, 1977 and 1981 respectively.

The Trio Lines also reached agreement on the key elements of the ships' specification so that they would be able to operate in a joint service. They should have a minimum capacity of about 1,800 TEU, (though this was increased in the light of experience) and the ship with the smallest capacity was 1,950 TEU,[11] a speed of not less than 26 knots, a beam not exceeding 106 feet (the maximum for passage

11 NYK's *Hakone Maru*, which inaugurated the Trio service.

through the Panama Canal) and they should rely on shore-based gantry cranes. These criteria meant that they would be over 900 feet long with a maximum draft in excess of 40 feet and would need specially designed and equipped terminals. The next problem facing BLC was where the ships should be built. We had not built outside UK since the days of the sailing ships built in Canada. Ellerman also had a long tradition of building in British yards, so William Thomson IV and Henry Paton, entrusted with ascertaining the available options, went first to them, but none was prepared to quote for such a large sophisticated vessel within our required time scale. We soon learned however that Howaldtswerke Deutsche Werft (HDW) in Hamburg, where Ben already had very satisfactory dry docking and repairing connections, would be glad to do business with us and were to build all the OCL ships designed for the Far East trade.

Holt's (or rather Ocean Fleets) had a large staff of ship designers headed by Mr Marshall Meek, and from the outset OCL had entrusted design, placing of orders and supervision of building of all OCL ships to them. Some costly mistakes had been made in the six OCL Encounter Bay class ships designed for the Australian trade, which were only 1,300 TEU and 21½ knots. These suffered from severe vibration, and there were also problems with gearing, turbines and boilers.[12] BLC were very fortunate in being able to learn from these mistakes, and in being allowed by Ocean Fleets to make use of their hull design for the Far East ships which were so much larger and faster.

BLC were fortunate in another way. We could not build in any British yard, but we could and did insist that the main engines and much of the ancillary machinery and equipment should be manufactured in UK. Each of the three containerships *Benalder* VI (1972), *Benavon* IV (1973) and *City of Edinburgh* (1973) (so named as a concession to our Ellerman partners) were powered by four turbines developing 88,000 shp driving twin screws to give them a speed of 26½ knots. Two sets of turbines were built by GEC Turbine Generators Ltd, Manchester and those for *Benavon* by English Electric-AEI, Manchester, by then part of GEC. Our national loyalty was rewarded because although we had a fixed price contract in marks with HDW they passed on to us the savings on these sterling

12 M. Falkus, *op. cit.*, p.366.

purchases caused by the catastrophic decline in the value of sterling against the mark which occurred soon after the orders were placed for the first two in 1969. Further savings were made by eliminating many of the 'belt and braces' features traditionally incorporated in ships built to Holt's class, which was superior to Lloyds requirements. Henry Paton on the engineering side and Captain Alex Paterson, assisted by Captain Ian Liston, on the deck side refined the specifications. The HDW yards in Kiel, which built *Benalder* and *Benavon*, and in Hamburg which built *City of Edinburgh* produced, on schedule, three very fine, reliable ships. Two former Ben Line captains, J. W. Mitchell and R. L. Chalmers, were stationed in Kiel and Hamburg respectively to ensure that the structures conformed with the steel plans and were properly constructed in accordance with the specification. The very good condition of these ships' hulls after twenty years of intensive service bears witness to the soundness of the basic design, the workmanship of the shipyard, and the labour of these two able and dedicated supervisors. Both had voluntarily decided that they were unable to take the continued strain of command at sea, but had been gladly retained as chief officers in the company's service.

Designing and building the ships was only one aspect. Deciding on the best mix of 20-foot and 40-foot containers, where they should be built and of what material was of vital importance. The box in its BLC livery would be carried exclusively in other Trio ships until the BLC ships had been delivered. Our initial orders were for over 7,000 boxes in a range of styles, in both 20-foot and 40-foot sizes, some made of aluminium and some of steel. BLC favoured galvanised steel for 20-footers and aluminium for 40-footers as being probably the most cost-effective. In those early days the durability and lifespan of the various types of box were largely a matter for speculation.

To make sure that we had containers in the right spot when the Trio service began these orders were shared between Japan, Hong Kong and UK. As the scope of the service expanded the number of BLC containers was increased to about 11,000 TEU and this 'fleet' was further augmented by hired boxes to cope with fluctuations in trade. Controlling the movements of such large numbers, ensuring that so far as possible they did not sit about empty, and were not purloined to serve as storage – even housing – was a mixture of science and art undertaken by a small International Container Control Unit in Edinburgh, whose proud boast was 'We've never lost a box'. Of course some got damaged and had to be repaired or condemned.

For inland transport in UK we were able to rely on the resources and experience of ACT Services, together with British Rail which introduced special 'Freightliner' trains connecting the inland containerbases set up at Glasgow (Coatbridge), Leeds (Stourton), Manchester (Urmiston), Liverpool (Aintree), Birmingham (Perry Bar), London (Barking) and Bristol (Weft) with the terminal at Southampton. UK was however only part of the problem; systems had to be set up on the Continent and in the Far East. We knew very little about the mechanics and economics of land transport and therefore recruited an expert in this field, Jonathan Tolson, who was later to become a director of the Ben Line in 1982. His appointment, initially to set up inland transport systems in the Far East, was an exception to our policy of teaching old dogs new tricks and preserving as far as possible our existing trained and trusted resources of staff both ashore and afloat. By contrast OCL hired in many experts and, it seemed to us, employed four or five people to do what we expected from one or two.

Six Technical Compatibility Committees (TCs), staffed by representatives of each of the Trio Lines, planned the coordination of various aspects of the service. The main task of TC6 was to negotiate the financial and operating agreements between the lines. Day-to-day operations were the responsibility of the Trio Tonnage Committee, likewise staffed by British, German and Japanese representatives. These essays in practical international cooperation worked much better than might have been expected, particularly since the committee members had generally been brought up to keep their own counsel and never to 'fraternise with the enemy'.

When the ships were ordered there were no terminals in our trading area that could handle them. BLC tried to keep its investment in terminals to a minimum, but there was a difference of approach between port authorities who were prepared to make the investment and lease the facilities to users, and those who looked to the users to design and construct their own terminals. In UK the Port of London Authority built a container terminal at Tilbury for the Australian trade, which the dock labour refused to operate from 1969 to 1972. During all that time cargo had to be transshipped via Rotterdam and Hamburg at enormous expense. For the Far East trade Trio decided to develop a terminal in collaboration with British Transport Docks Board at Southampton which would serve the whole of UK. Ben argued that putting all the eggs in one basket invited trouble from the dock labour and was strategically unsound. We tried to promote the idea of having at least one alternative, and advocated Greenock where the ships could berth at any state of the tide – as they could at Southampton. However Greenock was deemed to be too remote from the main sources and destinations of cargo and to be served by inadequate road and rail links. So we were overruled, and felt compelled to safeguard our position by taking a 35% interest in Solent Container Services at Southampton. A somewhat similar situation arose in Hong Kong were government was prepared to sell suitable land and leave its development to private enterprise. For this purpose Modern Terminals Ltd (MTL) was set up in which BLC took a 15% share. The other shareholders were OCL, Hapag and five leading local businesses.

I visited the Hong Kong terminal at Kwai Chung on the outskirts of Kowloon shortly before it was due to open in September 1972, expecting to see a feverishly active army of workers racing against time. But it was a holiday, the construction was on schedule and there was no need to work that day. On the vast empty expanse of the apron a solitary Chinese was pottering about with a small barrow and spade. This terminal opened on time and from the beginning its performance was outstandingly good, due in no small measure to the energy and efficiency of MTL's managing director Derek Lygo. MTL had enough land to build a second berth and this was subsequently constructed, primarily for use by third parties. The seaward approach to Kwai Chung was however made more difficult for a considerable period by an unexpected navigational hazard in the shape of the partially submerged wreck of the former *Queen Elizabeth*. This famous ship approximately the same size as our containerships, had been purchased by C. Y. Tung, chairman of Orient Overseas Line of Taiwan, to be converted into 'Seawise University' a floating educational institution. During the opulent conversion – 'CY' assured me that there would be real gold leaf on some of the ceilings – the ship caught fire and became a total loss.

The terminals at Tokyo, Kobe, Hamburg, Bremerhaven, Rotterdam and Southampton were all operating from the beginning of the Trio service, and these were the ports served direct until Singapore opened in August 1972 and Hong Kong a month later. The direct service was further extended to Kaohsiung in January 1973 and Port Kelang in August that year. Le Havre was added in April 1976, Busan in November 1978 and Jeddah in April 1979.

The Jeddah trade was unique in being one way, consisting of imports only. When Trio started to call eastbound in 1979 we made an arrangement with our ACT colleagues, Cunard, that they should market the BLC share in return for a fee on each container filled. Cunard Arabian Middle East Line (CAMEL) operated a service from Europe to Jeddah, Akaba and Hodeidah with chartered ships and in November 1980 we bought a 15% share in CAMEL but in the following year rates were driven down to uneconomic levels and we ended our association with CAMEL in 1983.

Of our main trades this left only the Philippines, Thailand and Indonesia. The Indonesian Government was opposed to that trade being containerised because they had four national lines equipped with conventional ships. In Thailand there was insufficient water depth and room for manoeuvre in the Bangkok river to enable the Trio ships to call, but BLC started a feeder service in March 1977 from Bangkok, feeding boxes to and from Singapore with chartered ships; that trade was fully containerised by the following January.

In the Philippines there was a demand, though limited in volume, for imports and exports to move in containers, and in any case the authorities showed a marked reluctance to provide port facilities which would have enabled the big containerships to call. We met this situation for a time by buying a small second-hand containership[13] in 1976 which fed containers between Manila and Hong Kong until 1978, when the transshipment port was switched to Kaohsiung which reduced the steaming distance by nearly a hundred miles. However this ship gave us a lot of mechanical trouble, so we sold her in 1980 and thereafter relied on chartered feeder ships.

Further experience of operating small containerships was gained

13 *Benrinnes* V, ex-*Neptune Fisher*, 193 TEU, built 1970.

when Sea Containers International Corporation gave us the management of their new *Jeddah Crown* in 1976, running between Europe and the Red Sea. We managed and crewed her until 1979 in which year E. G. Thomson (Shipping) Ltd took delivery of *Benvalla* II (420 TEU). The building of this very successful ship, the first bearing a Ben name to be built in Japan, was inspired by William Thomson IV chairman of E. G. Thomson (Shipping) Limited. *Benvalla* was employed in the Ben Asia Container Service (BACS) in a consortium of Japanese and British owners serving Japan, Taiwan, Singapore and West Malaysia in both directions. BACS had been inaugurated in the middle of 1974 but had hitherto used small chartered vessels.

There was considerable variation in efficiency between one terminal and another, often, though not invariably, reflecting the national, political and trade union mood of the territories in which they were located. The Japanese terminals at Tokyo and Kobe, and the Taiwan terminal at Kaohsiung began, surprisingly, by being much less efficient than expected. Hong Kong was outstandingly good, Singapore also worked very well. Nobody was much surprised that Port Kelang opened behind schedule and took a long time to get into its stride. Rotterdam, Hamburg and Bremerhaven were reliable and good. Bremerhaven is only about sixty miles from Hamburg, but German politics dictated that both should be included. At Southampton the terminal itself was excellently designed and equipped. It opened on schedule and began to perform well, but gradually deteriorated. The British workers were determinedly bloody-minded and disruptive. In 1978 and 1979 there were numerous expensive stoppages. Starting in February 1981 and continuing for some twelve months a series of labour disputes necessitated feeding boxes to and from Continental ports at vast expense. When the port was not closed altogether its performance fell far short of that for which Trio had contracted. Meanwhile Felixstowe, the terminal used by the Ace consortium (about which more below), demonstrated what could be achieved by private enterprise with good labour relations.

In UK we had to contend with many other disruptions during the seventies, mainly caused by trade unions abusing their power, though they, at least, could not be blamed for the precipitate move of head office to Leith a few weeks before the inauguration of the

Trio service, which is described elsewhere. The ASTMS union recruited a number of members among the staff of ACT Services, which moved from Ellerman's London Office to their own new building at Southampton in the latter part of 1973, and for some time efficiency was jeopardised by partial strikes and working to rule. We had foreseen the possibility of power strikes and had equipped the Leith office with its own generators so that we could be assured of sufficient electricity to run telex and computer machinery, and be provided with some heat and light. During the power strikes it became impossible to buy candles in UK and we imported stocks from Germany. Inland road transport was disrupted by a strike of drivers. To overcome postal strikes we set up our own courier services. These were particularly important to get BLC shipping documents to the Far East ahead of the ship carrying the cargo to which they related. On one occasion Killick Martin's Southampton office decided to send a Chinese courier to Heathrow where he was to hand over a parcel of documents to another courier. The latter waited anxiously as the time approached for his aircraft to depart until at last he saw a Chinese carrying a likely bag. That must be him! He rushed up and seized the bag but the indignant Chinese refused to part with it. The altercation prompted the airport police to arrest them, and by the time the misunderstanding had been explained both intending passengers had missed their connections. I told Killick Martin that next time they employed a Chinese courier the should dress him in a kilt.

We began 1974 with the three-day week in UK from which we, as an essential service industry, were exempted and there was a reduction in the availability of bunker fuel accompanied by a four-fold increase in price. To save fuel the speed of the Trio ships was reduced to 21 knots.

V

We could have done without these difficulties over which we had little or no control. We did have some control in overcoming the complexities of introducing the 'through cargo concept' implicit in the container operation. As Roderick MacLeod put it:

Instead of playing draughts we had to manipulate a Rubik's cube. One dimension was the BLC operation. Another was ACT where we worked closely with our erstwhile British competitors to set up a joint service operation which would help all of us develop our own container operations. The third dimension was the development of the Trio operation. I led the Trio committee which devised and negotiated the Trio Pooling and Operating Agreements – there were three of them in succession. By the end of that time most of us, even including the Committee Chairman, knew what pooling was about. The vital fourth dimension consisted of changing and reconciling the human attitudes and widely differing angles of approach of all those concerned. We had to train ourselves (and the shippers) in the new skills. And we had to do all this without jeopardising the operation of the conventional vessels for as long as they could trade successfully. This put a great load on all our Offices and Agents.[14]

There was yet another dimension – dealing with external and internal competition, about which more is said later in this chapter.

Our decision to market the BLC service in the Ben Line image was fully vindicated, and much of the credit must go to J. F. (Hamish) Muirhead, who had joined the Ben Line in his teens shortly after the Second World War and had spent his entire business career in the company. In 1971 he was brought back from managing the Hong Kong Office to join the board with the specific task of coordinating the marketing of both the container and conventional services. BLC consistently outperformed its Trio colleagues, in terms of its allotted percentage of the Trio share, and the Trio fleet could offer a more frequent, reliable service than anyone else. During the second half of 1973 Trio ships were running virtually full in both directions, much earlier than had been originally anticipated.

The Trio Lines' pooling system involved a settlement at quarterly intervals when the overcarriers paid the undercarriers. BLC reckoned it could afford to overcarry (thereby building up performance to justify some future increase in its share), since interest on its earnings would go a long way towards paying the compensation due to undercarriers. But it turned out to be not as simple as that. Earnings were in many different currencies which were fluctuating against sterling and each other. Sterling became spectacularly and progressively weaker against the German mark and Japanese yen. Manipulating the pooling system (always strictly within the rules) could involve placing more, or less, marketing effort on eastbound or

14 *Ben Bulletin*, no. 25, December 1982, pp.4,5.

westbound cargo, concentrating on one country of origin rather than another, even on one commodity rather than another. It was a measure of Hamish Muirhead's success that our offices and agents, working on commission, loyally accepted these changes of direction. They did, of course, earn commission on every ton booked, and did not have to contribute to the compensation paid to undercarriers.

During 1976 Trio was still running full westbound and about 70 per cent full eastbound, despite intense competition both external and internal. The main external competition came from the Trans-Siberian Railway which was able to attract cargo from Japan, South Korea, Hong Kong and Taiwan and in the reverse direction from Central Europe to those destinations. The strongest seaborne competition came from the Taiwanese line Evergreen which, starting from scratch, demonstrated that it was possible to operate a successful container service independent of anyone else.

Internal competition came from the ScanDutch partnership established in April 1972, who operated eight large, fast containerships, including one owned by Messageries Maritimes built by Howaldtswerke Deutsche Werft to the exact BLC specification.[15] A third multi-national consortium, Ace, established in 1975 was operating eleven containerships by 1980.

These were owned by the Belgian Far Eastern Line, the French Chargeurs Réunis, Kawasaki Kisen Kaisha ('K' Line), which had entered the Conference through a joint venture with the Danish Maersk Line, Singapore's national line Neptune Orient, Korea Shipping Corporation, Cho Yang Shipping Co. of Korea and the Taiwan-based Orient Overseas Container Line.

These alignments made necessary an Intergroup Agreement between Trio, ScanDutch and Ace about the respective shares of the trade which each should aim to carry. Equally important was the need to stop various forms of rate-cutting and malpractice to which some lines resorted in contravention of their Conference agreements. After protracted negotiations an Intergroup Agreement was reached in March 1978 but BLC were rightly sceptical about how far it would be honoured. This agreement expired in March 1980 and it

15 BLC allowed Howaldtswerke Deutsche Werft to use the specification free of charge for this ship, *Korrigan*.

was not until October 1981 that a further agreement was put together.

VI

By 1979 the price of bunker fuel had increased tenfold from what it had been ten years earlier. The effect was offset by a 20% reduction in the service speed of Trio vessels, but the likelihood of yet further price increases compelled us to examine the possibility of replacing the containerships' turbines with low consumption diesels. If each of the three ships were fitted with two 7-cylinder M.A.N. diesels, together developing 51,380 bhp they would be capable of a service speed of 23 knots on a consumption of about 140 tons per day. The turbines needed about 220 tons for the same speed at the same draft. A quotation from Kawasaki Heavy Industries Ltd of Kobe, was substantially better than any from Europe. We received two British quotations, but neither was remotely competitive. The work began in October 1980 on *City of Edinburgh* followed immediately by *Benalder* and then *Benavon*, which came back into service in January 1982 on schedule, as the others had done. During the five months which each ship spent in the shipyard, work was carried out to enlarge their carrying capacity by 8% from 2,804 to 3,028 TEU. This was achieved by increasing the deck load from eleven to thirteen containers across the breadth of the ship. The extra containers were supported on stools built between the hatch coamings and the ships' bulwarks. Stability was maintained by ballasting double bottom tanks and wing tanks, previously needed for oil to feed the hungry turbines.

Concurrently other turbine vessels in the Trio fleet were being converted, so we and our Trio colleagues chartered in a series of ships to maintain the service.

This whole operation was a quite remarkable feat of planning, coordination and cooperation, not only on the part of the shipyard, but of those responsible for scheduling the ships' arrival in Kobe, maintaining the Trio service, and re-integrating the converted ships into the service when the work had been completed.

As Roderick MacLeod reflected on the eve of his departure at the end of 1982 to become chairman of Lloyd's Register (where he was subsequently knighted):

[194]

It is not a matter of luck that Ben is one of the very few companies to step into the magic box and emerge clearly recognisable as the shipping company that went in. It went into containerisation with the industry being turned upside down and inside out and Ben not only survived it as an independent company but made a significant contribution to the general development. The success of Ben comes from a committed, enthusiastic independence, the product of history, leadership and style. It wasn't a restful experience but it was never dull and I was lucky to be in the thick of it.[16]

16 *Ben Bulletin*, no. 25, December 1982, p.5.

14
Death of the Conventional Cargo Liner

Of the thirty-three conventional cargo liners in the fleet during 1969 and 1970, twenty-seven were owned by the Ben Line Steamers Ltd and its subsidiaries.[1] The remaining six were chartered to the company, three being owned by E. G. Thomson (Shipping) Ltd, two by Sir Douglas Thomson and Partners, one by Sir Douglas Thomson and Others.

When the Trio container service got into its stride in 1972 we decided to sell five conventional ships to help pay for the investments in containerisation. With some reluctance we chose those ships which would command the highest prices: all five were motor ships capable of 20 knots or better. *Benvalla* I, built in 1962, was the oldest and the newest, *Benalbanach* III, was less than five years old. Two were bought by the People's Republic of China and three went to an Italian owner. The loss of these splendid ships was partially offset by the acquisition, relatively cheaply, of five second-hand cargo liners.[2]

By the end of 1973 the total conventional fleet had been more than halved to sixteen, though our carrying capacity had been increased by the delivery of BLC's three containerships. This left us with a surplus of senior officers, which we solved partly by offering early retirement to some masters who were nearing retirement age and partly by seconding officers to other companies for training in bulk carriers and tankers, with the intention of reabsorbing them in due course either in our own ships or those we hoped to manage for

1 The subsidiaries were Avon and Chine, companies bought up to utilise their accumulated tax losses.

2 Between 1970 and 1974 we exchanged two former Ellerman ships *Benedin* and *Benratha* for the larger, faster turbine-engined *Benvannoch* VI, ex-*City of Winchester*, and *Bencairn*, ex-*City of Brisbane*; we bought *Benledi* VII, ex-*Pando Cape*, *Benalbanach* IV, ex-*Pando Gulf*, *Benwyvis* V, ex-*Pando Point*.

other owners. Concurrently there was an industry-wide shortage of junior navigating officers which became so acute during 1973 that we were temporarily inhibited from seeking ships to manage.

The need for conventional ships in the Far East trade continued to shrink. In 1974 we were surprised to receive an approach from Ocean Transport & Trading Co. Ltd (as Holt's now styled themselves) who proposed that the conventional fleets of Blue Funnel, their subsidiaries Glen and NSM Oceaan, and Ben Line should run a joint service in the Far East trade. Negotiations, in which Sir David Thomson played a leading part for the Ben Line, resulted in agreement that the new joint service would start in early 1975 running seven sailings per month with between twenty-five and thirty ships which would continue to be crewed, stored and repaired by their respective owners, but the day-to-day operation of the fleet would be undertaken by the Ben Line in Edinburgh and would be known as the Ben Ocean service. In the *Chairman's Review* for 1974 I commented: 'There is a long history of friendly rivalry between the four fleets. We believe it will be possible to work harmoniously to our mutual benefit' – and that happened – but I added, 'This should ensure that the conventional service will continue profitably for a long time to come.' How wrong I was! When the service began in February 1975 we ran six sailings per month instead of seven and by the end of that year there was sufficient cargo for only four per month. The cream of the cargo was now being carried by the containerships, which were still using the Panama Canal or Cape of Good Hope routes. In July 1975 the Suez Canal was reopened for conventional ships and this increased a world surplus of shipping space.

During 1975 nine Ben Line ships were employed in the Ben Ocean service and the remaining six were chartered out, but in June there was a massive increase in wages and salaries to all seafarers which placed additional strain on our international competitiveness, particularly as regards conventional cargo liners, where crews' pay made up rather more than half the daily operating costs.

Crews of the ships which were chartered out had to accustom themselves to circumstances very different from those they were used to on the Far East run. Most masters enjoyed the extra degree of self-reliance needed to deal with strange agents at ports which they had never before visited and to care for cargo which was different from that carried in the Far East trade.

The enormous increase in the price of oil fuel was common to all shipowners, but bore more heavily on turbine ships than on motor vessels. By 1978 it had become impossible to charter out any conventional ship powered by turbines. The last such ship, *Bencruachan* III, built in 1968, continued in the Ben Ocean service until May 1980 when she was sold for breaking up. She was only twelve years old.

In July 1976 Ben Ocean inaugurated a monthly service from the Far East to the Red Sea. In order to circumvent severe congestion then affecting breakbulk cargo operations at most Red Sea ports, the ships discharged at the new port of Sharjah. Here general cargo was transferred to containers and oncarried by lo-lo (lift on-lift off) vessels operated by a company named Medtainers Ltd. In the following year the Sharjah experiment was abandoned and the Ben Ocean service called at Jeddah and Akaba direct, carrying as many loaded containers as could be accommodated and some breakbulk cargo. A major impediment to the profitability of these stratagems was the long empty voyage back to the Far East in ballast since there was no cargo moving out of the Red Sea ports. So, in 1979 it was decided to include direct calls at Jeddah and Akaba in the Ben Ocean vessels which served UK and Continental ports. It was a losing battle; more and more cargo was being carried in containers. London, which during the fifties and sixties had been Ben's most important port of call, measured by frequency of service and volume of cargo, ceased to be served on a regular basis in 1979. The Ben Ocean service between the Far East and Europe was reduced to one ship per month using four Ben ships and one Ocean, while the service calling at Red Sea ports used two Ocean vessels. Serving the Red Sea with conventional cargo liners was finally abandoned, but in 1980 a 'slot-hire' agreement was reached with NYK and Mitsui OSK whereby Ben Ocean made their own bookings for their own containerships which were then carried in the Japanese containerships. Attempts to make common cause with traditional rivals took place in the Indonesian trade. A joint service with the Dutch and Scandinavia lines in 1980 was replaced early in 1982 by a Hapag/Ben Ocean service, but this was abandoned seven months later.

In 1978, 1979 and 1980 there were further big increases in seafarers' wages and salaries. This did not deter the National Union of Seamen (NUS) and the Merchant Navy and Airline Officers Association (MINAOA) from seeking a massive increase in 1981. We told our seafarers that a settlement greater than that which the shipowners were prepared to offer would be likely to lead to earlier disposal of the remaining three conventional ships as well as making us less internationally competitive in the bulk carrier market and in managing ships for other owners. The 1981 settlement was reached only after an expensive NUS strike. Two conventional ships[3] were sold since we had no liner berth employment for them and could not have chartered them out at a loss of less than £1,000 per ship per day. The last conventional ship, *Benstac*, built in 1968 was on a long-term charter and when that expired she was sold to Greek owners in September 1982.

Disposal of the conventional ships at last confronted us with a situation already experienced by other British shipping companies, which we had so far largely avoided by creating new job opportunities and teaching old dogs new tricks. During 1981 we had to terminate the employment of 50 officers and 74 Chinese ratings. The officers were all seen individually by me and William Thomson IV, sometimes together, sometimes alone. Neither of us enjoyed the experience. The many spontaneous expressions of affection for and gratitude to the company were perhaps more emotionally demanding than the bitterness which might have been expected, but was entirely absent.

3 *Bendearg, Benarty* VI.

15

Diversification

In November 1970 the Ben Line fleet consisted of thirty-three conventional cargo liners. By November 1980 these had been reduced to three and the whole fleet of twenty-five units consisted of:

3 conventional cargo liners
3 containerships, each 2,750 TEU, of which 20% owned by
    Ellerman
1 containership 456 TEU
6 bulk carriers
1 moored drillship
2 semi-submersible drilling rigs
1 dynamically positioned drillship ⎫
1 drillship   ⎬ owned by Odeco
1 jack-up drilling rig   ⎭
3 chemical tankers, one owned 50% by Scotspark, a Charles
    Connell company
3 managed oil tankers.

In seeking for ways to diversify William Thomson said:

We set ourselves four principal guidelines. We were looking for activities which could be profitable, [secondly] related to what we were already doing so that we could, with retraining, make use of our existing manpower and expertise. [Thirdly] being in a cyclical business we had a preference for new business which would not necessarily follow the same cycles as liner shipping. And last but not least we were looking for high technology opportunities allied to heavy capital investment which would to some extent insulate us from competition from low cost operators.[1]

During the fifties and sixties we had been very conscious of our major dependence on the liner trade between Europe and the Far

1 W.R.E. Thomson, 'International Freighting Management', October 1982, reprinted in *Ben Bulletin*, no. 25, December 1982.

East. We chartered out occasionally, for example, to the British Government to carry stores and equipment to Christmas Island for the nuclear test in 1955, and there was a regular annual charter from New Zealand and Australia to carry wool and concentrates to UK. We also examined and discarded the possibility of investment in oil tankers, and of reviving our interest in the trade between the Pacific West Coast and Europe, useful to us in the inter-war years.

Sir Douglas was enthusiastic about air travel and air transport which he saw as a possible diversification. He formed, with Killick Martin, Atlantis Air Co. Ltd which in 1953 acquired a new De Havilland twin-engined Dove, whose first cost, including the most up-to-date navigational instruments, was about £24,000. The Dove, G-ANPH, was based at Croydon and managed by Morton Air Services which specialised in chartering out a fleet of De Havilland Doves and the larger four-engined Herons. When G-ANPH was not needed for Ben Line work she could be chartered out and the hire was credited against her operating costs. On one occasion she was chartered by Sir Winston Churchill, who used her to take Field-Marshal Lord Montgomery to Newmarket for his first ever race meeting. Our choice pilot, Captain Argles, remarked to me afterwards that he was jolly glad when he had landed those passengers safely. I replied that I hoped he was just as glad when he landed me! In fact I spent many happy hours in the Dove with few anxious moments. She was heated but not pressurised so one became rather breathless at heights between 5,000 and 10,000 feet, which meant flying through or round bad weather rather than over the top of it. I remember being slightly unnerved on a flight from Edinburgh to Hull through strong winds and heavy rainclouds when the pilot (on that occasion not Captain Argles) shouted from the cockpit 'This is totally unacceptable.' One was comforted by the knowledge that as a last resort the Dove could land in a field. On one occasion, carrying Sir Douglas and Percy Rogers from Edinburgh to London, she made an unscheduled stop at Newcastle, but that was to obtain a bottle opener, an essential implement which had been omitted when storing for the journey. Her maximum speed was 180 mph, slightly more with a following wind, considerably less against a head wind. The most frequent journeys were between Edinburgh and London (Croydon) where the length of tarmac runway was insufficient for even the Dove to take off without roaring at full throttle on to the grass outfield. When Croydon was eventually closed as an airport we used Bovingdon, Gatwick and occasionally Blackbush.

The Dove was particularly useful during the freight war against Mitsui (1953-56). As a member of the Conference Fighting Committee I flew from Edinburgh to London, Hamburg, Rotterdam, Antwerp, Paris and back to Edinburgh each on a succeeding day and was able to do a full day's work at each stop. This would have been impossible using scheduled air services as they were then.

G-ANPH was also useful in emergencies. *Benmacdhui* III, fully loaded outward bound, had to put into Lisbon with a distorted turbine rotor. The initial estimate by Lloyd's surveyor was that she would be delayed for several weeks and that there was no possibility of repairing the rotor locally. It was a bank holiday weekend and airlines were heavily booked, but the Dove was available. I abandoned my wife and family in a remote part of East Lothian, where we had just begun a much-needed summer holiday, and flew to Lisbon accompanied by Cecil Hutton.

With us on the flight to Lisbon came a senior engineer from David Rowan, who had built the engine, and an expert from Pametrada, who had designed the turbine. This formidable team in their various capacities exhorted and persuaded the bureaucrats, the ship repairers and the surveyors. Chief credit must go to the Pametrada expert who, when the rotor had been extracted and set up in the repair shop, working partly by instinct, partly by measurement to 1,000th of an inch, stroked the distorted metal with his heat torch for hours on end until it was restored to its true alignment. *Benmacdhui* resumed her voyage within a few days. On our return flight we stopped at Biarritz to refuel and have a celebratory lunch before flying home over the still visible remains of the Mulberry Harbour off Arromanches where *Bendoran* II had been deliberately sunk in 1944.

The Dove's slow speed was partly compensated for by her short take-off and landing ability. I remember arriving over Frankfurt one morning where already some fifty aircraft were stacked because of fog. As the Dove needed a visibility ceiling of only 200 feet she was brought through the stack and landed on schedule, long before her larger and faster competitors.

A partner could charter G-ANPH for £40 per hour, which was quite good value as she seated six passengers comfortably. If the plane was being used on business anyway many friends and relations benefited from free rides. In 1963 I chartered her to take my wife and four children from Edinburgh to Corfu. We refuelled in London, Lyons, Ajaccio (where we spent the night) and Brindisi. Captain Argles and Mr Pitt, our choice navigator, flew her back empty, but on our return from Corfu picked us up in Paris and flew us to Edinburgh.

On another occasion my wife and I had been holidaying in Spain. We were joined in Barcelona by Sir Douglas's sister-in-law and her husband and the Dove flew us to Nice to pick up Percy Rogers and his wife, who were likewise returning from holiday. True to form, Percy gave us a lavish dinner and insisted that we should all go to the casino afterwards. I have never enjoyed gambling, but my wife was keen to try it. After half an hour's play she was persuaded to stop, having won enough to pay for our holiday.

Percy Rogers persuaded us to place an order for the Dove's jet-engined successor, then known as the DH125, which cost double and rose year by year to £250,000. We eventually decided to cancel the order as Morton's said they could not give it priority for charters over their fleet of Doves and Herons, and it would have been difficult to justify such a large expenditure simply to save wear and tear on the executives who would have travelled in it. In any case scheduled air services had greatly improved by the mid sixties when we finally sold G-ANPH, which remained in service for several more years. Stripped of her passenger seating, we occasionally spotted her at Turnhouse, Edinburgh's airport, to which she carried cargoes of lobsters from the Western Isles. Atlantis Air remained dormant and was eventually wound up. It did not generate profits for the Ben Line, but it turned out to be our least unsuccessful venture into air transport. It did engender a certain amount of admiration and envy from our shipowning competitors who at that time, in common with many large public companies, had not equipped themselves with a private aeroplane.

Meantime Sir Douglas had become interested in Lloyd International Airways, which owned two second-hand Britannia aircraft struggling to make a living with cargo flights between Hong Kong and Europe. Besides Wheelock Marden the other major shareholder was Jaime Ortiz-Patino, chairman of what became Lloyd Airways Group, a Bolivian living in Switzerland (when he was not flying around the world), whose family had made a fortune from his native country's tin mines. The Ben Line took a 15% share at an initial cost of about £20,000 and vigorously set about offering our customers air freight as an alternative to sea freight, using our existing organisation of canvassers.

We were well acquainted with the regulatory practices of shipping conferences but soon discovered that the protectionist and obstructive policies pertaining to air transport were far more rigid. Lloyd International Airways had the advantage of being a registered Hong Kong company, but the restrictions on loading and discharging rights in other territories particularly UK, were formidable. The forerunner of British Airways, BOAC, was extremely obstructive and could rely on the support of the UK Civil Aviation Authority. Nevertheless good westbound cargoes of high-value goods were obtained and in 1969 the fleet was increased to four aircraft with two more second-hand Britannias.

By this time Sir Douglas had ceased to be able to contribute much to the direction of Lloyd's affairs and I was left as the senior Ben Line representative on its board. It was necessary to accommodate ourselves to a style of management to which we were unaccustomed. The managers were more addicted to flying than to thinking. They thought they were achieving something by flying off at a moment's notice to try to exploit some new opportunity, leaving themselves too little time when they arrived at their destination, sometimes arriving late for appointments and having to leave early. The Ben Line's shareholding was insufficient to offer decisive opposition to sudden changes in policy, and we resisted invitations to increase our capital investment because we realised that there was little prospect of obtaining less restrictive trading rights so long as British Government policy remained unchanged.

Lloyd Airways Group acquired two second-hand Boeing 707s on hire purchase terms in 1970, primarily to undertake transatlantic passenger flights on charter. The four Britannias continued cargo flights from the Far East and our staff, particularly in Hong Kong, Kuala Lumpur and Singapore, worked hard on their behalf, but the group became increasingly involved with passenger traffic to and from USA. Here they ran up against the discriminatory licensing system operated by the British and US Governments. In June 1972 the group decided that it could not continue trading, and receivers were called in to wind it up. This was particularly disappointing for the Ben Line since the cargo services, on which we had expended great efforts, were then doing well.

We were reluctant to abandon the experience we had gained in marketing air freight and attempted to exploit this by becoming general sales agents in Hong Kong, Singapore and Japan for Austrian Air Transport, but they decided to cease operations in the Far East at the end of 1974. We had also been appointed agents by the British company, Court Line, which was running pilgrimage flights to Mecca from South East Asia. But Court Line, which had diversified from shipping into air traffic, ran into financial difficulties and went out of business. In 1974 we finally decided that we would not involve ourselves in any more air ventures.

II

Our General Manager Far East, Richard Thorman, was appointed Director Far East in 1971 and in November the following year he joined the board in Edinburgh with a specific remit to investigate new projects consistent with the object of 'the continuing development of a vigorous, prosperous and independent Ben Line'. He soon identified what appeared to be an attractive opportunity which reflected the characteristics of doing difficult things well – like the Ben Line's earlier enterprise in carrying heavy, awkward cargo and explosives. The carriage of liquid chemicals, many of a toxic and hazardous nature, appeared to be a growing trade, particularly between European ports, and a recent revision of the international safety regulations created a requirement for specially designed vessels to replace those which the new regulations would make obsolescent. In 1973 we placed an order for a small chemical tanker with Nieuwe Noord Nederlandsche Scheepswerven of Groningen. *Benvenue* V was 256 feet long and had a deadweight capacity of 2,581 tons. Her Dutch 7-cylinder motor gave her a speed of 13 knots. BP Chemicals Limited undertook to charter her and the wife of the managing director accepted an invitation to be her sponsor.

The ship was built alongside a canal which led to the sea and was launched broadside on. The shipyard was very experienced – *Benvenue*'s yard number was 382 – but this particular launch did not go according to plan. The launching party were having their photograph taken with their backs to the ship when there was a horrible grinding noise followed by a tremendous splash. One of the last two wires holding her in position had parted. With great presence of mind a worker released the other wire and this minimised the damage to her keel as she somewhat inelegantly launched herself. She was brought alongside and the naming ceremony was completed in the traditional manner – with whisky.

The company and the charterers were well pleased with *Benvenue* and in 1976 we took delivery of two sister ships, *Benmacdhui* IV and *Bencleuch* VII. They were all manned by Ben Line crews, who received special training in the handling of chemical cargoes. Nobody was compelled to serve on a chemical tanker; there was no shortage of volunteers and they adapted themselves extremely well to a pattern of life very different from that to which they had become accustomed on the Far East run, though many hardened seafarers discovered a need for seasick pills until they got used to the little ships' wriggling movements in all but calm waters. The crew consisted of a master, two navigating officers, and sometimes a deck cadet, chief engineer, 2nd engineer and initially, though not latterly one other engineer officer, bosun (chief petty officer deck) and three deck ratings (SG1), one engine room petty officer (POM) a cook/steward, one JCR (junior catering rating - the new name for a galley boy), a maximum of fourteen in all. The smallness of the ship broke down the traditional barrier between officers and ratings without any loss of discipline, which had to be of the highest order when dealing with toluene, benzene, styrene monomer, acetone, methanol and many others sometimes in full cargoes, sometimes in separate parcels. Loading and discharging took place at terminals which for safety reasons were remote from port areas frequented by other shipping; there was neither time nor attraction for much shore leave. Crews were relieved at approximately six-week intervals for three weeks' leave. Most of the sea passages were in busy coastal waters, though longer voyages were made to the Baltic, Mediterranean and Black Sea.

BP Chemicals were our most consistent customer and chartered *Benvenue* continuously for a year at a time throughout the period covered by this narrative. In the eighteen months to the end of June 1976 *Benvenue* completed 220 coastal voyages.[2] *Benmacdhui* and *Bencleuch* operated partly on time charter, partly on the spot market, and did some contract work. The market for these ships was, however, generally less buoyant than we had expected and became particularly depressed in 1980 and 1981. In the latter year all three were badly affected by a National Union of Seamen's strike. *Benvenue* was off hire for four weeks; the other two were operating on the spot market, but charterers with ample choice of foreign flag vessels, preferred to avoid using our ships, which could not be guaranteed to complete their voyages.

This diversification was an undoubted technical success. Because the new international safety regulations were not enforced and obsolescent competitors remained in service, it was less financially successful than we had hoped, but not a disaster such as that which afflicted Bibby Line and Ocean (Blue Funnel)[3] with their related but much larger-scale ventures into the carriage of liquefied natural gas.

III

One of the obvious ways of exploiting our accumulated expertise in ship management, and providing employment for crews which might otherwise become redundant, was to manage ships for other owners. A separate company, Ben Line Ship Management (BLSM), was set up in 1972 in collaboration with Galbraith Wrightson (which had been formed by a merger between Galbraith Pembroke and Matthews Wrightson). In the following year Galbraith Wrightson transferred to BLSM the management of their *Vianna*, a giant OBO (oil bulk ore carrier) with a deadweight capacity of 101,450 tons and a speed of 15½ knots. She remained with BLSM until she was sold in 1976.

Meantime BLSM had acquired the management of two new

2 *Ben Bulletin*, August 1976, p.8.
3 The cost of Ocean's French-built LNG carrier *Nestor*, originally estimated at £25 million when she was ordered in 1970, had risen to nearly £63 million when she was delivered in 1977. She went into immediate lay up and remained there throughout the 1980s. Falkus, *op.cit.*, p.343.

tankers, *Grey Hunter* and *Grey Fighter*. They were nearly identical sisters of 123,894 deadweight tons and were both delivered to Bergen Shipping Partners (in which the Ben Line took a 5% interest) towards the end of 1974 by Mitsubishi Heavy Industries of Kobe. Two years later they were joined by an even larger tanker of 155,612 deadweight tons from the same yard. *Grey Warrior* was 920 feet long, with a beam of 176 feet (30 feet shorter but 70 feet broader than our big containerships). One consequence of her very broad beam was the spaciousness of her accommodation – the master's day room was the size of a large drawing-room. Her 10-cylinder Sulzer engine developed 29,000 bhp for a speed of 15¼ knots, fractionally slower than *Grey Hunter* and *Grey Fighter* which were powered by 9-cylinder Sulzer engines, all built under licence in Japan.

The Ben Line crews to man these vessels were trained on courses and by seconding them for training with other companies. Mobil were very helpful in this respect and our Glasgow neighbours, Denholm Ship Management Ltd, were cooperative, despite the fact that we were in direct competition with them for business.

We had examined the possibility of owning tankers more than once during the fifties and sixties but had concluded that the oil charter market was too volatile and uncertain. The big oil companies such as BP, Shell and Mobil owned tankers, but hedged their bets heavily by chartering on the open market. The wisdom of our decision to tie up minimal capital in ownership was borne out by our experience with these managed tankers in the seventies. *Grey Hunter* and *Grey Fighter* traded for a few months after their delivery, but in 1975 both were laid up at Molde in northern Norway. *Grey Fighter* traded again from January 1977 to July 1978 when she returned to Molde. *Grey Hunter* did not start trading again until December 1978 when she obtained a two-year time charter at a rate which showed her owners no profit, but which was less expensive than continuing to lay her up.

Grey Warrior fared little better. After her delivery in November 1976 she traded until June 1977 and was then laid up, together with many other tankers, in Brunei Bay until October 1978. New hope dawned at the end of that year and all three traded from then until 1981. In that year *Grey Warrior* was acquired by Murphy Petroleum Co. and renamed *Celtic Link*. BLSM retained the management, but the market weakened and she went to Molde where all three were laid up in 1982.

Molde Fjord, about a hundred miles south west of Trondheim, chosen by Bergen Shipping Partners as the best value for money, is reminiscent of a Scottish loch on a far grander scale. The ships lay off the south shore below peaks rising to around 4,000 feet, with a distant view of the town of Molde, some ten miles away on the opposite side of the fjord. Each ship was moored by the stern to two shore bollards, with two anchors out forward. When two ships were laid up they were moored close together so that it was possible to step across gangways from one to the other. Lloyd's Register and the Salvage Association inspected, and prescribed what tasks had to be carried out to keep a ship in class and to qualify for a reduction in the insurance premium which would have been payable if she had been at sea.

The crew numbered about seven per ship: a master, or chief officer with a master's ticket, could command two ships, backed up by a 1st or 2nd officer, a chief engineer, 2nd engineer and chief electrician. One cook and one galley sufficed for both ships and everyone did his own washing up and cabin cleaning. There was plenty of work to be done. The tanks were kept filled with inert gas from the vessel's own plant, both to avoid any explosion and to prevent corrosion of the tanks. Dehumidification plant was installed in the pump room, the engine room and on the bridge, powered by local electricity fed by a specially laid cable from the shore. Fresh water was also piped from the shore. Generators, radar and other equipment were run and checked regularly. Any spare time could be used in painting those surfaces most liable to corrosion. The owners, anxiously watching the market for the chance to make a fixture, which would at least mitigate the losses they were suffering, gave us, the managers, a variable notice of readiness within which the maintenance programme could be planned.

Some wives and families visited during the summer months; there was plenty of spare accommodation on board. There was no very close rapport with the local population, who perhaps resented this unprecedented intrusion, though the local grocer enjoyed an increase in business and at least one Norwegian girl became a crew member's bride. The authorities would not allow any duty free stores on board, and a small bottle of Norwegian beer cost £1, so we gave crew a compensating cash allowance. Small wonder that, apart from fishing either from the ship or a lifeboat, one of the most popular hobbies was brewing beer from kits imported from UK. I tasted some when I visited and found it a sorry substitute, but fresh young haddock caught by the anglers were delicious.

Some Ben Line crew took quite easily to this remote, stationary lonely life. One or two liked it so much that they asked not to be relieved; the usual practice was to relieve them every three to four months.

Only *Grey Warrior* had one period of lay-up in Brunei Bay. Here the ships were left totally unattended apart from regular visits by contract maintenance staff.

IV

If the containerships could supplant the conventional cargo liners they were clearly incapable of assuming the role of bulk carriers. In 1973 two such second-hand, British-built ships were acquired. They were both under ten years old and slightly under 30,000 tons deadweight.[4]

One of these ships, *Benvorlich* IV, was chartered to a new service inaugurated in 1973 in a 50/50 partnership with the East Asiatic Company of Copenhagen, our old allies in the trade between Europe and Thailand. The Ben/EAC Bulk service, directed on Ben's side by Sir David Thomson, began by loading one or two chartered ships a month with mainly timber and plywood from the Far East, particularly from Singapore, West Malaysia and the Philippines, to Europe and tramping back from Europe to the Far East. We found that a sharp fall in the bulk charter market made *Benvorlich* unprofitable, so we sold her in 1975 with delivery early the following year, but the Ben/EAC Bulk service was able to take advantage of low rates to charter ships for single westbound voyages and in the year to 31 March 1975 the Ben Line's share of the profits was slightly under £2 million. To make up for reduced tonnages from the Philippines and the Malay Peninsula the

4 *Benhiant* II (ex-*Wearfield*) whose name was changed to *Cramond*, a Thomson steamship name, in 1977 to avoid possible confusion if her charterers wished to trade her in the Far East, and *Benvorlich* IV (ex-*Ribera*).

service was extended to load in East Kalimantan and Sarawak. During 1977 we ran two, sometimes three, sailings monthly, though freight rates were forced down to very low levels owing to strong competition chasing the limited cargo available, and there was a loss on the year's operations. In the following year there was also a loss, exacerbated by strikes in Liverpool and Hamburg, and in early 1979 our partnership with East Asiatic was terminated by mutual consent.

During the partnership EAC had the prime responsibility for fixing the ships and, of course, they had their own merchant interests in the timber trade, while we had gained much experience in superintending the loading, and 'educating' the masters and crews of chartered-in bulk carriers, who often had little experience of how their ships could be loaded to best advantage. We felt that if we had sole responsibility for fixing and loading these bulk sailings, they could still be profitable. David Thomson was particularly enthusiastic and in 1978 had taken advantage of an upsurge in steel exports from Europe to the Far East to charter in, and also to use some of our own bulk tonnage, to carry mainly steel products but also some difficult and large pieces of general cargo which could not be accommodated in our containerships or in our remaining conventional ships. So when the Ben/EAC Bulk Service ended we set up Benbulk which operated one, sometimes two, sailings a month mainly with vessels which were chartered in. Besides carrying timber and plywood they lifted parcels of steel and ore from the Far East to Jeddah, Liverpool, North Continental and occasionally Mediterranean ports. Benbulk struggled on for some years, but if, as happened in 1982, the cost of chartering in tonnage continued to fall, the benefit was offset by fierce competition, falling freight rates and a depressed market for forest products.

A major involvement in the ownership of bulk carriers did not take place until 1976 when Ben Line Steamers acquired Sheaf Steam Shipping Co. Ltd of Newcastle. Sheaf and Ben had quite a lot in common. Though Sheaf was a public company, it was owned predominantly by the Souter family. They were our agents in Newcastle and there had been an exchange training scheme of deck officers and cadets so that ours could learn about bulk carriers and theirs could learn about general cargo. I got on well with their chairman, David Souter, whom I met regularly at meetings of the General Committee of Lloyd's Register of Shipping, on which we both served. This was a large committee representative of shipowners, shipbuilders and insurers. The meetings of this committee were not lengthy and there was always opportunity before, during or after an excellent lunch to talk shop, exchange gossip and meet interesting people who were prominent in their particular fields.

One day in the late summer of 1976 David Souter told me that Sheaf were thinking of selling up. They wanted a purchaser who would not only pay an acceptable price, but would as far as possible safeguard the livelihoods of their sea and shore staff. Might we be interested? Having examined Sheaf's structure and financial position we decided that we were. Agreeing a price at which to make an offer for Sheaf's 3.6 million shares was only one aspect of complex negotiations in which William Thomson IV and David Walker were helped by our merchant bank advisers, J. Henry Schroder Wagg, and our lawyers Norton Rose, Botterell & Roche, whose partner Douglas Hamilton was in this, as in previous and subsequent negotiations, a model of lucidity, industry and reliability. By December 1976 the deal had been finalised.

What we acquired were, firstly, four ships[5] ranging from a single tween-deck vessel of slightly under 15,000 tons deadweight to a newly ordered, gearless[6] bulk carrier of so called 'Panamax' size, (the largest which could transit the Panama Canal) with a beam of 106 feet and a deadweight capacity of 71,500 tons which was due for delivery from Sunderland Shipbuilders Limited in February 1978.

In addition the deal gave us a 51% interest in three fine, relatively new, gearless bulk carriers, all on good long-term charters, and one much smaller ore carrier nearing the end of a charter and of her useful life.[7] These four units were in a Sheaf subsidiary, Bamburgh

5 *Sheaf Field* 14,800 dwt, name unchanged, sold March 1978; *Sheaf Tyne* 51,735 dwt, name unchanged, sold March 1978; *Sheaf Royal* 38,711 dwt, renamed *Benvorlich* V August 1978, sold May 1984; *Benhope* II 71,500 dwt, delivered April 1978.
6 Without derricks or cranes, loading and discharging being carried out by shore-based appliances.
7 *Alnwick Castle*, renamed *Benwyvis* VI July 1981; *Dunstanburgh Castle*, sold June 1981; *Ros Castle*, renamed *Benledi* VIII February 1981; *Cheviot*, sold September 1977.

Shipping Co. Ltd, of which British Steel Corporation owned the other 49%. The small ore carrier was sold in 1977 and none of the others were given Ben names until after we had acquired British Steel's interest in them in 1980.

The third and last ingredient in the acquisition turned out to be the most significant for the Ben Line: 100% interest in Sheaf Drilling which, with Reardon Smith the Welsh shipowners, an Irish and a Mexican company, owned two semi-submersible drilling rigs under construction in Finland for delivery in March 1976 and March 1977. Negotiations resulted in the departure of the Irish and Mexican interests leaving Ben and Reardon Smith each owning one rig and each having a 50% interest in Atlantic Drilling, the company set up to manage these rigs.

As regards satisfying Souter's requirements to safeguard their employees, the Ben Line's interest and theirs happily coincided to a large extent. We did not have the trained manpower immediately available to crew the Sheaf and Bamburgh ships so it was arranged that their management should remain with Souter and be transferred progressively to the Ben Line one by one to correspond approximately with the forecast disposal of our older ships as they came to the end of their useful lives.

Bulk carriers operate in a complex of world markets. Those up to 20,000 tons deadweight have access to a wide range of loading and discharging ports but this range diminishes as the size of vessel increases. The market for a particular size is affected by the worldwide number of vessels available, which may be increased by speculative building, sometimes sponsored by governments wishing to boost their national shipbuilding industry. During the seventies much speculative building took place, particularly of 50,000-tonners. The market for this class became so low that we could not find profitable employment for *Sheaf Tyne* and she was sold in 1978 to Greek owners. Foreign flag owners, not subject to British rates of crew pay, could still make a profit. The numbers of ships available increased through the shortening of voyage times when the Suez Canal reopened in 1975 and when the problems of port congestion, particularly in West Africa and Jeddah, were progressively overcome. *Sheaf Field* proved to be mechanically very troublesome and she was sold in 1979. In purchasing second-hand ships we were confined to British flag vessels because it would have been prohibitively expensive to bring a foreign flag ship up to British statutory regulations. In 1981 we sold one that we had bought in 1977 and replaced her with a larger, newer vessel.[8] We could compete on equal terms with foreign flag operators as regards the cost of oil fuel and stores, and might even have an advantage over them through lower insurance premiums, but we could not control successive massive wage increases awarded to British seafarers in the seventies and early eighties. Like the dockers, British seafarers were pricing themselves out of jobs.

Crew costs were, however, much the same irrespective of the size of a ship and this was an important factor in our decision at the end of 1981 to place an order – the first order we had ever placed for a bulk carrier – for a giant of 150,661 deadweight tons, speed 14¼ kts,[9] particularly suited to participate in what appeared to be increasing worldwide coal movements. Few similar ships existed and there was less likelihood of supply exceeding demand owing to their high capital cost. British Shipbuilders Ltd, newly formed from the surviving major yards, declined to quote, and the order went to a new South Korean yard, Daewoo Shipbuilding and Heavy Machinery Ltd. At a first cost of about US$40M the price was very attractive, but it was a bold decision.

V

We could not ignore what was happening under our noses in the North Sea and Dick Thorman led investigations into various aspects of oil exploration and exploitation. In 1973 the Ben Line board decided to involve the company in this area, in collaboration with suitable partners. A new company was formed, Ben line Offshore Contractors Limited (BLOC). The Ben Line held the majority of the shares and the balance was held by North Sea Assets and Royal Bank Development Ltd, a company established by our bankers, who had been splendidly supportive when we took the plunge into containers.

The science and technology of offshore drilling had been developed

8 We sold *Bennevis* IV, ex-*Baron Dunmore*, 20,278 dwt, 16 kts; and acquired *Benalbanach* V (ex-*Eredine*), 60,907 dwt, 15¾ kts.
9 *Bencruachan* IV, delivered May 1983.

mainly in USA, so it was there that we looked for partners. In 1973 we approached Ocean Drilling and Exploration Company of New Orleans (Odeco) which had much experience, particularly in the Gulf of Mexico, and was already tackling the new problems of drilling in the harsher climate of the North Sea. We received a warm response. In the following year BLOC and Odeco formed a 50/50 company Ben Odeco Limited, to which Odeco transferred a self-propelled jack-up rig, *Ocean Tide*, built for them by Upper Clyde Shipbuilders, Clydebank in 1971, which was then working in the North Sea.

We were in business, but many of us had plenty to learn. What were the characteristics and capabilities of a jack-up rig, a semi-submersible rig, and the various types of drill ship which then existed? What were a kelly, marine riser, draw works? The men who worked the rigs had strange American titles: what were the functions of a toolpusher, a bargemaster, a roughneck and a roustabout?

On the other hand we had some things to offer. Bids to undertake exploration drilling in the North Sea might stand a better chance of being accepted if a British connection could be demonstrated. Furthermore we had qualified seafarers likely to become surplus to our requirements who were ready to adapt themselves to a new way of life. A master, or chief officer with a master's ticket, was admirably qualified to become an installation manager. Our qualified engineers, who were accustomed to cherish and maintain their machinery, were more valuable than their American counterparts, mostly unqualified, who were inclined to hit a malfunctioning part with a hammer and if it still did not work to chuck it overboard and order a new one. By 1981 some eighty Ben Line officers had been transferred to the company's oil-drilling business.

Seafarers were not the only ones to be given new responsibilities. Bryan Forman, an exceptionally gifted engineer, was posted from Hong Kong, where he was resident engineer superintendent covering the Far East area, to join Atlantic Drilling in 1977. In the following year he became operations manager for Atlantic. Jonathan Harris, who had joined the Ben Line as a graduate trainee in 1968, came back from our Tokyo office. He became commercial manager of Atlantic in 1977 and general manager in 1978. Henry Paton, chief engineer superintendent of the Ben Line since 1964,

[215]

and a director of Atlantic Drilling, joined the BLOC Board in 1982. In the same year Forman and Harris became directors of Atlantic Drilling.

Odeco were keen to acquire an interest in a very advanced dynamically positioned drill ship, built to a Dutch design. We agreed that the Ben Line's accumulated marine expertise combined with Odeco's drilling experience would make this a feasible proposition. With some difficulty, arrangements were made for Scotts of Greenock to build such a ship, under licence, capable of drilling down to 20,000 feet in water depths as great as 3,000 feet and able to stay in precise position during drilling operations without the use of anchors. Ben Odeco placed the order in 1974 for delivery in October 1976. It was decided to name her *Ben Ocean Lancer* and shortly after construction had begun she was chartered for two years from her delivery at a handsome rate to Chevron Overseas Petroleum Inc. Various difficulties and delays, partly caused by increasing the water depth at which the ship could drill from 1,000 feet to 3,000 feet in order to comply with the terms of the Chevron charter, resulted in delivery being postponed until March 1977. The charterers became impatient and attempted to cancel the charter. Fortunately the drilling contract contained no cancellation date and no penalty clause. Chevron thought they could use their considerable muscle to ignore these documentary deficiencies and see us off, but we took them to arbitration and soon after proceedings had started they climbed down. Thereafter *Ben Ocean Lancer* carried out her charter with conspicuous success, drilling off Spain, Nova Scotia, Labrador and Baltimore. She came back to Leith, her port of registry, to refit and seek employment in the North Sea, but was unsuccessful in competition with less sophisticated rigs of which there was by then an over-supply. She was expensive to man, needing a marine crew of about thirty, including a master, chief officer, three deck officers, two chief engineers, 2nd engineer, five other engineer officers and three electricians. All the marine crew came from Ben, whilst Odeco supplied the drilling crew.

In the meanwhile a much older and simpler drillship[10] had been added to the Ben Odeco fleet and in the following year, 1977, Ben (Ben Line Steamers) bought Reardon Smith's rig and their 50%

10 *Ben Ocean Typhoon.*

ABOVE *Ben box 290043 making acquaintance with a more venerable but more static Ben* BELOW *A BLC box in Bangkok.*

ABOVE Benvalla II *(1979-)* BELOW Benavon IV *(1973-) about to berth at Bremerhaven, July 1976.*

BEN LINE

BETTER SHIP BE...

	Singapore	Port Swettenham	Penang	London	Liverpool	Hamburg	Bremen	Rotterdam	Grange-mouth (Scotland)	Antwerp	Hull	Haw
CITY OF ADELAIDE	29 Feb/3 Mar	4/7 Mar	—	—	4 Apr	28 Apr	23 Apr	17 Apr	----	----	—	
BENHOPE	4/6 Mar	7/10 Mar	11/12 Mar	—	—	---	15 Apr	—	20 Apr	3 May	27 Apr	
BENREOCH (R)	6/8 Mar	----	—	11 Apr	—	8 Apr	---	---	----	----	—	
BENARMIN (R)	---	—	12 Mar	13 Apr	—	9 Apr	---	---	----	----	—	
BENVENUE	11/13 Mar	---	15/17 Mar	25 Apr	---	—	19 Apr	—	3 May	----	—	
BENARTY	---	29/30 Mar	—	29 Apr	---	8 May	---	----	----	----	—	
BENKITLAN	5/8 Apr	9/12 Apr	13/14 Apr	—	18 May	9 Jun	5 Jun	31 May	----	----	—	
BENDORAN (R)	4/6 Apr	---	----	6 May	---	14 May	---	----	----	----	—	
BENALLIGIN	6/8 Apr	9/12 Apr	13/14 Apr	—	—	—	---	----	24 May	19 May	30 May	
BENGLOE (R)	----	---	10 Apr	11 May	—	8 May	---	----	—	----	—	
BENLOMOND	8/10 Apr	11/14 Apr	15/16 Apr	15 May	—	2 Jun	29 May	----	—	—	----	25
BENDEARG	—	21/22 Apr	—	19 May	---	28 May	---	----	—	—	—	
BENVANNOCH (R)	3/5 May	6/9 May	10/11 May	—	—	—	10 Jun	—	16 Jun	—	23 Jun	
BENWYVIS (R)	4/6 May	---	—	2 Jun	---	10 Jun	—	----	14 Jun	----	—	
BENMHOR	—	8/10 May	—	—	13 Jun	5 Jul	30 Jun	26 Jun	----	—	—	
BENLAWERS (R)	—	—	10 May	7 Jun	—	3 Jun	—	----	----	----	- -	
BENCLEUCH	18/20 May	---	—	29 Jun	—	—	23 Jun	—	----	----	—	
BENSTAC (R)	—	21/22 May	—	18 Jun	—	26 Jun	---	----	----	----	—	
BENRINNES	31 May/2 Jun	3/6 Jun	7/8 Jun	—	—	—	11 Jul	—	17 Jul	—	24 Jul	

Ben Ocean
A joint service of Ben Line, Blue Funnel, Glen Line and NSMO

BEN OCEAN

A joint service of Ben Line, Blue Funnel, Glen Line and NSMO

The three major British Lines operating in the Far East have made the momentous decision to run a joint service with the day-to-day commercial management of the Service to be conducted by Ben Line of Edinburgh. The Principal Agents in UK will be Killick Martin & Co Ltd of London.

TOP *Detail from Ben Line schedule to Europe*
LEFT AND ABOVE *From a Ben Ocean card.*

ABOVE *About to board the Dove G-ANPH at London (Croydon) for Edinburgh (Turnhouse), 26 April 1954. L to r: Captain J. Liston, Captain W. O. Atkinson, J. O. Grieve, Sir Douglas Thomson, Bt* BELOW *Chemical tanker* Benvenue V *(1974-89) launching herself at Nieuwe Noord Nederlandsche Scheepswerven N.V., Groningen, November 1974.*

from 2nd May 1977

BEN LINE
Wm. Thomson & Co.

The Ben Line Steamers Limited ☐ Ben Line Containers Limited ☐ Ben Line Offshore
Contractors Limited ☐ Ben Line Ship Management Limited ☐ Ben Ocean Limited ☐
Ben Odeco Limited ☐ E. G. Thomson (Shipping) Limited ☐ E. G. Thomson
(Bulk Carriers) Limited ☐ Lombard Street Investment Trust Company Limited ☐ The Salmonier
Shipping Company Limited ☐ The Sheaf Steam Shipping Company Limited ☐
The Bamburgh Shipping Company Limited ☐ The Sheaf Drilling Company Limited

move to
33 St Mary's Street, Edinburgh EH1 1TN
Telephone 031-557 2323 P.O. Box 65 Telex 72611

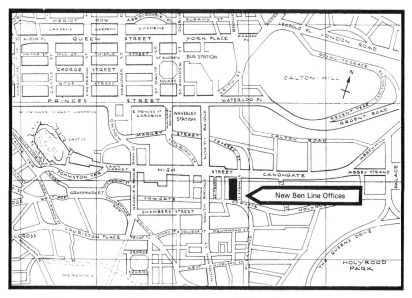

ABOVE *The move to 33 St Mary's Street, Edinburgh* BELOW, LEFT
Benvrackie VI (1976-), acquired as Atlantic I, *renamed 1981* BELOW, RIGHT
Benvorlich V (1976-), acquired as Sheaf Royal, *renamed 1978.*

Head Office, 33 St Mary's Street, Edinburgh.

Bencleuch VII (1976-89) at sea, a sister ship of Benvenue V (see illustration two pages back).

Benledi VIII (*1976-84*), *acquired as* Ros Castle, *renamed 1981.*

Ben Ocean Lancer (*1977-90*).

Board of the Ben Line Steamers Ltd, 1980. L to r: Sir David Thomson, Bt,
D. W. B. Walker, R. Thorman, W. R. E. Thomson, M. F. Strachan, CBE,
H. R. MacLeod, Hon. N. D. G. Galbraith, J. F. Muirhead, W. A. C. Thomson.

interest in Atlantic Drilling, thus making Ben the sole owner of the management company and of a second new semi-submersible rig.[11]

Reardon Smith had been anxious that Atlantic's head office should be located in London on the grounds that this was where most of the potential customers operated. For the sake of continuity, particularly since some of the staff were based in the south, the office remained in London until 1981 when it joined the Ben Line's Head Office in Edinburgh. As both the Atlantic rigs were working in the North Sea it had been necessary to establish a shore base in Aberdeen in 1977 and this moved into purpose built offices and store in 1981.

Worldwide depression in the rig chartering market, caused by an over-supply of rigs and a reduction in exploration, characterised 1977. The depression continued into 1978, but there was a steady improvement the following year and in 1980 it became apparent that demand had outstripped supply. The upward movement continued and profit from our oil-related activities exceeded that from the container service, which, at that time, had been running very profitably for ten years.

By the end of 1982 Ben Odeco owned:

2 drill ships (*Ben Ocean Lancer* and *Ben Ocean Typhoon*).
1 jack-up drilling rig (*Ocean Tide* which had worked continuously, apart from drydocking, since 1974 mainly in the Gulf of Suez).
1 semi-submersible drilling rig (*Ocean Benloyal*, ex-*Sea Conquest*, a sister of *Bendoran* V and from the same Finnish yard).

In addition Ben Line Steamers owned:

1 drill ship (*Benlomond* VII, ex-*Fredericksburg*)
2 semi-submersible drilling rigs (*Benvrackie* VI, ex-*Atlantic* I and *Bendoran* V, ex-*Atlantic* II.
1 enhanced semi-submersible rig, *Benreoch* II, under construction by Daewoo Shipbuilding and Heavy Machinery Ltd, South Korea for delivery in 1983.

Ben Odeco joined with British National Oil Corporation (BNOC) in December 1981 to build with Scott Lithgow Ltd, Port Glasgow, a

11 *Atlantic* I, and *Atlantic* II were renamed *Benvrackie* VI and *Bendoran* V in 1981.

dynamically positioned semi-submersible, self-propelled rig capable of drilling in 4,500 feet of water for delivery in 1986. Ben Odeco managed this rig on behalf of the joint venture and it was contracted to Britoil (formerly BNOC) for 6½ years from delivery.

In 1982 some weakening in what had been an extremely strong market was caused partly by the numbers of new rigs, but mainly by an over-supply of oil, and a consequent softening in the price of crude. Most of the units in which Ben Line had an interest were, however, temporarily protected: *Benvrackie* and *Bendoran* had worked throughout the year on contracts which extended well into 1984. The drill ship *Benlomond* had also worked throughout the year off Sabah and Western Australia on a long-term contract which had another year to run. *Benreoch*, still building in South Korea, had been fixed to work for about a year off New Zealand after delivery.

Ocean Tide and *Ben Ocean Typhoon* had continued working in the Gulf of Suez and were also contracted into 1984. Only *Ben Ocean Lancer*, which had spent 1982 drilling for Chevron off California, was about to be laid up without work. This was disappointing because she had performed very satisfactorily in environments as diverse as Brazilian and Chilean waters and, during the short season when it was possible to drill from June to October, in Arctic waters off Baffin Island. There it was necessary to keep a constant lookout for icebergs. If one or more approached on a dangerous course attendant tugs might deflect it by running a rope round it and pulling. If that proved ineffective – and bergs could be up to 4 million tons weight – *Ben Ocean Lancer* was able to detach herself, manoeuvre, and reposition again when danger was past. Preserved in the archives is an advertisement in the Inuit language for Eskimo workers, and a photograph of some of those who responded and became part of the crew for the season.[12]

VI

Throughout the seventies and on into the eighties we examined numerous new projects. Most were turned down because we thought they would not be profitable, (we decided that the expense of converting *Benstac* into a passenger ship would be too great), or would be too risky, or were not sufficiently closely allied to what we

12 *Ben Bulletin*, no. 16, September 1979, p.5.

were already doing. Some were progressed, with expenditure of time and money, but did not come to fruition. A joint venture with another Scottish company, Liquid Gas Engineering, fell into this category. Throughout the seventies enormous quantities of gas, resulting from drilling operations in the North Sea, were flared into the atmosphere. If, instead, this gas could be captured and fed into a fractionation plant on a VLCC (very large crude carrier), settled on the seabed in an appropriate water depth in a relatively sheltered spot, probably in the Orkneys, we believed that the operation could be commercially viable, and environmentally beneficial. We were a few years ahead of our time in taking the environment into account, but others had observed the commercial possibilities, and in 1980 the project was overtaken by the gas-gathering scheme to be developed in a joint venture by the Gas Council, Mobil and BP.

A few of the projects examined became active ventures. In addition to those already described we took in 1975 a small interest, 5%, in a consortium to drill a well in the Dutch Sector of the North Sea, but the well was dry. In 1981 a new company, Ben Energy Ltd, was set up to invest in on-shore oil and gas in USA. In the nature of things those ventures which were actively pursued met with varying financial results. We had our share of disappointments and setbacks, but we also had our strokes of luck. The easiest money we ever made was a US$1 million cancellation fee from a Japanese company, Sanko, who in the early seventies had ordered about fifty new tankers, against long-term charters at a low fixed rate. Our brokers, offering us one of these charters, had told us that it was 'a licence to print money', always a dubious form of bait, but when Sanko had to admit that they could not perform their side of the bargain it turned out for once to be true.

16

Epilogue

So it seemed in 1982 that the Ben Line had survived the container revolution, had preserved its identity and a fair measure of independence. In contrast Ocean (Blue Funnel) was diversifying out of shipping and its subsidiary Glen Line had completely disappeared. Of the other components of OCL, British & Commonwealth had become an investment company and was shaping up for catastrophe; Furness Withy had been taken over by the Taiwanese Tung Group. P & O had survived as a shipping company, with large property interests acquired by its reverse takeover of Bovis. As regards our fellow members in ACT, Cunard had been taken over by Trafalgar House, Ellerman were soon to change hands and were in due course destined to be taken over by Cunard. Only Blue Star and T. & J. Harrison retained their independence.

Mr Ted said that if 50% of one's business decisions turned out to be correct no great harm would occur. That, alas, disregards the fact that the repercussions of individual decisions may be large or small. It disregards sudden economic changes, and government intervention – or lack of it. It takes no account of the decline in business ethics.

Against adverse influences can be pitted courage, perseverance, integrity and self denial. These qualities may succeed in overcoming them, but charting the rough waters of the late eighties and beyond must be left to some subsequent historian, who may also exercise his critical judgement on this partial sketch of the Ben Line's previous long and honourable history.

APPENDIX

The following listings are believed to be accurate within their respectively defined limits. Some staff, ashore and afloat, who attained senior rank after the 1956 compilation in George Blake, *The Ben Line,* pp.183-5, had retired or died before this appendix was prepared. Some of these are mentioned in the text of the present book, but there were others whose names do not appear, so this is not in all respects a comprehensive record.

PARTNERS 1825-1964

A. & W. Thomson

ALEXANDER THOMSON 1825-47   WILLIAM THOMSON I 1825-47

Wm. Thomson & Co.

WILLIAM THOMSON I 1847-70

WILLIAM THOMSON II
  1861-1911

JAMES WISHART THOMSON
  1862-1907

WILLIAM THOMSON III
  1890-1940

SIR JAMES WISHART THOMSON
  KBE 1892-1929

H.M. THOMSON 1911-19

E.G. THOMSON 1911-64

R. McARTHUR 1911-25

J.D.W. THOMSON (LATER SIR
  DOUGLAS 2nd BT.) 1928-64

A.M. MITCHELL 1928-47

J.O. GRIEVE 1943-64

J.M. MILLER 1947-64

M.F. STRACHAN 1950-64

H.R. MacLEOD (LATER SIR
  RODERICK) 1959-64

W.R.E. THOMSON (WILLIAM
  THOMSON IV) 1963-64

F.D.D. THOMSON (LATER SIR
  DAVID 3rd BT.) 1963-64

DIRECTORS THE BEN LINE STEAMERS LIMITED 1919-1982

WILLIAM THOMSON III 1919-41
  (CHMN. 1919-29)

SIR JAMES WISHART THOMSON
  1919-29

H.M. THOMSON 1919-20

E.G. THOMSON 1919-1966
  (CHMN. 1929-66, PRESIDENT
  1966-76)

ALEXANDER MITCHELL
  1919-34

A.M. MITCHELL 1934-47

SIR DOUGLAS THOMSON 2nd BT.
  1941-72 (CHMN. 1966-70)

A.C. HILL 1947-68

J.O. GRIEVE 1961-64

M.F. STRACHAN 1964-82
  (CHMN. 1970-82)

H.R. MacLEOD (LATER SIR
  RODERICK) 1964-82

W.R.E. THOMSON (WILLIAM
  THOMSON IV) 1964-
  (CHMN 1982-)

F.D.D. THOMSON (LATER SIR
  DAVID 3rd BT.) 1964-

HON. N.D.G. GALBRAITH 1968-

R. THORMAN 1971-

J.F. MUIRHEAD 1971-

D.W.B. WALKER 1975-

W.A.C. THOMSON 1978-

J.H. TOLSON 1982-

THE BEN LINE STEAMERS LTD. & BEN LINE CONTAINERS LTD.
SENIOR STAFF 1982

Accountants G. CRAYTHORNE, K. J. GORDON, D.C.R. GRAHAM, A.M.B. MACLEAN, M.J. PRETTY

Averages I.S.A. SKINNER

Bunkering J.W. TAYLOR

Cashier H. COLE

Chartering D.C. MONRO

Chemical Tankers P.I. EWART

Claims G.E. INGLIS

Conferences A.M. FAIRBAIRN, D.M. TULLOCH

Container Operations C.J. KIRSOP, J.E.C. MITTELSTEIN, J.P. YOUNG

Female Staff Supervisor MISS E.J. UNDERWOOD

Fleet Personnel Manager S.S.C. MARWICK, J.W. MAUL

Freight Manager R.B. HOWELL

Marketing D.W. McCULLOCH

New Business T. CLARK, P.B. ELLIS

Property Manager G.M. CAMERON

Public Relations A.M. PEILL

Red Sea Service A.J. RAIT, W.L. WOOD

Staff Manager W.D. LAWRENCE

Superintendents, Cargo D.J. CRANNA, J.W. SHIELDS, R.G. FAULKNER, J.L. GILMOUR, D.D. HUME, E.J. NESBIT, E.H. TRAVERS

Superintendents, Engineer (BASED IN EDINBURGH) H. PATON, A.H. BROWN, J.M. CLARK, J. SYME (DESIGN ENGR.). (BASED IN LONDON) S.J. REID, R.C. STEWART, A.M. BANNISTER, A.W. WALKER, W.J. PATRICK (ELECTRICAL), J.W. SIMPSON (ELECTRICAL).

Superintendents, Marine A.P. PATERSON (RET'D 1982), A.M. WATTERS, D.E. ROSS, J.E. ATKINSON.

Systems T.H. KELLY

Trio Tonnage Centre A. SYME, W.E. DUN, R. LOGAN, G.W.F. WALKER

ATLANTIC DRILLING CO. LTD. SENIOR STAFF 1982

Directors R. THORMAN (CHMN.) B.J. FORMAN, J. HARRIS

Chief Accountant T.D. BURKE

Marine Superintendent A.J. JOHNSTON

Engineer Superintendents N. ROSS, T. KENNEDY, G. PORTER (SUB. SEA), P.H. REYNOLDS (ELECTRICAL)

Drilling Superintendents J.O. BANKS, M.J. FREEMAN, W.R. MILLAR, R.A. SMITH, D.E. WATSON

Aberdeen Office Mgr G.M.J. STRACHAN

Safety Officer B. NOBLE

Purchasing Mgr J.G. HOWELL

SEA-GOING STAFF, SENIOR MEMBERS, 1982

Masters S. I. BARBOUR, T.P. BARR, C.P. BROWNE, A. BURNETT,
J.M. CAMPBELL, R.E. COWIE, W.D. COWIE, R. DICK, T. FYFE,
E.P. GIBB, H.G. GRAY, A.S. HAMILTON, O. HENDERSON,
H.H. McINTOSH, A. McKENZIE, A. MacLEAN, W.A. MASON
G.D. MUTCH, J.E. PRITCHARD, J.D. PRYDE, A.S. RANKIN,
G. REID, J.S. SCHOFIELD, I.A. SHEPHERD, W.C.S. SPENCER,
M.P.F. TENNANT, S.A. WALKER, J.L. WALTERSON, W.C. WATSON.

Chief Officers F.G.J. ANDERSON, H.A. BLAIN, J.I. BROWN,
G. BYERS, R.S.A. COLES, J. FLEMING, F.I. HOGG, M.D. HUMBY,
W.M. KAY, D. KEILLOR, J.D. LEWTHWAITE, A.I. MacFEATE,
J.N. MacNISH, I.G. MORRISON, G.A. NOBLE, J.S. PHILLIPS,
J.E. ROBERTSON, M.J. SIMPSON, B.C. SPAVEN, D.M. STAFF,
J.H. STEEL, D.D. SUTHERLAND, P.C. THOMPSON, N.M. WIGHT.

Chief Engineers W. ALLAN, L.H. ANDERSON, M.M. BROWN,
W.L. CAMPBELL, A. CLARK, M. COWIE, R.B. DALE, J. GILLON,
A.G. HENDERSON, S. HERRON, J. HOLMES, J.A. LAWS,
G.F. MacDONALD, J. McGEEVER, D.C. McOWAT, D. McVICARS,
J.A. MAGUIRE, W. MAIR, P. MANN, E.L. MATTHEWS,
T.F. RICHARDSON, C. RUTHERFORD, N.J.S. SANDERSON,
K.C. SCOBIE, P. SIMPSON, A.J. THOMSON, J.G. WALKER,
D.B. WOOD.

OFFSHORE DRILLING STAFF, SENIOR MEMBERS, 1982

Senior Toolpushers A.L. CLARK, D.M. IRELAND, G.C. MENEAUD,
J.M. NAYLOR, T. NEEDHAM, M. RENDALL, T. RYAN, J.L. VALLEJO.

Masters A.A. DAVIDSON, I.W. JAMES, G. KELL, A.T.L. KEMP,
R. McPHEE, J.R. MILNE, N. NAIL, G.A. NOBLE, R. SHAW,
D.I. WALKER, A.J.M. WILSON.

Chief Engineers F.K.F. ANDERSON, W.J. ARKLEY, P.H. CURTIS,
S. DONNELLY, T. FREER, B.C. JACKMAN, P.B. LAURIE,
C.A. LINDSAY, W. MacRATE, W.M. MAINLAND, C. RICHARDSON,
H.A. RITCHE, C.L. TOUGH, W.W. WATKINS.

[223]

Far East Management
General Managers: A.S. KINNEAR, 1957-63. R. THORMAN 1963-72;
 D.O. SMITH 1972-82; D.N.A. FARGUS 1982-.
Deputy General Managers: G.S. ALLAN 1972-75;
 M.J. ALLWOOD 1975-78.
Financial Controller: D.C.R. GRAHAM 1975-80.
Marine Superintendents: CAPT. W.O. ATKINSON 1951-57;
 CAPT. A.C. McMASTER 1957-74; CAPT. D.J. CRANNA 1974-81.
Engineer Superintendents: S.J. REID 1963-65; D.K. TAPPIN 1965-67;
 B.J. FORMAN 1967-77; D. CRAWFORD 1977-79;
 P.J. DAVIES 1979-.
Hong Kong Managers: D.O. SMITH 1957-58; R. THORMAN 1958-62;
 J.F. MUIRHEAD 1962-71; M.J. ALLWOOD 1971-75;
 I.H. MOYES 1975-82; D. KEITH-WELSH 1982-.
Singapore Managers: A.S. KINNEAR 1951-57; F. CESSFORD 1957-62;
 R. THORMAN 1962-63; J. SIBREE 1963-64;
 J.L. GILMOUR 1964-69; G.W. WATSON 1969-73;
 S.C. PEACOCK 1973-82; J.B. MATTINSON 1982-.
Malay Federation Owners' Representatives: C.B. BARR-SIM 1957-62;
 F. CESSFORD 1962-72; R.M. HURST 1972-74.
West Malaysia Managers: J.B. MATTINSON 1975-77;
 N. MACDONALD 1977-79; D. KEITH-WELSH 1979-82;
 S.J. FORBES 1982-.
Bangkok Managers: A.H.J. O'CONNELL 1959-66; R.E. LYNN 1967-70;
 L.N.C. DALE 1970-74; A.AITKEN 1974-75; R.W. MIALL 1975-78;
 J.B. MATTINSON 1978-82; N. MACDONALD 1982-.
Japan Owners' Representatives: S.G.R. MORRISON 1961-62;
 I.S.A. SKINNER 1962-67; G.S. ALLAN 1967-70.
Japan Managers: G.S. ALLAN 1970-72; P.C.M. THOMPSON 1972-78;
 R.W. MIALL 1978-.
Indonesia Owners' Representatives: I.H. MOYES 1970-75;
 R.A.M. RAMSAY 1975-.
South Korea Owners' Representatives: G.M.J. STRACHAN 1978-79;
 P.B. ELLIS 1979-81; D.M. TAYLOR 1981-.

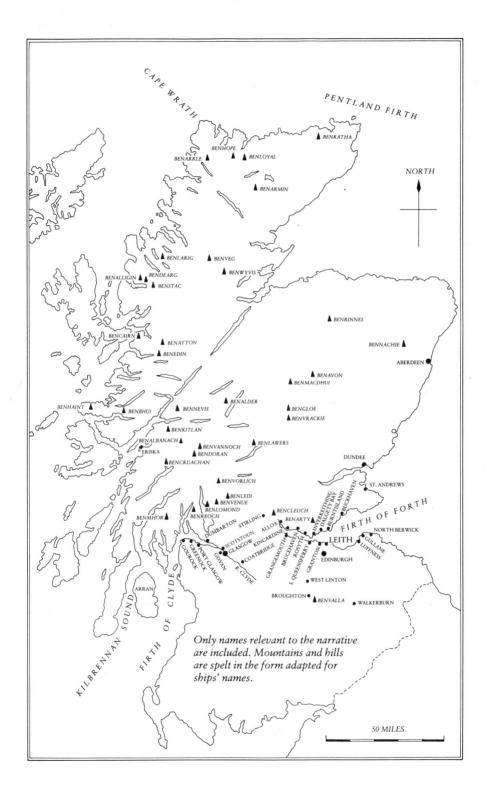

CAPE WRATH

PENTLAND FIRTH

NORTH

BENRATHA

BENHOPE
BENARKLE
BENLOYAL

BENARMIN

BENLARIG
BENVEG
BENWYVIS

BENALLIGIN
BENDEARG
BENSTAC

BENRINNES

BENCAIRN
BENATTON
BENEDIN

BENNACHIE

ABERDEEN

BENAVON
BENMACDHUI

BENHAINT
BENBHUI
BENALDER
BENNEVIS
BENGLOE
BENVRACKIE

BENKITLAN

BENALBANACH
ERISKA
BENVANNOCH
BENLAWERS
DUNDEE
BENDORAN
BENCRUACHAN
ST. ANDREWS

BENVORLICH

BENLEDI
BENVENUE
BENCLEUCH
BUCKHAVEN
BENMHOR
BENLOMOND
INVERKEITHING
DALGETY BAY
BENREOCH
BENARTY
BURNTISLAND
DUMBARTON
STIRLING
FIRTH OF FORTH
SCOTSTOUN
ALLOA
GLASGOW
KINCARDINE
NORTH BERWICK
GOVAN
COATBRIDGE
GRANGEMOUTH
LEITH
GULLANE
GREENOCK
R. CLYDE
BRUCEHAVEN
LUFFNESS
PORT GLASGOW
ROSYTH
GOUROCK
S. QUEENSFERRY
GRANTON
EDINBURGH

ARRAN

WEST LINTON

BROUGHTON
BENVALLA
WALKERBURN

KILBRENNAN SOUND

FIRTH OF CLYDE

*Only names relevant to the narrative
are included. Mountains and hills
are spelt in the form adapted for
ships' names.*

50 MILES

Only place names relevant to the
narrative have been included.

NORTH

C. WRATH

SHET

ORKNEY

NORT

DUNDEE   ABERDEEN

GLASGOW

EDINBURGH

NEWCASTLE

BELFAST   SOUTH SHIELDS

SUNDERLAND

BLYTH

MIDDLESBROUGH

DUBLIN

LIVERPOOL   LEEDS

MANCHESTER   HULL

IMMINGHAM

CARDIFF   BIRMINGHAM

AVONMOUTH   BRISTOL

BATH   LONDON   FELIXSTOWE

TORQUAY   SCHEVENINGEN

SOUTHAMPTON   ROTTERDAM

FALMOUTH

PORTLAND BILL

DUNGENESS   DUNKIRK   ANTW

BREST

HAVRE

ARROMANCHES

PARIS

ST. NAZAIRE

ATLANTIC OCEAN

BORDEAUX

LEIXOES   OPORTO   BIARRITZ

LYONS

MARSEILLES

LISBON

BARCELONA

AJACC

ALGARVE

VALENCIA

JEREZ

GIBRALTAR

MEDITERRANEAN

500 MILES

ALGIERS

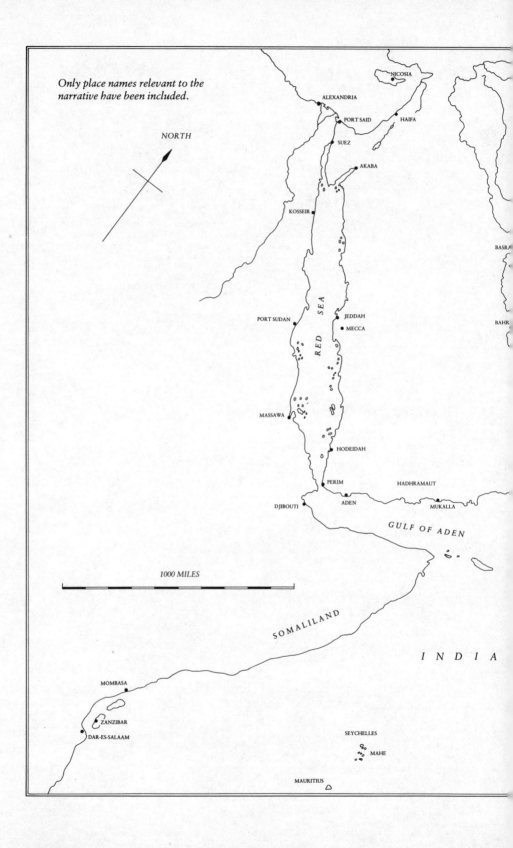

Only place names relevant to the narrative have been included.

NORTH

NICOSIA

ALEXANDRIA

PORT SAID   HAIFA

SUEZ

AKABA

KOSSEIR

BASRA

RED SEA

PORT SUDAN   JEDDAH

MECCA

BAHR

MASSAWA

HODEIDAH

PERIM   HADHRAMAUT

DJIBOUTI   ADEN   MUKALLA

GULF OF ADEN

1000 MILES

SOMALILAND

INDIA

MOMBASA

ZANZIBAR

DAR-ES-SALAAM

SEYCHELLES

MAHE

MAURITIUS

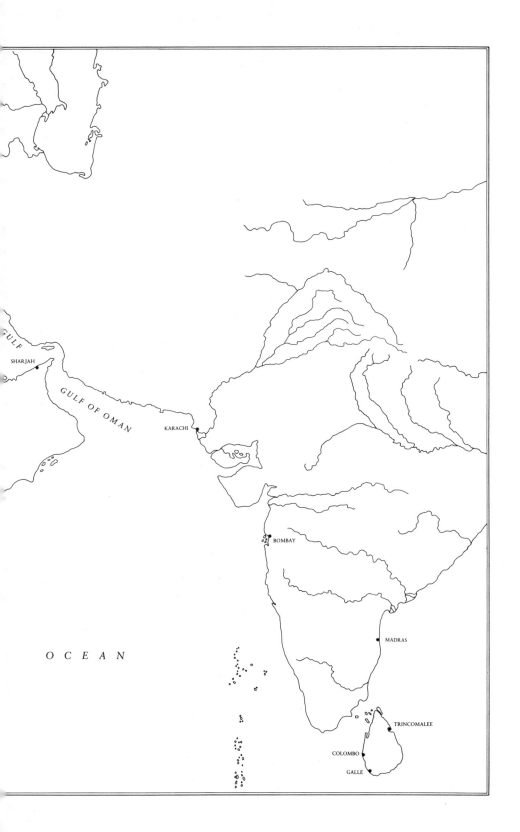

GULF

SHARJAH

GULF OF OMAN

KARACHI

BOMBAY

MADRAS

OCEAN

TRINCOMALEE

COLOMBO

GALLE

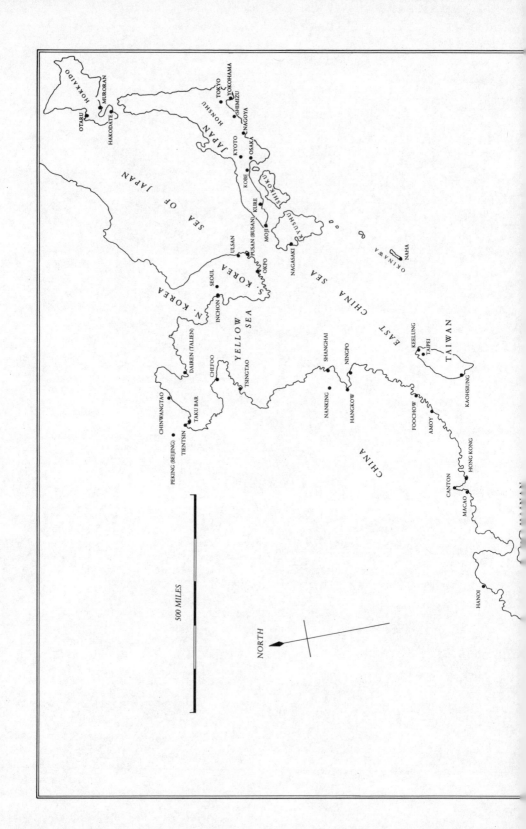

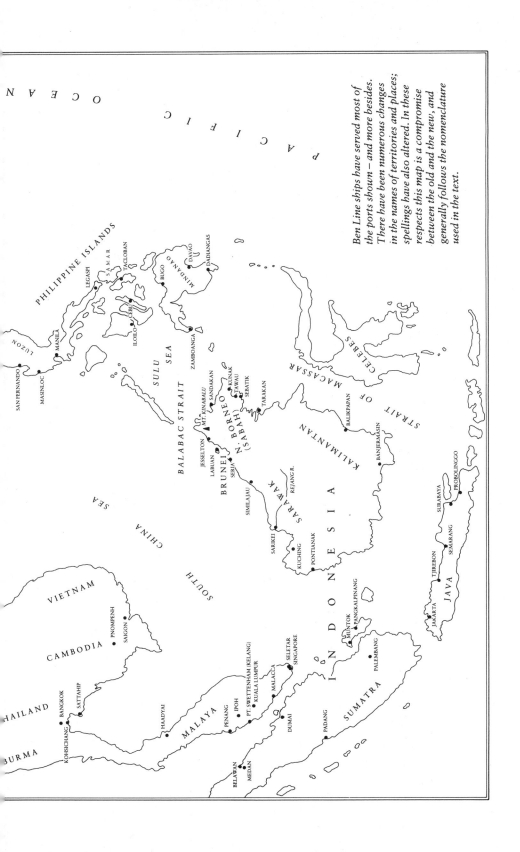

Ben Line ships have served most of the ports shown – and more besides. There have been numerous changes in the names of territories and places; spellings have also altered. In these respects this map is a compromise between the old and the new, and generally follows the nomenclature used in the text.

PACIFIC OCEAN

PHILIPPINE ISLANDS

LUZON

SAN FERNANDO
MASINLOC
MANILA

LEGASPI
SAMAR
TACLOBAN

CEBU
ILOILO

BUGO
DAVAO
DADIANGAS

MINDANAO

ZAMBOANGA

SULU SEA

BALABAC STRAIT

CELEBES

STRAIT OF MACASSAR

MT. KINABALU
JESSELTON
SANDAKAN
KUNAK
TAWAU
SEBATIK
TARAKAN

N. BORNEO (SABAH)

LABUAN
BRUNEI

SERIA
SIMILAJAU
REJANG R.
SARAWAK
SARIKEI
KUCHING
PONTIANAK

BALIKPAPAN
BANJERMASIN

KALIMANTAN

INDONESIA

SOUTH CHINA SEA

VIETNAM

PNOMPENH
SAIGON

CAMBODIA

THAILAND
BANGKOK
SATTAHIP
KOHSICHANG

BURMA

HAADYAI
PENANG
IPOH
PT. SWETTENHAM (KELANG)
KUALA LUMPUR
MALACCA

MALAYA

DUMAI
BELAWAN
MEDAN
PADANG

SUMATRA

MUNTOK
PANGKALPINANG

SELETAR
SINGAPORE

PALEMBANG

JAKARTA
TJREBON
SEMARANG
JAVA
SURABAYA
PROBOLINGGO

Index

Date after a ship's name is year in which she joined the owned fleet

[232]

onions, 127

Oranje, 69

Orkney Is., 63, 219

ore, chorme, 129; ilmenite, 129; iron, 154; lead, 133

Orient Overseas Container Line, 193

Orinoco R., 154

Ortiz-Patino, J., 204

Osaka, 101

Osaka Shosen Kaisha Line, 161, 166; *see also* Mitsui OSK Line

Oslo, 160

Otaru, 98, 132

Oughtred & Harrison Ltd, Hull, 87

Overseas Containers Ltd (OCL), 46, 47, 89, 169, 174 ff

Oxley Studios, 112n

P & O, 5, 7, 15, 33, 39, 41, 46, 86, 89, 121, 130, 159, 160, 162, 163, 168, 175, 179, 181, 220

Pacific West Coast, trade with, 15-16, 201

Pakistan, 47

pallets, 48, 173

palm oil, 58, 96, 129

Palmyra (1873), 6n

Pametrada turbine, 48, 202

Panama Canal, 128, 168, 197

paper-making, Scottish, 9

Paris, 101, 163, 164

Park, T.R., 142-3

Parker, G., 38

Parsons Marine Steam Turbine Co, 39

passengers, 9, 40, 56, 63, 69-71, 75, 149-50, 153

Paterson, Capt. A.P., vii, 14n, 17, 38, 81-2, 148, 177, 186, 222; Mrs Paterson, 17

Paterson, W.A., naval architect, 42

Paterson Simons & Co Ltd, 90

Paton, H., OBE, vii, 82-3, 185, 186, 215, 216, 222

Patrick, Eng. Supt. W.J., 222

Payne, J.G., 178

Peacock, S.C., 224

peas, dried, as cargo, 132

Peebles Hydro Hotel, 163

Peill, A.M., vii, 107, 109, 116, 119, 222

Peking, Treaty of, 1860, 5

Penang, 5, 69, 101, 134

Pentland Firth, 4

Perim Is., 69

Peru, 4

Petersburg I (1878), 8; II (1891), 8, 9

Petrograd Steamers Ltd, 9n, 10

pets, 75, 100, 135

Philippine Is., 8, 16, 66, 67, 93-4, 189, 210

Phillips, Ch. Off. J.S., 223

phosphate, bulk, 121

Pickthorn, Sir Kenneth, Bt, 20

pig bristles, 124

pigs, as food, 15; as cargo, 134-5

pilferage, 55, 123, 148, 173

pilots, 65-6

pineapples, 129, 167

Pitt, Mr, air navigator, 203

Plenderleith, Capt. A., 96n

plywood, as cargo, 210, 211

Poltock, D., 92

polythene, 151

Poon Lim, 18-19

pornography, 74

Port Kelang, *see* Port Swettenham

Port Line, 176, 178; *see also* Cunard

Port of London Authority, 84, 85, 187

Port Said, 16, 63, 68-9, 121, 127

Port Sudan, 127

Port Swettenham, 69, 75, 90, 129, 132, 133, 189, 190

portage bills, 58, 78

Porter, Eng. Supt. G., 222

Porter & Henderson, Hull, 87

Portland Bill, 159

Portsmouth, L.C., 86

postage stamps, 112-13

postcards of ships, 112

potatoes, as cargo, 127

Powell, Rt Hon J. Enoch, MBE, 118, 162

Prentice, Service & Henderson Ltd, 101

Pretty, M.J., 222

Prince Line, 121

Pritchard, Capt. J.E., 155, 158, 223

Pryde, Capt. J.D., 223

Puerto Ordaz, 154

Quebec, 4

Queen Elizabeth, 188

Queen Mary, 45

radio officers, 62

Rae, Nina (Mrs J.O. Grieve), 23n

Rae, Mr, 179n